SO-BBA-264

Unlocking the Garden

Unlocking the Garden
A Feminist Jewish Look at the
Bible, Midrash and God

NAOMI GRAETZ

GORGIAS PRESS
2005

BS
1199
.W7
G73
2005

First Gorgias Press Edition, 2005.

Copyright © 2005 by Gorgias Press LLC.

All rights reserved under International and Pan-American Copyright Conventions. Published in the United States of America by Gorgias Press LLC, New Jersey.

ISBN 1-59333-058-8

GORGIAS PRESS
46 Orris Ave., Piscataway, NJ 08854 USA
www.gorgiaspress.com

Printed and bound in the United States of America.

Library of Congress Cataloging-in-Publication Data

Graetz, Naomi, 1943-
  Unlocking the garden : a feminist Jewish look at the Bible, midrash and God / Naomi Graetz.— 1st Gorgias Press ed.
      p. cm.
  Includes bibliographical references.
  ISBN 1-59333-058-8
  1. Bible. O.T.—Feminist criticism. 2. Feminism—Religious aspects—Judaism. 3. Women in the Bible. I. Title.
  BS1199.W7.G73 2005
  296.3'082——dc22
                                          2004022873

היושבת בגנים חברים מקשיבים לקולך השמיעיני.

"My friends who sit in the gardens of Omer listen to my voice and
encourage me to speak out."
(adapted from Song of Songs 8.13)

Thou that dwellest in the gardens, the companions hearken for thy
voice: cause me to hear it. R. Nathan said in the name of R. Aḥa:
God is like a king who was angry with his servants and threw them
into prison. He then took all his officers and servants and went to
listen to the song of praise which they were chanting. He heard
them saying: 'Our lord the king, he is the object of our praise, he is
our life; we will never fail our lord the king.' He said to them: "My
children raise your voices, so that the companions who are by you
may hear.'... The word 'companions' denotes the ministering
angels—and take good heed that ye do not hate one another nor be
jealous of one another, nor wrangle with one another, nor shame
one another."... Bar Kappara said: Why are the ministering angels
called companions? Because there is among them no enmity nor
jealousy nor hatred nor quarrelling nor heresy nor altercation
(*Song of Songs Rabba*, 7:13).

CONTENTS

CREDITS

Several of the articles in this book have appeared in various versions in periodicals and edited collections.

"Miriam, Guilty or Not?" *Judaism* 40:2 (Spring 1991): 184-192. Reprinted as "Did Miriam Talk Too Much?" in Athalya Brenner (ed.), *A Feminist Companion to Exodus to Deuteronomy* (Sheffield UK: Sheffield Academic Press, 1994): 231-242. Reprinted in Rebecca Schwartz (ed.), *All the Women Followed Her* (Mountain View, CA: Rikudei Miriam Press, 2001): 142-155.

"Akeda Revisited," *Judaism* (Summer 1991): 322-323. Reprinted in Naomi Graetz, *S/He Created Them: Feminist Retellings of Biblical Stories* (Chapel Hill, NC: Professional Press, 1993).

"The Haftara Tradition and the Metaphoric Battering of Hosea's Wife," *Conservative Judaism* (Fall 1992): 29-42. Reprinted as "God is to Israel as Husband is to Wife," in Athalya Brenner (ed.), *A Feminist Companion to the Latter Prophets* (Sheffield UK: Sheffield Academic Press, 1995): 126-145. Also as "A Prophetic Metaphor: God is to Israel as Husband is to Wife— The Metaphoric Battering of Hosea's Wife," in Naomi Graetz, *Silence is Deadly: Judaism Confronts Wifebeating* (Northvale, NJ: Jason Aronson, 1998): 35-52.

"Dinah the Daughter," in Athalya Brenner (ed.), *A Feminist Companion to Genesis* (Sheffield UK: Sheffield Academic Press, 1993): 306-317.

"Feminist Jewish Reconstruction of Prayer," *At The Crossroads*, 4 (June 1994): 43-45.

"Jerusalem the Widow," *Shofar* 17:2 (Winter 1999): 16-24.

"Is *Kinyan* Only a Metaphor? Metaphor and Halakha: The Metaphor of *Kinyan*," in Brad Horowitz (ed.), *Proceedings of the Rabbinical Assembly, Ninety-Eighth Annual Convention* Volume LX (New York: Rabbinical Assembly, 2000): 175-186.

"Response to Popular Fiction and the Limits of Modern Midrash," *Conservative Judaism* 54:3 (Spring 2002): 106-110.

"A Passover Triptych," in Sharon Cohen Anisfeld, Tara Mohr, Catherine Spector (eds.), *The Women's Seder Sourcebook* (Woodstock, VT: Jewish Lights Publishing, 2003): 164-166.

"A Midrashic Lens on Biblical Women: A Review Essay," *Conservative Judaism* (Winter, 2004): 77-85.

"Will the Real Hagar Stand Up," *Hagar: International Social Science Review* 4:1-2 (2003): 203-213.

PREFACE

What does it mean to be a Feminist Jew who is unlocking the garden? To help myself answer the question I turned to the Internet and searched for the words 'Feminist Jew' and 'Jewish Feminist' to see if I could find a clear distinction between the two terms. I found 7,360 entries for the latter and 51 entries for the former. Clearly the more common usage is the latter and in describing myself as a feminist Jew I am making a statement. I tried to distinguish between the two terms. I think it is a matter of priorities, though many would no doubt disagree with me. I have been told by Jewish feminists that they are not sure what they would do if their Jewishness and Feminist agendas were engaged in mortal combat. It has often been the experience of Jewish feminists that when national, ethnic, religious concerns are at stake, all women are expected to rally around the flag and "momentarily" put aside their own agendas for the sake of commitment and loyalty to their group. I often feel this tug, but have come to terms with it—and possibly may be accused of being a traitor to the cause.

What is the garden that this feminist Jew is engaged in unlocking? Alicia Ostriker shares with us: "If the Bible is a flaming sword forbidding our entrance to the garden, it is also a burning bush urging us toward freedom. It is what we wrestle with all night and from which we may, if we demand it, wrest a blessing."[1]

It is my impression that feminists are now going through less of a wrestling stage—that there is more conciliation and that the inchoate anger of the 70s and 80s (when we were all discovering how "bad" patriarchal texts were for women) is now being channeled into a forum where we ask: "so…what can we

---

[1] Alicia Suskin Ostriker, *Feminist Revision and the Bible* (Cambridge, MA: Blackwell 1993): 86.

constructively do with all this anger?" Jewish texts were home to me before I grew into feminism. Yet I became equally committed to Jewish and Feminist teaching, and was never prepared to give up on Judaism. My approach was always to "reclaim" the texts. One way I made these texts mine was to read unconventionally, against the grain. In his commentary on Song of Songs, Rashi says that *gan na-ul* (the locked garden) refers to the modesty of the daughters of Israel, who don't engage in forbidden sexual activity. Instead of seeing these women as wearing some form of chastity belt I decided to widen the net and think metaphorically as to what is inside these gardens (and orifices) that women are told to guard so carefully. Not only are they to cross their legs so that nothing gets in, but their mouths are also to be stuffed and silenced so that nothing comes out. I rebelled against this image.

The image of the garden or the *pardes* in which we plant seeds, then add water and fertilizer until the seeds flower, is more congenial to me. The *pardes* is what was taken away from humanity because God was threatened by knowledge. The *pardes* is the place to which we often aspire to return and then burn our hands in the process of unlocking and re-entering what has been closed to us for so long.

This lasting image of forbidden fruit from the garden is found in the Talmud and Midrash[2] about the four sages who entered the *pardes* (garden).

> Ben Azzai peered into the mysteries and became demented; Ben Zoma looked and died; Elisha b. Abuya [or *Aḥer*] "lopped off the branches," i.e. defected and apostatized; R. Akiba, came in peace and left in peace, i.e. departed unhurt. Of him it is said, *The King* [metaphorically God] *has brought me into his chambers* (Song of Songs 1.4).

Feminists are often accused of "lopping off the branches." I grew into feminism using the lens of Judaism as a guide. When I am confronted with a conflict between my feminism and Judaism, I very often will push as far as I can go, but will not abandon my Jewishness, even if I cannot resolve an issue to my feminist satisfaction. Thus in my academic writings I continue to challenge

---

[2] B. *Hagiga* 14b; *Song of Songs Rabba* I.4:1. In the Talmud the names of Ben Azzai and Ben Zoma are reversed.

the traditional approach to our canonical literature, but have not abandoned ship. I situate myself between those who come in peace without asking questions and those who flex and bend the branches.

Being a feminist (religious) Jew in Israel is even more of a problem. Feminism is still an "F" word in Israel. To feminists in Israel, being a religious Jew (or identifying as a Jew rather than as an Israeli) is equated with sleeping with the enemy. Since I am affiliated with the Masorti branch of Judaism I do not have an outlet for my views in the new wave of feminism in modern Orthodoxy. Finally, since I have chosen not to become a rabbi, I do not necessarily fit into, or represent, the official line of my own movement. Thus I often experience the sense of being unwelcome in many groups either because of my affiliations or the lack of credentials.

I began to look at midrash from an academic perspective by chance. I wanted to share my midrashim at a conference being organized by Penina Peli: *The First Jerusalem International Conference on Women and Judaism* (1986). She suggested instead that I write about what rabbinic midrash had to say about women in the Bible. Since I had just finished writing about Dinah's rape, I chose to write about "Rabbinic Attitudes towards Women: The Case of Dinah." Although the paper was first presented in Jerusalem and later in Ireland (July, 1987) at the *Third Interdisciplinary Congress on Women*, it was only published in 1993. That too was by chance, when Atalyah Brenner called to ask if she could republish my articles on Miriam and Hosea in a collection that she was editing for Sheffield Press. Over the phone I told her that I had an unpublished article about Dinah. The book was going to press soon, but since she did not need to get permission to print it, she asked me to send it to her a.s.a.p. and thus it appeared in one of her first volumes, *A Feminist Companion to the Bible.*

Most of the articles in this book have been previously published. The opening article, "A Feminist Jewish Interpretation of the Bible," was meant to be the introduction to a book entitled *Introducing Jewish Feminist Approaches To The Hebrew Bible* in a series entitled Introductions in Feminist Theology. For personal reasons, I withdrew my participation in this important series and I thank Mary Grey, one of the series editors for Sheffield Academic Press, for her forbearance, understanding and patience. Some of the articles appear in slightly different versions. Some are shorter or longer. I take full responsibility for any errors when changes have been made.

A word about the computer and technology: I must admit to the fact that I would not be a writer were it not for the ease of writing. I still remember when twenty years ago my husband brought home our first computer from Radio Shack. I was in ecstasy when I discovered the delete button and then later the cut and paste function. Fortunately for me (though not our budget), we were always the first on the block to upgrade our computers. As I moved from various models of Atari computers and on to the PCs I believed that the word processor was to me what the cuneiform block must have been to the ancients. It was my way of leaving many marks and my scratching and scribbling are much easier because of this new technology.

There are many who have contributed to my growth as a writer. There are people who have supported me, inspired me, criticized me and, worse, ignored me. It has been difficult writing from Israel (Omer no less) far away from where the action is taking place. Once e-mail became common this was somewhat alleviated. When Gorgias Press accepted my book for publication, I did not realize how painstaking and creative an editor, Lieve Teugels was going to be. We were back and forth daily. There is nothing like sending an entire book as an attachment to an editor and getting an instant reply followed by critique. When response takes more than a day, it seems endless. In the past, it was weeks or even a month until one received a snail letter of acceptance or rejection. Besides my fortune in Lieve as an editor, I would like to thank my cousin by marriage, Jim Eng, for donating his talents to make my cover so meaningful.

I have been exceedingly fortunate in having a wonderful support group of friends and family. I first came to Omer thirty years ago right after my father died in 1974—I used to smile at everyone, just in case they knew me. Omer has grown and I am less friendly, but it is still a village where all are concerned about each others' welfare. Once a year, on Memorial Day, we all gather to commemorate our fallen soldiers. I know most of the families. It is a town where I and my family have thrived. I dedicated my previous books to my parents, my husband and my family. I would like to dedicate this book to all my friends in Omer who have sustained me through both the lean and fruitful years and who have encouraged me to unlock the garden.

Omer, February 10 2004
(The date of my father's thirty year *yahrzeit* which coincided with the birth of my third grandson Uriyah Avshalom Graetz).

INTRODUCTION

The first article in this section "A Feminist Jewish Interpretation of the Bible" was originally written as the introduction to a book which I was unable to complete. In it I explore what is the state of the art of feminist Jewish interpretation of biblical texts. "Dinah the Daughter" and "Did Miriam Talk Too Much?" exemplify clearly that in rabbinic midrash there is no unanimity among the sages about biblical women and men. The same women and men are depicted as good and bad, depending on the circumstances. I demonstrate that there are certain criteria that are used to decide when a particular biblical woman is to be portrayed positively and when the same woman is to be portrayed negatively.

"Metaphors Count" and "Is *Kinyan* Only a Metaphor" stress how much our thinking about Jewish marriage is conditioned by metaphors. I suggest that there is a strong connection between ownership or purchase of women and jealousy. "The Metaphoric Battering of Hosea's Wife" deals with the danger of the marriage metaphor which describes God and Israel in an abusive husband and wife relationship. This article played an important part in my book on wifebeating.[3]

In "Will the Real Hagar Please Stand Up?" I show how Hagar, who is favorably treated in biblical sources, is then treated very negatively in midrashic sources. She is the battered women and also foreshadows Israel as a battered nation. The reconciliation (happy ending) is that when Abraham remarries after Sarah's death, his new wife Ketura is identical with Hagar according to the midrash. This article also hints at the political realities in Israel.

In the "Review Essay of Sisters at Sinai and Midrashic Women" I connect the academic and creative aspects of my own writing while reviewing two very important books.

---

[3] Naomi Graetz, *Silence is Deadly: Judaism Confronts Wifebeating* (Northvale, NJ: Jason Aronson, 1998): 35-52.

1

Much of my writing has been inspired by holiday settings both in the home and synagogue. "Jerusalem the Widow" started out as a lesson given to the Jerusalem Rosh Hodesh group founded by Alice Shalvi and was given several times at different venues on the Ninth of Av (Tisha B'Av). I finally worked it into a paper for a conference in Tucson and found myself addressing the theological problem of God's responsibility for Israel's suffering. The midrash that appears in the "The Barrenness of Miriam" was a direct result of my active participation in the synagogue. The explanation for why I "needed" to write it is an integral part of the article. The midrash, which was written in Hebrew, appears at the end of the article.

Since prayer has become problematic for me over the years, I am constantly struggling with my changing concepts of God and the manner in which God should be addressed. In the mid-80s I was asked by *Tikkun* to submit a response to an article by Marcia Falk. Although the comments were not published then, they were later published by an ecumenical journal in the form of "Feminist Jewish Reconstruction of Prayer." To this day I am not sure if I prefer an immanent or a transcendental God since both of them remain problematic for me. Some of my views of prayer and theology are also found in "Modern Midrash Unbound: Who's Not Afraid of Goddess Worship?"

"Akedah Revisited" is my personal confrontation as a believing Jew in the choices we (and our fore-parents) were offered. The Yiddish expression "ist schwer tzu sein a yid" (it's hard to be a Jew) comes to the fore here, especially for one who is also feminist who lives in Israel.

In "Vashti Unrobed" I incorporate all the characteristics of Jews who were forced to stand at the stake for their ideals into this proud woman, who although not Jewish, could certainly serve as an exemplar for us. "A Passover Triptych" looks at the sibling rivalry of Moses, Miriam and Aaron in their personal, and my imagined, retellings of their life histories. This triptych has been included in *The Women's Seder Sourcebook* and has been used as a ritual at our annual Passover Seder.

A FEMINIST JEWISH INTERPRETATION OF THE BIBLE[4]

The Hebrew Bible[5] is a sacred text to many peoples and religions. Each group and religion has its own religious agenda, and these agendas influence their approaches to the Bible. Before discussing what a Feminist Jewish approach to the Bible is, it is necessary to attempt to draw a portrait of elements that constitute or typify a Jewish approach to the Bible.

WHAT CONSTITUTES A JEWISH APPROACH TO THE BIBLE?

The Torah is "a living tree to those who uphold her, and whoever holds on to her [instructions] are happy" (Prov 3.18). The Torah includes the story of the birth of the Jewish people and the origins of the Jewish legal system. For those following a literalist approach, the five books of the Torah were revealed by God to Moses at Mount Sinai. The words of the Torah are not merely a record of the past, but the expression of God's will, and therefore Torah is the ultimate source of authority in this Jewish view. For those who follow this approach, one may protest or question God's will, but it remains the final source of authority as it is written in the Torah.

---

[4] This article was given as a plenary talk at the Fourth Annual Women's Studies Conference at Valdosta State University in March, 1999.

[5] Since I am writing from the perspective of a Jewish feminist who views the Hebrew Bible as "THE" Bible and not the Old Testament, I will use the term Bible, Torah (which can either be the Five Books of Moses (Pentateuch) or a general term expressing the meaning of "Teachings") or Tanakh (which is a specific term that includes the Five Books of Moses [Torah], The Prophets [Nevi'im] and the Writings [Ketuvim]) rather than use the expression Hebrew Bible, which for me is a euphemism, a politically correct term which is awkward for me to use. Another term that is often used is Scripture.

Thus, little effort can be made to eliminate abuses against women that exist in the Torah by radically overhauling the entire received system. Indeed, this view may lead to denying that any such abuses exist in the Torah altogether. The view is that God's will would not do anything to harm women. If we perceive abuses, the fault must be in the way we understand Torah. This view, thus, is capable of generating explanations of Torah law which "explain away" what appear to be abuses against women in the Torah.

Those who take a more anthropological approach, view the Torah as a human creation which, like any human creation, must be studied and understood in its socio-historical context. From the perspective of this view, there is no inherent authority in the Bible text. Thus, abuse and women's disabilities in biblical law derive from the social status of women at the time. If, in our time, biblical law translates into disabilities for women, we need to effect a radical transformation and rethinking of Judaism.

A third view takes a more middle ground. These are feminists, like me, who, because of our religious orientation, respect the authority inherent in the traditional text. However, since feminism is inseparable from our religious orientation and is viewed as part of our concepts of spirituality and holiness, its teachings must be integrated. We bring to the texts questions from our time and seek to uncover meanings that we believe are dormant in the text, that relate to these questions. Unlike the anthropologist, we slough over the question of the authority of the Bible, since we anchor our creativity within the text. Authority evolves out of the dialectic process of closely studying a text and simultaneously interpreting its meaning in terms of our own feminist and religious consciousness.[6]

Whatever the approach to the Torah, Jewish feminists consider the Torah to be our primary book, our heritage. The

---

[6] One can consider Blu Greenberg to be a representative of the first approach and Judith Plaskow of the second approach. See Blu Greenberg, *On Women and Judaism* (Philadelphia: Jewish Publication Society, 1982); Judith Plaskow, *Standing Again at Sinai: Judaism from a Feminist Perspective* (San Francisco: Harper & Row, 1990). Although Phyllis Trible is Protestant, her article "Depatriarchalizing in Biblical Interpretation," in Elizabeth Koltun (ed.), *The Jewish Woman: New Perspectives* (New York: Schocken, 1976): 217-240 is a key to understanding the third or "middle" approach.

physical scroll is kept in a sacred space in the synagogue and it is dressed with a covering and silver ornaments. When it is removed from the ark it is treated with honor, and blessings are recited by those who read from it. When it is returned to the ark we sing the phrase from Proverbs 3.18, quoted above, referring to its being a living tree.

The question is what makes this a living book. To be alive, means not to be ossified, to grow, to branch out, and to be open to new interpretation. Even within the Tanakh itself, one can discern change of viewpoints,[7] internal commentary on earlier books,[8] moral development,[9] and change in women's status.[10] The issue of memory is very important: As Yosef Hayim Yerushalmi explains, the guide for the continuous historical journey of the Jews is the imperative to remember (*zakhor*), a command given repeatedly in the Bible.[11]

Not only is there on-going internal commentary on the text, but after a portion of the Pentateuch is read in the synagogue every week, there is an additional reading of a portion from the Prophets, called the Haftarah, which serves to elucidate and comment on the weekly portion. The association of the Torah with the synagogue is further reinforced because of the extensive use of biblical phrases and allusions to events, places, and people from the Bible in the prayers and blessings found in the Siddur, the Jewish prayer book. Quotations from The Book of Psalms constitute the introduction to the Shaharit service, the daily Morning Prayer. The values of the

---

[7] E.g., the centrality of Jerusalem is a later development; hinted at perhaps in Deuteronomy, when sacrifice is to be made at a central place, rather than at a local site.

[8] See Michael Fishbane, *The Garments of Torah: Essays in Biblical Hermeneutics* (Bloomington, IN: Indiana University Press, 1989).

[9] The prophets prefer moral activity and downplay sacrifice of animals: "For I desire goodness, not sacrifice; Obedience to God, rather than burnt offerings" (Hos 6.6).

[10] See Calum Carmichael, *Women, Law and the Genesis Traditions* (Edinburgh: Edinburgh University Press, 1979) for a compelling argument that the book of Deuteronomy serves to change the Genesis stories vis à vis women.

[11] Yosef Hayim Yerushalmi, *Zakhor: Jewish History and Jewish Memory* (New York: Schocken, 1989).

land of Israel, justice, and compassion are all found in these quotations.

Jewish people are expected to be literate, so that we can read and understand our sacred texts. This text study is the meaning of religious experience, even the experience of "revelation." The ideal is that the text represents a continuous medium on which Jews base their relationship with, and their supplication to God. Certain events which are central to Jews are biblically based such as the Sabbath and the three main pilgrimage holidays (Succot, Passover, and Shavuot). God gave the Sabbath to His people; this is enshrined in the Ten Commandments (Exod 20.8-11). Each of the three pilgrimage holidays is associated with biblical texts and biblical events. Thus the Bible is read and interpreted through actions.

When Jews build a Succah (booth), we do it because we are commanded to sit in the Succah for seven days to reenact God's protection of Israel while wandering in the desert. When we observe the Passover Seder, we do so because we commemorate God's Redemption, Rescue, and Delivery of Israel from the Land of Egypt where we were slaves. We are commanded to relate to this historic event as if we were still slaves—we are a re-living enactment of our history once a year. On Shavuot, we recall and relate to an agricultural holiday when we bring the First Fruits to the Temple and read the pastoral Book of Ruth. The settlement on the land of Israel and the sustenance found by working the land, is symbolized by the sacrifice of the bringing of the first grain. Later Jewish commentary connects this festival to the day when the Torah was given to the people of Israel at Mount Sinai.[12]

The question of the biblical text as a site of authority is a complex one. There is both a narrative and a legal aspect to the Bible. The narrative parts of the Bible may serve as moral exemplars (though not necessarily if we think of King David's adultery), but the behavior patterns found there are not legally

---

[12] In the State of Israel there are constant reminders of the fact that the Bible is living in the consciousness of its people. The foremost example of this is the Hebrew language used in modern literature, popular songs, political statements and stances (where biblical allusions are a commonplace). Moreover, there are many street names named after the prophets, the 12 sons of Jacob, the matriarchs, etc. The names of cities, settlements often have biblical origins.

binding. At most, legislation is occasionally derived from them. The legal parts of the Bible are one of the major sources of Halakha, Jewish legislation and as such have influence on Jewish ethical, moral and practical behavior. Many Jews consider the legislation, Halakha, to be literally binding. Laws such as: no work on the Sabbath, Kashrut (the Dietary laws), menstrual purity, marriage and divorce, as practiced in Jewish religion, are all biblically based.[13]

Although the Bible is authoritative, that does not mean that we are in such awe of it that we are not allowed to criticize it. Although biblical criticism may possibly contradict the idea of literal divine authorship, many Jews consider themselves blessed that the tools of biblical criticism enable them to understand their tradition in the greater context of history, linguistics, and culture. The Jew who uses these tools still views the text, within the lens of her own norms, as a means to discovering what she believes to be true. The critical stance, for many, embraces the religious experience associated with studying the Bible. David Blumenthal writes that:

> the traditional Jewish world view is an approach to text that is both logocentric and plurisignificant; it is univocal and multivocal at the same time. Text, even sacred text, is the result of intertextuality—with other preceding texts and contexts…Yet text always has authority…that provides intellectual, spiritual, and social coherence.[14]

Jacob Neusner suggests that a Judaic tendency or approach includes three major characteristics: first, "Jewish scholars take up texts neglected by others or study them in a different context";

---

[13] It should be noted of course that these laws have been subject to interpretation in the Mishnah and later in the Talmud and even later in the Codes and Responsa literature. See Elliot Dorff and Arthur Rosett, *A Living Tree: The Roots and Growth of Jewish Law* (Albany, NY: State University Press of New York, 1988) for an expansion of this. The Bible is so important that there is a concept *de-oraita* (stemming from the Torah) as opposed to *de-rabbanan* (stemming from rabbinic strata) in which laws which have Toraitic origin are considered superior to those which have been derived from rabbinic interpretation.

[14] David R. Blumenthal, "Many Voices, One Voice," *Judaism* 47:4 (Fall 1998): 465-474.

then "they draw from a corpus of exegetical traditions and a deep mastery of Hebrew"; and thirdly, "Judaic perspectives on ancient Israel lead to a distinctively and particularly Judaic inquiry into a biblical text or problem...so that we can recognize beyond doubt (even without names) 'that the author is Jewish.'"[15]

Having written all this, we must ask, is there a difference between a Jewish and non-Jewish approach? I think there is. Let us examine the three pilgrimage holidays, and the Scrolls read on these holidays. In addition, to these three scrolls, Jews read the Scroll of Esther on Purim, to celebrate Jewish survival from disaster, and the Scroll of Lamentations on Tisha B'Av to commemorate the destruction of the First Temple. These books are read in a synagogue setting. Thus it is natural that the Jewish reader of such texts will read them differently than the Christian or agnostic reader of the Bible. Edward Greenstein discusses the need for a Jewish reading of Esther, pointing out that Jews love the book, whereas Christians dismiss or tolerate it. It even has a different place in the Christian Bible (as part of the chronological history) whereas in the Jewish Scriptures, the book's place is determined by "its function in Jewish liturgy" as part of the five scrolls "chanted in the synagogue in the course of the liturgical calendar." Thus for the Jewish reader, "Esther belongs to Purim. It is in the context of Purim that Jews hear the book...more importantly, Jews have read in the story...a paradigm of their people's vulnerability to racist hatred."[16]

I have referred to the fact that Jewish scholars are familiar with the midrash, an exegetive tradition not necessarily familiar to non-Jewish scholars. Alan Levenson writes,

> Midrash invites the sort of strong readings which empower the interpreter to heal and make whole... Referencing midrash also serves the function of putting oneself in dialogue with a Judaic tradition... Despite the use of rabbinic interpretation of the Bible, Jewish

---

[15] Jacob Neusner, *Judaic Perspectives on Ancient Israel* (Philadelphia: Fortress Press, 1987): xii as quoted by Alan Levenson, "Jewish Responses to Modern Biblical Criticism," *Shofar* 12:3 (Spring 1994): 103-104.

[16] Edward L. Greenstein, "A Jewish Reading of Esther," in Jacob Neusner et al., *Judaic Perspectives on Ancient Israel* (Philadelphia: Fortress Press, 1987): 225-226.

scholars don't necessarily use the Apocrypha to do the same, whereas Christian scholars do.[17]

Another difference has to do with God. The doctrine that God is One, that there is neither a trinity nor even a major prophet such as Jesus or Mohammed associated with Judaism is a central tenet in Judaism. It abhors foreign gods and goddesses. Even though we have prophets and rabbis, there are no direct intermediaries between God and the people, such as the Pope or Saints.[18]

Certain historic events and observances which are unique to Judaism have been altered in other religions. Passover, the deliverance of Israel from Egypt is not celebrated by other peoples; the Sacrifice of Isaac is not a foreshadowing of Jesus' sacrifice by his father, as it is in Christianity, nor is Isaac to be supplanted by Ishmael, as he is in Islam. The doctrine of original sin does not exist for Judaism, although women are blamed for the expulsion from the Garden of Eden.

Lurking in the background is also the Jewish mistrust of Higher Bible Criticism which was labeled by Solomon Schechter as "Higher Anti-Semitism."[19] This led perhaps to the apologetic and polemical tone which often pervades much of modern Jewish scholarship.[20] Thus we often find acerbic comments directed at those who dare to question the Bible's historicity.[21]

---

[17] Alan Levenson, "Jewish Responses to Modern Biblical Criticism," *Shofar* 12/3 (Spring 1994): 106.

[18] Though note the growing tendency among the Lubavitch Hassidim to give Messiah status to Menachem Mendel Schneerson who died in 1994. See David Berger's critique of this in *The Rebbe, the Messiah and the Scandal of Orthodox Indifference* (Oxford, UK: Littman Library of Jewish Civilization, 2001). Among Moroccan Jews there is something verging on this in the "worship" of Baba Sali at his shrine in Netivot.

[19] Solomon Schechter, "Higher Criticism—Higher Anti-Semitism," *Seminary Addresses* (New York, 1959).

[20] Alan Levenson, "Jewish Responses to Modern Biblical Criticism," *Shofar* 12/3 (Spring 1994): 104.

[21] An example of this might be Hershel Shanks's comments directed at an archaeologist he takes issue with as being prejudiced with an anti-biblical bias. Shanks seems to feel that one's starting point should be one of faith in the authenticity of the Bible and not one that is skeptical at the

WHAT CONSTITUTES A FEMINIST APPROACH TO THE BIBLE?

While I have presented some general characteristics of a "Jewish" approach to the Bible, there are many more identifiably different characteristics which typify a feminist approach. In this section I will consider the most important aspects of what characterizes a "feminist" approach, and show that, as the Jewish approach is not univocal, neither is the feminist approach. The most important characteristic is that a feminist interpretation challenges the very notion of objectivity, that there is "no such thing as a neutral, historical-critical, scientific, objective interpretation of the Scriptures,"[22] or in Adrienne Rich's words "objectivity is really male subjectivity." Tikva Frymer-Kensky points out that the paradigm shift, from the perception that a text has one correct meaning to the perception that there is a value-neutral way of reading the Bible, was not caused by Women's Studies. Yet this shift has developed an openness and expectation that women can provide new perspectives to the biblical text.[23]

This leads to feminists approaching the Bible critically as a "resisting reader rather than an assenting reader and, by this refusal to assent, to begin the process of exorcising the male mind that has been implanted in us."[24] What this means is to view the canon with a "hermeneutics of suspicion."[25] This stance sees the

---

outset. Hershel Shanks, "Dever's 'Sermon on the Mound,'" *Biblical Archaeology Review* 13:1 (March/April 1987): 54-57.

[22] Elizabeth Achtemeir, "The Impossible Possibility: Evaluating the Feminist Approach to Bible and Theology," *Interpretations* XLII: 1 (January 1988): 50.

[23] Tikva Frymer-Kensky, "The Bible and Women's Studies," in Lynn Davidman and Shelly Tenenbaum (eds.), *Feminist Perspectives on Jewish Studies* (New Haven: Yale University Press, 1994): 16-17.

[24] Judith Fetterly, *The Resisting Reader: A Feminist Approach to American Fiction* (Bloomington and London: Indiana University Press, 1978): xxii. Fetterly's approach did not really address the omission of women from canonical text, only the need to reread those texts as a resisting reader.

[25] See Elisabeth Schussler Fiorenza, *In Memory of Her* (New York: Crossroad, 1989): xxiii, where she introduces the expression and 108 ff., where she discusses the methodological rules for a feminist hermeneutics of suspicion. She introduced the term in an earlier work: Elisabeth Schussler Fiorenza, *Bread Not Stone* (Boston: Beacon Press, 1984): 15-22.

androcentricity of the text, which predicates "that to be human is to be male,"[26] and notes that in the Bible, the woman is marginal, the other. The condition of a woman in the Bible is "that of a prince[ss] cast out. Forced in every way to identify with men…she undergoes a transformation into an 'it,' the dominion of personhood lost…"[27] The feminist viewing the Bible knows that in the hierarchy of humanity, woman is on the bottom of the totem pole and that this is connected to the fact that the Godhead is usually depicted as male, be He father or husband.

Once feminists have analyzed the problem, we have to struggle with the question of how to move from a text which is androcentric to the process of putting women back into the text. One way is to highlight the importance of women—to give them equal time. There are forefathers and the four mothers. Another is to speculate that there was a matriarchal structure, which may or may not have included goddesses, that predates the biblical period and to rediscover this structure and reconsider it in a favorable light.[28]

Another way is to imaginatively re-discover these biblical women after questioning their absence. On a very basic level, we begin by naming. If a woman is referred to anonymously, without a name of her own, we give her one. Mieke Bal names Jephtah's daughter "Bat," Alice Bach names Potiphar's Wife "Mut-em-enet." By doing this, they both, on a very elementary level "give voice to the female figure in the text and seek to escape being seduced by the narrator into accepting his view" which includes naming men and leaving women nameless.[29]

---

[26] Judith Fetterly, *The Resisting Reader: A Feminist Approach to American Fiction* (Bloomington and London: Indiana University Press, 1978): ix.

[27] Idem.

[28] Carol Meyers has written about this in "The Roots of Restriction: Women in Early Israel," *Biblical Archeologist* 41 (1978): 91-103; "Procreation, Production and Protection: Male-Female Balance in Early Israel," in Charles E. Carter and Carol L. Meyers (eds.), *Community, Identity and Ideology* (Winona Lake, IN: Eisenbrauns, 1996): 489-514 (Reprinted from 1983); and Carol Meyers, *Discovering Eve: Ancient Israelite Women in Context* (New York: Oxford University Press, 1988).

[29] Alice Bach, "Breaking Free of the Biblical Frame-Up: Uncovering the Woman in Genesis 39," in Athalya Brenner (ed.), *A Feminist Companion to Genesis* (Sheffield UK: Sheffield Academic Press, 1993): 319; Mieke Bal,

The feminist who reads the Bible constantly questions the traditional understanding of women's place or role in the private, familial, sphere. She will highlight situations where women appear in the public sphere: she will over-emphasize the roles of the prophets, the judges, the sages. Although there is no prophetic book of Huldah—she may have been a minor prophet—the feminist scholar rediscovers her, and situates her as an important figure who was a female Jeremiah, a genuine spokesperson of Yahweh or possibly a prophet of the banned goddess, Asherah.[30] This will be justified on the grounds that since women have been written out of history, their stories have to be re-covered and re-placed. When the emphasis on the heroine who controls her own destiny becomes commonplace, the old view of women as property, whose anatomy is destiny, fades from prominence. The new view stresses the importance of leaders such as Miriam, Deborah, and the newly named or uncovered wise women and sages.

Although we can be cynical about this process or even call it an apologetic approach (because it deflects us from the "real" facts that women are marginal in the Bible) this re-memory and revision is crucial for the feminist. In Adrienne Rich's words revision is for women "more than a search for identity...more than a chapter in cultural history; it is an act of survival."[31] Catherine Simpson writes,

---

Death and Dissymmetry: The Politics of Coherence in the Book of Judges (Chicago: University of Chicago Press, 1988): 43ff. I do this in my midrash on Elisheva, Aaron's wife, when I create a daughter for her and then give her the name "Bityah." Naomi Graetz, "When Will it be My Time?" *S/He Created Them: Feminist Retellings of Biblical Stories* (Piscataway, NJ: Gorgias Press, 2003): 105-110. Then there are those who would argue that women do NOT need to be named—that it may even add strength to their being archetypes. See Adele Reinhartz, "Anonymity and Character in the Books of Samuel," *Semeia* 63 (1993): 117-141 and also her book *Why Ask My Name?: Anonymity and Identity in Biblical Narrative* (New York: Oxford University Press, 1998) which includes men.

[30] See 2 Kings 22.14-20 and 2 Chronicles 34.22-28 where Hulda prophesies. cf. Diana Edelman, "Huldah the Prophet—Of Yahweh or Asherah?" in Athalya Brenner (ed.), *A Feminist Companion to Samuel and Kings* (Sheffield UK: Sheffield Academic Press, 1994): 231-250.

[31] Quoted by Fetterly in her preface, Judith Fetterly, *The Resisting Reader: A Feminist Approach to American Fiction* (Bloomington and London: Indiana University Press, 1978): viii.

"There is no identity without memory…the very act of trying to summon up and organize memories establishes a sense of psychic, cultural social presence."[32]

The feminist quest is a dangerous one. First of all, it is interdisciplinary in its nature. It knocks on and knocks down the walls of the academy: "By asking questions in terms of women (and not in terms of a particular framework such as psychology or history, for example), feminists moved beyond some of the limitations which are imposed by 'compartmentalization.'"[33] The feminist critic is urged to "deny the temptation of trying to produce a universal truth, a univocal meaning. Feminist criticism must remain fluid, not fixed…"[34] But more dangerous than the attack on the academy, is the urgent need for change that the feminist demands. This is where the battle is taking place.

By definition, a feminist approach demands action. Tikva Frymer-Kensky writes that "feminist studies of the Bible cannot remain isolated from the political implications of their research…if one does not consciously address a problem, one becomes part of the problem."[35] It is not enough to stay in the ivory tower and analyze the problems. In addition to re-writing and re-interpreting there is a general question about patriarchy that may lead to reverse sexism—in validating woman's position, it may be taken as invalidating man's position. This approach may follow from Socialism or Marxism—which has lead women to want to "restructure completely the reproductive and preservative functions of human society in other ways than that of the

---

[32] Catherine R. Simpson, "The Future of Memory: A Summary," *Michigan Quarterly Review* 26:1 (1987): 259-265.

[33] Dale Spender (ed.), *Men's Studies Modified: The Impact of Feminism on the Academic Disciplines* (New York: Pergamon, 1981): 2. See Hillel Halkin's "Feminizing Jewish Studies," in *Commentary* (February 1998) in which he attacks those of us who do exactly this: "In good postmodernist fashion, objective historical truth is, for them, an epistemological illusion, the past being an inevitable 'reinvention' of the present by self-interested and conceptually predisposed observers" (40).

[34] Alice Bach (ed.), *The Pleasure of Her Text: Feminist Readings of Biblical and Historical Texts* (Philadelphia: Trinity Press International, 1990): ix.

[35] Tikva Frymer-Kensky, "The Bible and Women's Studies," in Lynn Davidman and Shelly Tenenbaum (eds.), *Feminist Perspectives on Jewish Studies* (New Haven: Yale University Press, 1994): 19.

traditional family, an extreme to which few societies are willing to go."[36] This approach is sometimes referred to as radical feminism, or rejectionism, as throwing the baby out with the bath water. But is it? If the waters are so polluted, the "radical" feminist asks, how can we continue to bathe in them? By rejecting the Bible as not being useful, the feminist is also rejecting religious tradition, saying that it is unredeemable. The main advocate of this alternative was Mary Daly in *Beyond God the Father*.[37]

WHAT CONSTITUTES A JEWISH FEMINIST APPROACH?

The Jewish feminist is influenced by general feminism—but tries to remain loyal to her sense of being Jewish. She[38] may define herself as a feminist Jew or a Jewish feminist. She may feel that Judaism and Feminism are two competing "ism"s, but she persists in seeing value in both. As a feminist she might be tempted to reject Judaism in its entirety—when the stakes get very high—but she too, like the non-Jewish feminist, considers this throwing out the baby with the bath water. Rebecca Alpert recognizes that "Exile from one's Jewishness is not necessarily the answer to the feminist dilemma…[on the other hand,] All of Judaism is called into question by feminism…"[39]

The Bible is not just another book to the Jewish feminist and she will criticize those who treat it as such. For instance, Ilana Pardes, despite her debt to Mieke Bal, the influential feminist scholar, unsympathetically criticizes her Christian biases and her statement that the Bible's message is only an issue for those who attribute religious authority to these texts "which is precisely the

---

[36] Carolyn Osiek, "The Feminist and the Bible: Hermeneutical Alternatives," in Adela Yarbro Collins (ed.), *Feminist Perspectives of Biblical Scholarship* (Chico, CA: Scholars Press, 1985): 95.

[37] Mary Daly, *Beyond God the Father: Toward a Philosophy of Woman's Liberation* (Boston: Beacon, 1973).

[38] Although I use the female gender to describe a feminist, I recognize that there are male feminists such as Mayer Gruber, Daniel Boyarin, and Arthur Waskow.

[39] Rebecca Trachtenberg Alpert, "Sisterhood is Ecumenical: Bridging the Gap between Jewish and Christian Feminists," in *Response: A Contemporary Jewish Review* XIV: 2 (Spring 1984): 12.

opposite of what I am interested in."[40] The baby referred to above, the canon, has to be treated with care, if it is not to be abandoned.

According to Levenson, we "Jewish feminists are in the awkward position of having to revision a biblical legacy while at the same time debunking tendencies to place the blame for the patriarchy, the West's oppression of women, and even the Holocaust on the "biblical" (read) Judaic heritage."[41] We are aware, on the one hand, that "Israel was neither the creator of patriarchy nor the worst perpetrator in the ancient world, [and that] the patriarchy of Israel was part of an inherited social structure…nevertheless, we make a profound statement when we acknowledge that the Bible is patriarchal."[42]

Feminism makes us suspect the authority of our texts, since we have been written out of the texts and we suspect that God was not necessarily speaking through those men who are responsible for a sexist type of Judaism. Yet the feminist Jew is very much in a relationship with Judaism—even if the relationship is acrimonious. She may be angry; she may be apologetic; BUT she strongly identifies with her Jewishness and wants to either change it or live with it (or both)—either in a state of conformity or rebellion. In other words, she hasn't written off her tradition. She may threaten the status quo; the establishment might view her as heretical—but she considers herself a member of the fold, even if there are attempts by the establishment to marginalize or silence her voice. She believes that by her efforts, and those of others, Judaism can (and should) be transformed. Our view of patriarchal Judaism is that, if we look at it with fresh (read feminist) eyes, we can change it.

The relationship between feminism and Judaism can be described as one in which two different world views collide. The

---

[40] Ilana Pardes, *Countertraditions in the Bible: A Feminist Approach* (Cambridge MA: Harvard University Press, 1992): 26-33; Mieke Bal, *Lethal Love: Feminist Literary Readings of Biblical Love Stories* (Bloomington, IN: Indiana University Press, 1987). Cited by Alan Levenson, "Jewish Responses to Modern Biblical Criticism," *Shofar* 12:3 (Spring, 1994): 107.

[41] Alan Levenson, "Jewish Responses to Modern Biblical Criticism," *Shofar* 12:3 (Spring, 1994): 109.

[42] Tikva Frymer-Kensky, "The Bible and Women's Studies," in Lynn Davidman and Shelly Tenenbaum (eds.), *Feminist Perspectives on Jewish Studies* (New Haven: Yale University Press, 1994): 18.

feminist values relatedness, connection, togetherness, sisterhood, whereas Judaism posits separation and holiness. The Jew is commanded to set himself apart from other nations in order to be holy. The rationale behind it is stated explicitly in Leviticus 19.2: "You shall be holy, for I, the Lord your God, am holy." Holiness consists of both ritual purity and separation. To retain the chosen status, the nation is commanded, among other things, to separate itself from other gods (and goddesses), from idol worship, from foreigners (the gentiles), from forbidden foods, from women after childbirth, and from menstruating women.

The Sabbath is a day which separates itself from the rest of the week and the Jew is commanded to observe this day, to set it apart and to engage in a totally different relationship to all of creation. Part of this change of mindset includes restrictions on "weekday" behavior. The Havdalah ceremony, which marks the end of the Sabbath, sanctions hierarchy and separation. The priestly laws assume a patriarchy: God on top, the High Priest as intermediary (only he can go into the Holy of Holies to sacrifice), the lesser priests below, and still downwards, the Levites. Further down are the normal Israelites and below them are their wives and children.

To retain the chosen state, men are required to be circumcised, which separates them from the gentiles and, of course, from women, who are often seen as being ritually polluted or impure, that is, the other. Part of the separation involves the creation of boundaries. One group is defined as being inside or chosen, they constitute the patriarchy. They are often in a hierarchical relationship to one another.

Thus, when a feminist approaches a Jewish text, and rejects the separation inherent in patriarchy, she threatens the traditional Jewish reading of the text. She comes to it bearing anti-hierarchical and anti-patriarchal biases. She notices gaps in the texts—those that leave women out; those that do not name women; those that misrepresent women or punish uppity women. She will challenge those who want to minimize the possibility of multiple meanings of text, those who ignore the findings of source and form criticism, archaeology and linguistics. She will align herself with the forces of modernity and against those of tradition.

She will want to read women back into the text, missing a woman's presence, when the traditional reading has not noticed her absence. She will uncover the "texts of terror" that have served as warnings to women to stay in their place: the acrimonious relationship of Abraham's wives, Hagar and Sarah; the sibling rivalry between Sister Leah and Sister Rachel; the non-participation of Dinah in her rape; Jepthah's nameless daughter; the sex sirens and temptresses: Delilah, Potiphar's (nameless) wife; the story of the suspected adulteress (Sotah) and the most frightening story of what can happen to an unprotected woman in a lawless society (the concubine at Gibeah).[43]

She will have noted that the people (and the land and the cities) of Israel are depicted with feminine metaphors—often uncomplimentary ones—and are all at the mercy of the ruling god who is sometimes depicted as an angry husband. If she thinks that Goddess worship has a legitimate place in the pantheon, she will find that the Bible has tried to wipe out all traces of Asherah (a sacred grove, tree, or tree-sculpture, cf. 1 Kings 15.13), Anat, Astoret (Esther), and that the prophets depict as evil those men who worship goddesses and foreign gods.

We have seen that the relationship between feminism and Judaism has many points which can be described as points of conflict. It might seem that within these parameters, the relationship of the feminist to the Bible is hopeless. Yet there are those who are committed to tradition, who choose to make the Bible a text that they can live with because there are many points of spiritual and intellectual value that concur with their needs.

In what ways can a Jewish approach be more compatible with a feminist approach? Is it possible to treat feminism and Judaism as capable of harboring similar systems of value? If we look at the writings of Jewish feminists we find that they are unwilling to give up on Judaism; they try and point to similarities rather than emphasize differences. How do they (we) do it?

Perhaps the most obvious way is to take an apologetic, whitewashing approach. Rather than admit that there is something wrong with our tradition, we engage in comparison with other religions, seeing ours as less sexist than others, or look at historical context—contending that gender was not an issue for our

---

[43] Phyllis Trible, *Texts of Terror: Literary-Feminist Readings of Biblical Narratives* (Philadelphia: Fortress, 1984).

forefathers. The danger of doing this is that it can lead to acceptance of what is and encourage lack of effort to make change.

Cynthia Ozick verges on the border of apologetics when she argues that the ethical passion against instrumentality, that is, woman as instrument, derives not from the Enlightenment, not from humanism, but from Genesis 5.1 where we are told that human beings are made in the likeness of the Creator, who has no likeness to man, woman, or beast. This she feels is meant to free us from the dictum that anatomy is destiny—that it gives both men and women access to the world, based on merit. She argues for the Jewish vision, for "In the Jewish vision, and only in the Jewish vision, the nature of the Creator is dissociated utterly from the biological: because the biological is the fount and origin of instrumentality... This is the power of Torah—that it declares against instrumentality." She has created a distinction between "power of Torah," for example, Genesis 5.1, which seems to be anti-instrumental and all the other parts of the Torah and Bible which are clearly instrumental. This is surely a questionable move. She claims that if "Jewish feminism does not emerge from Torah, it will disintegrate. For Jews the Enlightenment is an idol that will not serve women as it did not serve Jews..." Yet Ozick defines herself as a feminist, albeit NOT a classical feminist. She prefered to define issues, not as being women's issues but, as societal issues. In 1984, she felt that classical feminism had failed because it advocated segregation (separate destinies) and psychological separateness. Ozick had not given up on the rabbis—but did argue that the ideal would be "a congruence between the souls of the rabbis and the soul of Torah—a time when the rabbinate is not politicized, when religious values are not hierarchical."[44]

Tikvah Frymer-Kensky also borders on apologetics when she writes that the Bible does not justify the subordination of women by portraying them as subhuman or as other. She writes that "the Bible is not essentialist on gender; it does not consider differences between the sexes to be innate.... The Bible inherited its social structure from antiquity and did not radically transform it. At the same time, the Bible did not justify social inequality by an ideology of superiority or otherness." For those of us who think differently

---

[44] Cynthia Ozick, "Torah as Feminism, Feminism as Torah," *Congress Monthly* (September/October 1984): 9.

she has an answer: it is the Greek influence which "treats women as categorically 'other.' Nevertheless, this later development should not obscure the fact that pre-exilic Israel has no ideology of gender differences."[45]

Another approach is to ask "who owns the tradition?" What is authentic? What is inauthentic? Who decides? In this approach we take an anti-monolithic approach to text. Levenson calls this "pluriformity." There are majority and minority opinions. Both are preserved, not only in the Talmud, but in the Bible as well. There are more ways of reading the text than can be imagined and there is no one right way to relate to the sacred traditions. In fact one can argue that the rabbinic tradition of interpretation was just continuing to make this point in its multiple readings of the Bible. The rabbis encourage us to read and reread the Bible: "Turn it and turn it again, for everything is in it." This is the basis of a midrashic approach to text. Although midrash was mostly created by male rabbis, there is nothing to stop the modern writer and reader of the Bible from creating new midrash which re-examines texts that may be unfavorable and unsafe for women and re-fashions, re-interprets, and revises them. One can also un-cover and re-cover women's stories and re-focus the stories so that women take their proper and rightful places. This approach can harmonize the Bible and feminism because it views the Bible not in its fixed text but as "work in progress."

For example, we can look at similarities between Jewish experience and female experience and point to both groups being identified as an oppressed people. Just as the Jew was endangered by anti-Semitism and assimilation; so are women threatened by sexism and the need to conform to male values. In this view of seeing the similarities, women become natural allies to the Jews rather than enemies (much as the blacks sought analogy in the Jewish experience and women in the black experience). In Rebecca Alpert's opinion, the "feminist priority has deep roots in Jewish tradition. The Torah, the prophets, and the authors of rabbinic Judaism all expressed concern about the conduct of human relationships and the need to incorporate people who were

---

[45] Tikva Frymer-Kensky, "The Bible and Women's Studies," in Lynn Davidman and Shelly Tenenbaum (eds.) *Feminist Perspectives on Jewish Studies* (New Haven: Yale University Press, 1994): 23-24.

considered marginal, often referred to as 'the stranger, the widow, and the orphan.'" She sees as priorities the end to war, poverty, reallocation of scarce resources and sees these goals as "rooted in Jewish values and Jewish sources." [46]

We can model ourselves on the rabbinic approach to text which often presented the very biblical texts that dictate the hierarchy of priests and kings as texts which mandate learning and knowledge as keys to power. Although there may be some debate as to whether women should partake of the democratic pursuit of learning—the opening has always been there and it is up to women to grab the opportunity.[47] Part of the democratic preaching of the rabbis is the relationship to others which is often sympathetic— "we should not do to others as we would despise being done to ourselves,"[48] a powerful message which can be translated to include women. The Jewish world claims that its purpose of being a chosen people is not to conquer but to engage in *tikkun olam* (perfecting the world). This is totally compatible with feminism. Then there is the democratic message of monotheism—we all share the same God and come from the same place.

Finally it is possible to look at certain constructs which on the surface seem to be inimical to equality and see them as being grounded in feminist concerns like empathy in relationships. Marcia Falk has suggested the potential of Shabbat, which has separate categories of work and rest; and kashrut, separation of milk and meat, to be originally anchored in a concern for humanity and the environment. She writes that "as feminist theory applies

---

[46] Rebecca Trachtenberg Alpert, "Sisterhood is Ecumenical: Bridging the Gap between Jewish and Christian Feminists," *Response: A Contemporary Jewish Review* XIV: 2 (Spring 1984): 12-13.

[47] In *B. Sotah* 20a there is a debate between R. Eliezer and Ben Azzai about whether women need to study, should be encouraged to study or should be barred from study altogether. Ben Azzai states that a father should teach his daughter Torah so that if she has to drink [of the bitter waters testing to see if she is an adultress] she may know that the merit suspends the effect. Rabbi Eliezer says that whoever teaches his daughter Torah teaches her nonsense or obscenity [*tiflut*]. The debate is not whether she should be taught at all, but how much. Should women's education be based on need to know, i.e., enough to lead a proper Jewish life, or should they be taught the underlying meanings and reasons of Jewish law?

[48] Attributed to Hillel (*B. Shabbat* 31a).

itself to Jewish culture, it need not argue against the maintenance of all ideas and practices that separate Jews from other peoples. Rather, it ought to distinguish between those rituals which hierarchize a 'self-group' in relation to 'other-groups,' and those which affirm meaningful differences and appropriate boundaries in the world." Thus she argues that not all "dualistic separations built into Jewish rituals" are necessarily harmful. She feels that we can choose what to keep, what to let fall by the wayside, what to re-create so that they "reflect our experiences as women and our values as feminist Jews." [49]

In the articles in this section I hope that I have exemplified the possibilities of making Judaism compatible with feminism. Often my choice is conscious, but sometimes I take it for granted. My approach to the Hebrew Bible has been affected by and has emerged out of struggle with, feminist thought. No doubt the Jewishness of my choice is in conflict with my feminism (or vice versa) and both directly affect my interpretation of text. Often the spark of an idea has come from reading the text in a religious setting and may therefore fuel the passion with which I read the text. This is certainly the case with both the articles on Hosea's Wife and Lamentations.

Among the Jewish/Feminist women (men*) who have informed my thinking are the theologians Ellen Umansky, Judith Plaskow, Rachel Adler, Naomi Goldenberg, Michael Graetz*; the Bible scholars Tikvah Frymer-Kensky, Athalyah Brenner, Adele Berlin, Carole L. Meyers, Mayer I. Gruber*, Susan Niditch, Marc Brettler*; the midrashists Aviva Gottlieb Zornberg, Mary Gendler, Adrien Janis Bledstein, Savina J. Teubal, Devora Steinmetz, Jill Hammer, Arthur Waskow*, Judith R. Baskin; and those who take a literary approach such as Nehama Aschkenazy, Esther Fuchs, Ilona Rashkow, Alice Bach, Ilana Pardes, Lori Lefkowitz.

Some of the topics that are dealt with in this section are hierarchy and its patriarchal assumptions, both female and male metaphors of God, woman as other, the suffering and self-sacrifice of women, positive and negative role models, and the ambivalence of women's legal status.

---

[49] Marcia Falk, T. Drorah Setel, et al, "Roundtable: Feminist Reflections on Separation and Unity in Jewish Theology," *Journal of Feminist Studies* 2:1 (1986): 122-123.

The following are different approaches to the biblical text that many Jewish feminists take in treating the topics mentioned above. They are not necessarily mine, but should be noted.

The so-called scholarly, objective, *Wissenschaft* approaches of source and form criticism, that is, the historical methods of research, are less in fashion today than was once the case, although the influence lingers on. James Crenshaw goes as far to write: "A purely historical analysis of the literature cannot yield satisfactory results. Efforts to specify dates for biblical books are doomed…no satisfactory history of the literature can be written…every indication points to extremely active editorial work in updating ancient traditions."[50]

There are many who use archaeology and philology, the offspring tools of the historical approach. There are those who also engage in apologetics as a polemic against the scholarly historical approach and more recently against the feminist critique.

What is in vogue is synchronic paradigms of study which view the "Bible as a contained system of structurally related components."[51] Greenstein identifies three reasons for its attractiveness to the modern reader. 1) "It interprets what we have—rather than a reconstructed version of it… [And] many feel more comfortable with the received text."[52] 2) "We find the sense of a text…to be more significant or fuller by studying it in terms of its shape and function than by studying its historical evolution." 3) "Its practice requires fewer accessory disciplines than historical investigation. That is, one does not have to be as well educated in languages, scripts, archaeology, history and historiography, textual criticism, and comparative Semitic philology to analyze the biblical text within a synchronic paradigm… In order to perform synchronic analysis on the Bible one needs know only Hebrew, or even no Hebrew at all."[53] More importantly, Greenstein points out the authoritarian or hierarchical view of those who use the historical method. The synchronic approach is more democratic

---

[50] James L. Crenshaw, *Story and Faith: A Guide to the Old Testament* (New York: Macmillan, 1986): 2.

[51] Edward L. Greenstein, "Biblical Studies in a State," in Shaye J. D. Cohen and Edward L. Greenstein (eds.), *The State of Jewish Studies* (Detroit MI: Wayne State University Press, 1990): 34.

[52] Idem: 35.

[53] Idem: 35-36.

and its more egalitarian political agenda includes both the teacher and student engaged in a common quest to understand text and not engage in academic one-upmanship.

Some of the approaches which follow from this are structural anthropology;[54] literary criticism;[55] the psychoanalytical approach to text;[56] narratology;[57] a midrashic approach to text, including both exegesis and eisegesis;[58] a radical feminist approach with the goal of overthrowing patriarchy;[59] and finally deconstructionism, the postmodern approach to text versus the belief in a determinate, fixed and univocal meaning of text.[60]

There are still those who engage in the literal reading of text, who see text as revelation and therefore authoritative.

THE MANY ROLES OF WOMEN IN THE BIBLE

Biblical women interact, converse with and pray to God. They include Eve, Sarah, Hannah, Manoah's Wife, and Miriam. Yet women are clearly the other. They are behind the *parochet* (curtain)! Does the covenant apply to women? Were women at Mt. Sinai? Women are often expected to make self-sacrifice and to live for others. In addition they are often cast in the roles of immigrants and displaced persons who follow their husbands; victims of abuse:

---

[54] Edmund Leach and D. Alan Aycock, *Structuralist Interpretations of Biblical Myth* (Cambridge UK: Cambridge University Press, 1983) following in the footsteps of Claude Levi-Strauss.

[55] Robert Alter, *The Art of Biblical Narrative* (New York: Basic Books, 1981).

[56] Ilona N. Rashkow, *Taboo or Not Taboo: The Hebrew Bible and Human Sexuality* (Minneapolis: Fortress Press, 2000).

[57] Mieke Bal, *Narratology: Introduction to the Theory of Narrative* (Toronto: University of Toronto Press, 1985), *On Story-Telling: Essays in Narratology*, David Jobling (ed.), (Sonoma, CA: Polebridge, 1991); J. Cheryl Exum, *Tragedy and Biblical Narrative: Arrows of the Almighty* (Cambridge: Cambridge University Press, 1992).

[58] See e.g., David Stern, *Parables in Midrash: Narrative and Exegesis in Rabbinic Literature.* (Cambridge, MA: Harvard University Press, 1991).

[59] Naomi Goldenberg, *Changing of the Gods: Feminism & the End of Traditional Religions* (Boston: Beacon Press, 1979) and Judith Plaskow, *Standing Again at Sinai: Judaism from a Feminist Perspective* (San Francisco: Harper & Row, 1990).

[60] Daniel Boyarin, "Reading Androcentrism Against the Grain: Women, Sex, and Torah-Study." *Poetics Today* 12 (1991): 29-53.

rape; incest, neglect. In the book of Lamentations and some of the prophets, the suffering woman is an exemplum of the people Israel. Characters who are known for their suffering include Rachel, Hannah, Hagar, both Tamars.

The issues concerning women of the Bible most discussed by feminist writers include role models, both negative (witches, widows, temptresses) and positive (leaders, warriors, prophets, mourners, cultic leaders). Often there is an ambivalent attitude to them as in the cases of the witch of En Dor or tricksters. There are many images of woman who misbehave sexually (the Sotah, Bat Sheva), who worship foreign gods (Queen Athalyah), who are temptresses (Delilah), who are clearly negative role models. Positive women include the "woman of valor" in the Book of Proverbs; the daughters of Zelophad (Book of Numbers). Then there are some ambivalent role models for Jewish feminists which include Esther, Deborah, Miriam, Vashti, Eve—and have feminists writing on both sides of the fence about them.

Some of the most discussed women are those whose status is by virtue of their relationship to others. They have no intrinsic worth of their own. They are sisters, daughters, wives, grandmothers, widows; they include Ruth and Naomi; the *imahot* (mothers); Leah and Rachel; Jeptah's Daughter; Elisheba. Often they do not have names of their own or a genealogy. If they are identified, they are often referred to as the wife of, as opposed to the daughter of (e.g., Lot's wife, Manoach's wife or Deborah, Lapidot's Wife).

The bottom line of women's legal status is that they have to be controlled: They can be bought and sold; their status is conferred by marriage; by their virginity. They are sex objects; concubines. They are pure or impure. They can be divorced; if widowed, they may have to be released from a levirate marriage. They are in a *koy* state (see Judith Romney Wegner)[61]: neither animal nor fully human.

Is there a way to summarize what the State of the Art is and what is necessary for the future? Because of the demands of academic research, constraints have been put upon feminists to be

---

[61] For elaboration on this term, see Judith Romney Wegner, *Chattel or Person? The Status of Women in the Mishnah* (New York: Oxford University Press, 1988): 7-8, and "Tragelaphos Revisited: The Anomaly of Woman in the Mishnah," *Judaism* 37 (1988): 160-172.

objective. Therefore a communication gap exists between those in academia and those who are able to be more creative, revolutionary, and activist-oriented because of their "independent" status. It seems that some institutions are allowing and encouraging creative efforts and thus the future is open-ended. In my work I have always tried to relate to both by combining feminist critique with references to alternative midrashic solutions and interpretations. The next four articles in this volume can serve as exemplars to this approach.

DINAH THE DAUGHTER

It is safe to generalize that in all patriarchal societies, daughters are less valuable than sons. In such societies, daughters have value primarily on the marriage market and in their potential to bear children.[62]

The daughter's monetary value is a function of her sexual purity. If she violates the sexual code by losing her virginity prior to marriage, this transgression constitutes a loss of face to the family. Therefore the father's primary responsibility is to protect his daughter in his home. It would seem that the daughter is a burden to her father in all matters relating to her sexuality because of the potential threat it poses to the family's honor.

It is understandable why fathers and brothers breathe a sigh of relief when their daughters and sisters are safely married and off their hands. The only acceptable role for a girl is wife and mother, whereas "daughter" is a temporary and dangerous status.

This describes well the attitude in the biblical period. There are many daughters mentioned in the Book of Genesis, but the only one to retain the permanent status of daughter, who never marries or has children, is Dinah. When an individual woman such as Dinah acts contrary to the role expected of her by society, there are surface irregularities or loose ends in the text. This anomaly can be corrected through the process of interpretation, or midrash.

I plan to show how interpretation is an on-going process, utilizing five biblical sources relating directly and indirectly to the case of Dinah from the specific vantage point of Dinah as a victim. Then I will go on to look at two different post-biblical attitudes towards daughters in general, before moving on to show rabbinical attitudes toward Dinah. Finally, I will conclude by mentioning

---

[62] Nancy Williamson, "Daughter Preference," *Sons or Daughters: A Cross-Cultural Survey of Parental Preferences* (Beverly Hills, CA: Sage Publications, 1976): 103-105.

several modern interpretations which focus on Dinah as a subject, not as an object.

In the Book of Genesis there are two sources in which the treatment of Dinah is ambivalent. It begins with the very description surrounding the circumstances of her birth. The phrase *wattahar watteled* ("she conceived and bore") and an explanation of their names accompanies the description of the birth of each of Dinah's brothers—Jacob's twelve sons. But when Dinah's origin is accounted for, the text reads merely as follows: "Lastly, [Leah] bore him a daughter, and named her Dinah" (Gen 30.21). Was she conceived? What is the source of her name? The Bible chooses not to say.

This ambivalence continues in the tale of Dinah herself, who was raped[63] by Shechem. Shechem, son of Ḥamor, fell in love with Dinah after he had raped her and wanted to have her hand in marriage. Jacob's immediate reaction is silence; he waits for his sons to return from the fields. The brothers reaction is anger since Shechem "had committed an outrage (*nevala*) in Israel by lying with Jacob's daughter—a thing not to be done" (Gen 34.7). But both Jacob and the brothers agreed, on condition that Shechem and all the townspeople of Shechem were circumcised. However, on the third day when the Shechemites were hurting from the circumcision, Simeon and Levi killed the defenseless men and laid waste to the town. In response to their act of violence, Jacob said: "You have brought trouble on me, making me odious among the inhabitants of the land" (Gen 34.30), thus implying that they had "muddied" his heretofore clean reputation.[64] The brothers' answer

---

[63] Ariella Deem, "The Goddess Anath and Some Biblical Hebrew Cruces," *Journal of Semitic Studies* 23:1 (1978): 25-30, shows that *innah* in certain contexts means rape (cf. Judg 19.24; 20.5; 2 Sam 13.12, 14, 22, 32; Ezek 22.11; Lam 5.11). See, however, Moshe Weinfeld, *Deuteronomy and the Deuteronomic School* (Oxford: Clarendon Press, 1972) who disagrees, writing that *innah* in piel form in the passages cited above may "connote sexual intercourse in general rather than rape" (286). However, in a footnote, he concedes that *innah* might refer to sexual intercourse which involves "an element of imposition upon the woman. It might then still refer to seduction" (286, n. 5).

[64] cf. *Gen. Rabba* 80:12: *And Jacob said to Simeon and Levi: 'Ye have troubled me'* (34.30). The Rabbis commented: The vat was clear, and ye have muddied it... R. Judah b. Simon said: [They answered]: 'The vat was

to Jacob is in the form of a rhetorical question: "Should our sister be treated like a whore?" (Gen 34.31). The message is that our sister is not to be "made" (*ya a seh*) into an object of scorn. The text, which does not explicitly criticize the brothers for their violent act of revenge or Jacob for being a silent father, is left wide open to interpretation.

The two direct sources on Dinah (Gen 30 and 34) are highlighted by three additional intertexts. Jacob has the last word in our third source—his deathbed scene—when he says:

> Simeon and Levi are a pair; their weapons are tools of lawlessness... When angry they slay men, And when pleased they maim oxen. Cursed be their anger so fierce... I will divide them in Jacob, Scatter them in Israel (Gen 49.5-7).

This passage is usually understood by most exegetes to be a commentary on the episode in Genesis 34.

The Bible's attitude to such a story is more explicit in our fourth source: The Book of Deuteronomy. In contrast to the law pertaining to the seduction of an unbetrothed virgin in Exodus 22.15-16, whose object is "to protect the financial interests of the father," the author of Deuteronomy is "concerned with rectifying the moral and personal wrong committed against the maiden."[65]

> 28) If a man comes upon a virgin who is not engaged and he seizes her and lies with her, and they are discovered, 29) the man who lay with her shall pay the girl's father fifty <shekels of> silver, and she shall be his wife. Because he has violated her, he can never have the right to divorce her (Deut 22.28-29).

The seducer pays the father the money as a fine for violating the virgin, not as compensation to the father.

---

muddied, and we have purified it.' *And They Said: 'Should One Deal With Our Sister As With A Harlot?'* (34.31) 'Will they treat us as common property,' they exclaimed. What caused all this? The fact that 'Dinah went out' (34.1)." See further on this below.

[65] Moshe Weinfeld, *Deuteronomy and the Deuteronomic School* (Oxford: Clarendon Press, 1972) 284-285.

Shechem was willing to obey the law of the land as decreed by Mesopotamian legal sources.[66] He behaved according to the norms in his willingness to marry Dinah. The brothers, according to The Book of Deuteronomy, interfered with his obligation to marry her and were wrong to cut off her only chance of marriage. The law of Deuteronomy can thus be considered an internal commentary on the story of Dinah.

The fifth intertext addresses itself in circuitous fashion to Dinah's plight. The commentary—the story of Amnon and Tamar in 2 Samuel 13—is expressed by the recognition of linguistic analogies. The story is similar to Dinah's except that the rapist is Tamar's half-brother, David's son Amnon. Amnon pretends to be sick and refuses to eat unless Tamar feeds him. When he gets her alone he tells her to lie with him. She refuses, saying: "Don't brother. Don't force me. Such things are not done in Israel! Don't do such a vile thing (*nevala*)! Where will I hide my shame?"(2 Sam 13.12-14).

In clear contrast to Shechem, who fell in love with Dinah after he had raped her and wanted her for his wife, Amnon cannot stand the sight of Tamar after the rape and tells her to get out. Unlike Dinah—who has no personality of her own whatsoever in the biblical text, and is not heard from at the time of the rape (or after, for that matter)—Tamar pleads: "Please don't commit this wrong; to send me away would be even worse than the first wrong you committed against me" (2 Sam 13.16). But he kicks her out and she goes away screaming hysterically, dramatically tearing her tunic and putting dust on her head as a sign of mourning. Her brother Absalom keeps his hate to himself until it later explodes in an act of murder, in contrast to the immediate devastation which Simeon and Levi visit on the town of Shechem.

The parallels are clear: Tamar's anguished reaction (using the word *nevala* [outrage] and almost identical wording of the brothers in Genesis) makes it clear that the narrator wants us to think she was aware of Dinah's fate, one which she did not want to be her own. The story takes into account the pain a woman feels at being raped and the indignity of being thrown out. Yet, despite the echo

---

[66] J. J. Finkelstein, "Sex Offenses in Sumerian Laws," *Journal of the American Oriental Society* 86 (1966) writes "Midrashic authors were fully sensitive to the overtones of the verb *yasa* in the Dinah story, as their amplifications of it clearly show" (note, 363).

of her screams, Tamar, daughter of David, is not heard from again in the Bible—just like her counterpart, Dinah, daughter of Jacob. Finally, the two stories feature two daughters, and their two fathers who failed in their primary responsibility to protect their daughters from harm.

Before we look at what the rabbis of the third century had to say about Dinah the daughter and Jacob her father, it is worth looking at Ben Sira's view of daughters and fathers.

Ben Sira's work "Ecclesiasticus" was written in 180 BCE. It is part of the apocryphal literature which did not enter the canonized Jewish and Protestant versions of the Old Testament. However, despite the rabbinic ban on his work,[67] the rabbinic commentators knew it well and quoted him extensively. Ben Sira singles out all that is negative about women and spews it out in concentrated form. The worst examples of his personal negative bias against women have to do with daughters.

> [9]A daughter is a secret cause of sleeplessness to her father, and his concern for her robs him of his rest; in her youth, for fear she will pass her prime, and when she is married, for fear she will be hated.

> [10]When she is a girl, for fear she will be profaned, and be with child in her father's house; when she has a husband, for fear she will transgress; and when she is married, for fear she will be childless.

> [11]Keep a close watch over a headstrong daughter, for fear she will fill your enemies with malignant joy, and make you the talk of the town and notorious among the people, and disgrace you before the multitude. In the spot where she lodges let there be no window, or place overlooking the entrance round about.

> [12]Let her not expose her beauty to any male, and let her not take counsel among women.

---

[67] R. Akiva in particular. cf. the debate in the Babylonian Talmud, *Sanh.* 100b. Adin Steinsaltz, in his commentary on the tractate *Hagiga* (13a, p. 58), writes that despite the fact that the rabbis considered Ben Sira's book apocryphal, they quoted it at length and viewed it with distinction. Some even considered it part of The Writings. According to Steinsaltz it was excluded from the canon because it was often confused with the Alphabet of Ben Sira, a popular book of the time.

¹³For from the garment comes the moth, and from a woman comes a woman's wickedness.

¹⁴Better is the wickedness of a man than the goodness of a woman, and a daughter causes fear regarding disgrace more than a son (Ecclesiasticus or The Wisdom of Sirach 42.9-14).[68]

In a similar vein, Ben Sira writes elsewhere: "Do you have daughters? Protect their body, but do not let your face shine upon them" (7.24). This advice serves as a reminder of "the ancient reality that a daughter's marketability as a wife and her virginity were unquestionably related."[69] Daughters are nothing but trouble. Ben Sira is equally explicit in another passage, when he complains that: "A daughter is born to [the father's] loss... She who disgraces is a grief to him who begot her" (22.3-4). The worst thing she can do is cause her father public disgrace by surrendering her virginity or becoming pregnant while unmarried, for then he will lose face before his enemies. His reputation, like Jacob's, will become tarnished.

Had Ben Sira presumed to give advice to Dinah's father, he no doubt would have told him to guard her to the extent that she not have a room with windows—to prevent others from looking in. A daughter who deliberately exposes her beauty is guilty of seductive behavior. On the other hand, if she accidentally exposes herself, she might be raped. Therefore a father must do all he can to avoid being disgraced.

In a midrash, whose context is "when man began to multiply and daughters were born to them" (Gen 6.1), we can see that Ben Sira is part and parcel of a long line of tradition.

> The wife of R. Simeon b. Rabbi gave birth to a daughter. When R. Ḥiyya the Elder met him, he said to him: "God has begun to bless you."... When R. Simeon went to his father he asked him, "Did the

---

[68] The first half of the text is from Edgar J. Goodspeed, *The Apocrypha: An American Translation* (New York: Vintage Books, 1959): 306-307. From verses 11-14 the translation is from Trenchard, see footnote 69 below. Goodspeed does not include the lines about the window.

[69] Warren Trenchard, "Woman as Daughter," *Ben Sira's View of Women: A Literary Analysis* (Chico, CA: Brown Judaic Studies 38, 1982): 131-132 and 129-166 for a detailed discussion of his translation.

Babylonian [R. Ḥiyya] congratulate you?" "Yes," he answered, "and he said thus to me." "Nevertheless," he [Rabbi] observed, "both wine and vinegar are needed, yet wine is more needed than vinegar; both wheat and barley are needed, yet wheat is more needed than barley. When a man gives his daughter in marriage and incurs expense he says to her, 'May you never return hither'" (*Gen. Rabba*, 26:4).[70]

The message is clear: daughters are less valuable than sons. Fathers breathe sighs of collective relief only after their daughters are safely married, out of their homes and preoccupied with children.

We have seen the attitude of Ben Sira and Rabbi[71] towards daughters in general. Let us look at the next midrash and see what is its attitude to Jacob's daughter.

Most of our midrashim use the following phrases as their prooftext:

Dinah, the daughter whom Leah had born to Jacob, [*went out* to visit] the daughters of the land. Shechem son of Hamor the Hivite, chief of the country, saw her, and took her and lay with her by force (Gen 34.1-2).

Since girls of marriageable age did not normally "go out" to visit friends in the city, it is possible that the text itself criticizes Dinah's behavior by using the verbal stem *ytz*, "to go out," which has a long history of implying promiscuity.[72] One can read into Dinah's unconventional behavior a desire for freedom or self-fulfillment that is alien to the times and threatening to the patriarchal structure of biblical society.

Despite the possible undertone of disapproval of the text towards Dinah's behavior, there are a sizeable number of rabbinic commentators who are uncertain whether Dinah was responsible for the act. There are those rabbis (influenced by Ben Sira perhaps) who assumed the worst—namely that she was guilty of deliberate exposure and, therefore, of her own seduction. Then there are

---

[70] All English translations are from H. Freedman and M. Simon (eds.), *Midrash Rabba* (London: Soncino Press, 1983).

[71] 'Rabbi' is Rabbi Yehuda ha-Nasi, the Patriarch.

[72] For more on this see J. J. Finkelstein, "Sex Offenses in Sumerian Laws," *Journal of the American Oriental Society* 86 (1966): n. 59.

those who assumed she accidentally exposed herself and was raped. Both groups of rabbis follow the legal argument in Deuteronomy, in which there is a clear distinction between a woman who protests her rape and one who does not.

> ²³In the case of a virgin who is engaged to a man—if a man comes upon her in town and lies with her, ²⁴you shall take the two of them out to the gate of that town and stone them to death: the girl because she did not cry for help in the town, and the man because he violated his neighbor's wife. Thus you will sweep away evil from your midst. ²⁵But if the man comes upon the engaged girl in the open country and the man lies with her by force, only the man who lay with her shall die, ²⁶but you shall do nothing to the girl. The girl did not incur the death penalty, for this case is like that of a man attacking another and murdering him. ²⁷He came upon her in the open; though the engaged girl cried for help, there was no one to save her (Deut 22.23-27).

A woman who is raped in town, where one can prove whether she cried out, has to be judged according to the criteria of her having cried out or not. A woman who does not cry out for help is assumed not to have been raped. However, a woman who is raped in the country cannot prove whether she cried out, thus is presumed innocent. Those rabbis who see Dinah as going out to see the big city of Shechem made negative comments about her which state that "she went out..."(Gen 34.1) and got what she deserved. You can see instances of this trend below:

> And whoso breaketh through a fence, a serpent shall bite him: i.e. Dinah. While her father and brothers were sitting in the House of Study, she went out to see the daughters of the land (Gen 34.1). She brought upon herself her violation by Shechem the son of Hamor the Hivite, who is called a serpent and he bit her... (*Eccl. Rabba* 10:8).

> And Dinah the daughter of Leah went out (34.1) Behold, everyone that useth proverbs shall use this proverb against thee, saying: "As the mother, so her daughter" (Ezek 16.44)... Resh Lakish asks Kahana: "What is really the meaning of this verse?" "A cow does not gore unless her calf kicks; a woman is not immoral until her daughter is immoral," he replied. "If

so," said he, "then our mother Leah was a harlot!"
"Even so," he replied: "because it says, 'And Leah went
out to meet him' (Gen 30.16), which means that she
went out to meet him adorned like a harlot"; therefore
"And Dinah the daughter of Leah went out (*Gen. Rabba*
80:1).

Most rabbis do not follow the view that daughters deliberately
expose themselves when they go out and are therefore asking for it.
There is a second group of rabbis—who are not convinced it was
her fault, because they see her as one who was raped in the
countryside. They see her as one who accidentally exposed herself
to Shechem, and thus they have second thoughts about Dinah's
fate. These rabbis have her resurfacing as the mother of Asenath,
who is adopted by Potiphar and then marries Joseph. There are
midrashim that have Dinah married to her brother. According to
Ginzberg who retells the story:

> Dinah bore her brother a son and from her union with
> Shechem sprang a daughter, Asenath by name,
> afterward the wife of Joseph. When this daughter was
> born to Dinah, her brothers wanted to kill her, that the
> finger of men might not point at the fruit of sin. But
> Jacob took a piece of tin, inscribed the Holy Name
> upon it, and bound it about the neck of the girl, and he
> put her under a thorn-bush and abandoned her there.
> An angel carried the babe down to Egypt, where
> Potiphar adopted her as his child, for his wife was
> barren. Years later, when Joseph was viceroy, the
> maidens threw gifts at him to make him look at them.
> Asenath had nothing that would serve as a present, so
> she took off the amulet from her neck and gave it to
> him. Thus Joseph became acquainted with her lineage,
> and he married her, seeing that she was not an
> Egyptian, but one connected with the house of Jacob
> through his mother.[73]

Alternatively, these rabbis with second thoughts have Dinah
turning up as Job's wife (*Gen. Rabba* 57:4), and also have created a

---

[73] Louis Ginzberg, *The Legends of the Jews* (Philadelphia: Jewish
Publication Society, 1909, 1968): vol. 2: 38. Ginzberg's retelling of the tale
is a composite version of many midrashim. The sources of this retelling
are available in his very detailed footnote in vol. 5: 336-337.

midrash where she is betrothed to her own brother Simeon (*Gen. Rabba* 80:11).

One might ask why the second group of rabbis needed to stray so far from the text. My conjecture is that these rabbis had misgivings. Perhaps they thought she was innocent and had an uneasy conscience about her fate. Thus by filling in the gaps—the silence of the biblical text—these rabbis accounted for Dinah's whereabouts and destiny after the rape. In doing so they supply the tale with closure or a prototype "happy ending."

We have seen that there are two ways to view Dinah's fate. One blames her for "going out"; the other views her as pure victim. The midrash reflects the values of its time. On the one hand there was the historical necessity which dictated that women remain locked in a role of stereotypical passivity. This role was dictated by the genuine concern of a people whose physical and spiritual survival was at stake. Rabbis were (and still are) a product of their society's conditioning, and "could not conceive of any alternatives for women."[74] Theirs was a social reality in which "women [were] inferior to men in economic power, social standing, legal rights, and religious role and importance."[75] Thus they glorified the mother-wife role, and denigrated any signs of female initiative or other deviations from the norms of the period. This attitude continues to prevail in some circles in our supposedly modern society.[76] Traditionalists continue to depict negatively those women who are interested in self-fulfillment.[77] They do not encourage individual expression. Collective survival is still their overriding concern.[78] In contrast, the secularists claim not to need tradition at all, scoffing at those who reject modernity.

What should be our attitude towards the text? There is another religious position in Judaism, which "recognizes no

---

[74] Linda Kuzmack, "Aggadic Approaches to Biblical Women," Elizabeth Koltun (ed.), *The Jewish Woman: New Perspectives* (New York: Schocken Books, 1976): 251.

[75] Rachel Biale, *Women and Jewish Law* (New York: Schocken Books, 1984): 14.

[76] Moshe Meiselman, *Jewish Woman in Jewish Law* (New York: Ktav Publishing House, 1978).

[77] Ruth Wisse, "The Feminist Mystery," *The Jerusalem Report* (January 9, 1992).

[78] David Bleich, "Halakha as an Absolute," *Judaism* 29 (1980): 30-37.

stratification of human beings, no inferiority of women to men...
In ultimate moral and spiritual terms Judaism recognizes that a
woman's life is equal to a man's."[79] If we accept this viewpoint and
agree that physical and spiritual survival no longer dictate that
women fulfill stereotypical roles, the social role ascribed to women
has to be revised.

Feminists reflect these views, and seem to be divided into two
camps. A view which is similar to the secularist viewpoint is the
ascendancy view of feminism. It aims "primarily at exposing the
androcentric bias or oppressive intention operative within a text, to
show the text to be unalterably patriarchal and, therefore, without
authority or value."[80] In its confrontation with tradition the
ascendancy view throws out the baby with the bath water.

Then there is the apologetic or equality position which
attempts "to highlight the social, religious, and political power of
women which has been ignored, overlooked, or hidden by
patriarchal hermeneutics."[81] This approach bridges the traditional
male-oriented and the secularist viewpoints.

My position as a religious feminist Jew is that we have the
obligation to write women back into the tradition by continuing the
process of midrash, which insures that the Bible remains relevant
to all its readers.

I refuse to accept the extreme position of a feminist who is so
locked into the ascendancy view that she criticizes "a modern
biblical scholar" for not considering Dinah's rape and the
destruction of the town of Shechem equally heinous crimes. Judith
Ochshorn asks:

> Is the rape of a woman not a "heinous crime," and was
> Dinah not also helpless? Do the friendships and pacts
> among men assume greater moral weight than sexual
> violence committed against women? Is the sense of
> outrage over the rape of Dinah insufficient provocation
> for her brothers's anger? Are the lives and integrity of

---

[79] Rachel Biale, *Women and Jewish Law* (New York: Shocken Books, 1984): 14.

[80] Mary Ann Tolbert, "Defining the Problem: The Bible and Feminist Hermeneutics," *Semeia* 28 (1983): 119.

[81] Idem.

women dispensable and subordinate to the alliances among men?[82]

She implies that one woman's rape justified the wholesale killing of an entire town. In saying this she follows in the tradition of her namesake, Judith, a radical feminist of the second century BCE who glorified Simeon's and Levi's deed as an act of pious retribution (Book of Judith 9.2ff.).

What about Dinah? Is she only an object—to be used to make a point? By whom? By traditionalists? By extreme feminists? Does no one care about her pain? None of the traditional midrashim takes into account what Dinah the daughter thinks about her plight.

Most modern Jewish feminists have chosen to avoid this story for a good reason.[83] To them, Dinah symbolizes "the radical separation of women from the mainstream of Jewish life; the silence of women; woman as sexual commodity."[84]

In 1985, during a professional crisis, I turned to the story of Dinah for solace. To effect a "self-cure" and distance myself from my own plight, I wrote a modern eisegetical tale[85] about Dinah describing my feelings of betrayal by the institution for which I had worked for 10 years. These feelings, I later discovered, were identical to those shared by some victims of injustice. These

---

[82] Judith Ochshorn, "Sex Roles and the Relation of Power to Gender: Biblical Narratives," *The Female Experience and the Nature of the Divine* (Bloomington, IN: Indiana University Press, 1981): 207.

[83] In an unpublished paper delivered at the First Jerusalem International Conference on Women and Judaism: Halakha and the Jewish Woman (1986), I reviewed several twentieth century sources on Dinah, written for the most part by men. At this conference I also publicized my tale about Dinah "A Daughter in Israel is Raped" which appears in Naomi Graetz, *S/He Created Them: Feminist Retellings of Biblical Stories* (Piscataway, NJ: Gorgias Press, 2003): 69-72.

[84] Jeffrey Salkin, "Dinah, the Torah's Forgotten Woman," *Judaism* (Summer, 1986): 289.

[85] Since then, there has been a great interest in Dinah. Women are now confident enough to face this story and build on it. cf. Deena Metzger, *What Dinah Thought* (New York: Viking Penguin, 1989); Ellen M. Umansky, "Beyond Androcentrism: Feminist Challenges to Judaism," *Journal of Reform Judaism* (Winter 1990): 25-35; Anita Diamant, *The Red Tent* (New York: Picador USA, 1997); Phyllis Chesler, "The Rape of Dina: On the Torah Portion of *VaYishlah*," *Nashim* 3 (2000): 232-248.

feelings were of a person "who no longer shared a sense of control...[who]...had become uncertain about her ability to control her environment and to care for herself in it..." Ironically this quotation comes from an article entitled "Rape: A Family Crisis."[86] What Dinah and I shared is silence.

I wondered whether Dinah's [and my] silence was really a stifled scream. Are we women so traumatized that we are unable to speak up for our rights? Would I, the victim of circumstance, have behaved differently if I were a man?

I depicted a Dinah who tried to shrink into herself, for she did not trust her environment. Her life had been ruined by the rape since women who did not marry in biblical times usually had no other options for self-fulfillment. Her parents betrayed her; her brothers killed the only person she could marry—a man who clearly loved her and repented his violent act. Her body was no longer hers. Despite her despair, she concluded her woeful tale with (what to me at least was) a rhetorical question. Dinah asked, "Do I want to be left alone to sit on the sidelines of life? Forever?"[87]

Since I wrote this midrash, several other midrashim have been published about Dinah. The purpose inherent in these revisionings is to inspire our daughters who may still be sitting silently and patiently on the sidelines of Jewish life, waiting for external forces to liberate them:

> Unlike the biblical Dina, growing numbers of Jewish feminists are refusing to remain silent. If we are to create, or attempt to create, a non-patriarchal, non-androcentric Judaism—a Judaism in which the experiences of both women and men are seen as central—we Jewish women need to reclaim our voices. In so doing, we need to imagine what our foremothers, like Dina, might have said, if only they had spoken.[88]

---

[86] Leslie Feinauer, "Rape: A Family Crisis," *The American Journal of Family Therapy* 10:4 (1982): 35.

[87] Naomi Graetz, "The Rape," *Genesis Retold: Aggadot on Sefer B'reshit* (Beersheba: Schichpul Press of Ben Gurion University, 1985): 78.

[88] Ellen M. Umansky, "Beyond Androcentrism: Feminist Challenges to Judaism," *Journal of Reform Judaism* (Winter 1990): 33.

Rather than decry "the patriarchal structure of the Bible—we should attempt a reading that penetrates beneath the surface to uncover the awareness that the biblical narrator was either not fully conscious of or took pains not to reveal..."[89] Readers such as these tend to view Dinah in a different light. They do not see her as a "passive, submissive woman who was raped, crushed, and marked for the rest of her life."[90] Dinah's story has the potential to demonstrate that liberation must come from within, often after great suffering and struggle; that although our past influences us, it neither governs us nor permanently cripples us. Our past is a far more "liberating environment than the pseudo-past created by male-chauvinist mythographers who invoked a past that never was."[91]

---

[89] Nechama Aschkenasy, "A Non-Sexist Reading of the Bible," *Midstream* (June/July 1981): 51.

[90] Ita Sheres, "The Other Story: The Unredacted Version," *Dinah's Rebellion: A Biblical Parable for our Time* (New York:: Crossroads, 1990): 136.

[91] Personal communication conveyed to me by Professor Mayer Gruber of the Bible Department at Ben Gurion University.

DID MIRIAM TALK TOO MUCH?

At the beginning of Numbers 12 we read: "Miriam and Aaron spoke against Moses because of the Cushite woman he had married…" (Num 12.1). The Rabbis wonder why the Hebrew word used for "spoke," *wattedabber*, is in the singular form, rather than *wayyedabberu*, in the plural form, since the text says that Miriam and Aaron spoke. They also ask why Miriam, a woman, precedes Aaron, since "ladies first" was not a principle in ancient times. The chapter is problematic, and many questions can be raised upon studying it. First let us consider it:

> ¹When they were in Hazeroth, Miriam and Aaron spoke against Moses because of the Cushite woman he had married: "He married a Cushite woman!" ²They said, "Has the Lord spoken only through Moses? Has He not spoken through us as well?" The Lord heard it. ³Now Moses was a very humble man, more so than any other man on earth. ⁴Suddenly the Lord called to Moses, Aaron, and Miriam, "Come out, you three, to the Tent of Meeting." So the three of them went out. ⁵The Lord came down in a pillar of cloud, stopped at the entrance of the Tent, and called out, "Aaron and Miriam!" The two of them came forward; ⁶And he said, "Hear these My words: When a prophet of the Lord arises among you, I make Myself known to him in a vision, I speak with him in a dream. ⁷Not so with my servant Moses; he is trusted throughout My household. ⁸With him I speak mouth to mouth, plainly and not in riddles, and he beholds the likeness of the Lord. How then did you not shrink from speaking against My servant Moses!" ⁹Still incensed with them, the Lord departed. ¹⁰As the cloud withdrew from the Tent, there was Miriam stricken with snow-white scales! When Aaron turned toward Miriam, he saw that she was stricken with scales [leprosy]. ¹¹And Aaron said to

41

Moses, "O my lord, account not to us the sin which we committed in our folly. [12]Let her [Miriam] not be as one dead, who emerges from his mother's womb with half his flesh eaten away." [13]So Moses cried out to the Lord, saying, "O God, pray heal her!" [14]But the Lord said to Moses, "If her father spat in her face, would she not bear her shame for seven days? Let her be shut out of camp for seven days, and then let her be readmitted." [15]So Miriam was shut out of camp seven days; and the people did not march on until Miriam was readmitted. [16]After that the people set out from Hazeroth and encamped in the wilderness of Paran.[92]

Some of the questions that arise about this text are the following:

1) Who was this Cushite woman to whom Miriam and Aaron referred?

2) Why was Moses silent when accused by Miriam and Aaron?

3) Why did God have to defend Moses' honor in such a drastic way?

4) Why was only Miriam punished and not Aaron?

5) Why leprosy?

6) Does the Bible downplay Miriam's importance to keep the focus on her brother, Moses?

7) Finally, did Miriam and Aaron pose a real threat to Moses?

I suggest that Miriam was punished with leprosy because women in the biblical world were not supposed to be leaders of men, and that women with initiative were reproved when they asserted themselves with the only weapon they had, their power of language: a power which could be used viciously and was, therefore, called *lashon ha-ra*, literally, evil tongue.

Miriam is recalled in Deuteronomy where it is stated: "Remember what the Lord your God did to Miriam on the way as

---

[92] *Tanakh: A New Translation of the Holy Scriptures* (Philadelphia: Jewish Publication Society, 1985).

you came forth out of Egypt" (Deut 24.9). She is "a marked woman, a warning for generations to come," a woman so important "that detractors tabooed her to death, seeking to bury her forever in disgrace."[93] Yet she is also a woman whom the Rabbis chose to see as a positive role model: an advocate of the biblical command to mankind to "be fruitful and multiply," specifically, in criticizing Moses for not having sexual relations with his wife, and in encouraging the Israelite males to marry while in Egypt despite Pharaoh's decrees against Jewish male babies.

EXAMPLES OF PRAISE

First, let us look at the many examples of the Miriam whom the Rabbis admire. One instance is their explication of Numbers 12.14f., where it is written clearly that it was the people who did not journey until Miriam was returned to them. The Rabbis, however, say it was the Lord who waited for her. Not only that, but the "Holy One, blessed be He, said: 'I am a priest, I shut her up and I shall declare her clean'" (*Deut. Rabba* 6:9)! If God, portrayed as a concerned doctor, intervenes in Miriam's case and personally treats her illness, surely it follows that Miriam was someone to be reckoned with.

There are many midrashim which have to do with Miriam's "well," which is said to have been one of the ten things created during the twilight before the first Sabbath of the creation (B. *Pesahim* 54a). One of the few songs of the Bible, an obscure fragment of an ancient poem, is read by many Rabbis as referring to this well:

> Spring up, O well—sing to it—
> The well which the chieftans dug,
> Which the nobles of the people started
> With maces, with their own staffs.
> (Num 21.17-19)

Since the verse, which comes after Miriam's reported death (Num 20.1), is followed by a statement that there was no water for the congregation (20.2), the Rabbis write that Miriam's gift to us after her death was her song, which could cause the waters of her well to flow. The proviso was that the right person had to know

---

[93] Phyllis Trible, "Bringing Miriam Out of the Shadows," *Bible Review* 5/1 (February, 1989): 23.

how to address the well to get it to give water. Moses, who knew
only how to hit the rock, was not that person; clearly a woman's
touch was needed. The Rabbis actually located her well in Tiberias,
opposite the middle gate of an ancient synagogue which lepers go
to in order to be cured (*Deut. Rabba* 6:11).

Miriam is called a prophet in Exodus 15. Though the Bible
does not relate any examples of her prophesies, the Rabbis
interpret the passage "And his sister stood afar off" (Exod 2.4), to
mean that she stood afar "to know what would be the outcome of
her prophecy," because she had told her parents that her "mother
was destined to give birth to a son who will save Israel." That
prophecy, they say, is "the meaning of: 'And Miriam the
prophetess, the sister of Aaron, took a timbrel'" (Exod 15.20).[94]

A fifth midrash concerns the virtuous midwives who saved
the Israelite babies from the wicked Pharoah. The Rabbis decided
that the Hebrew midwives, Shifrah and Puah, were none other than
Yocheved and the very capable five-year-old Miriam. In this same
midrash her father, Amram, is shown as a coward who stopped
having intercourse with his wife, and even divorced her because of
Pharoah's decree to kill the baby boys who were born to the
Israelites. In this story, Miriam pointed out to him that "your
decree is more severe than that of Pharaoh; for Pharoah decreed
only concerning the male children, and you decree upon males and
females alike." As a result, Amram took his wife back, and his
example was followed by all the Israelites (*Lev. Rabba* 17:3). In this
midrash, Miriam is praised for outsmarting her father, and for
encouraging the people to be fruitful and multiply so that they will
survive.

To the Rabbis, Miriam is a perfect role model, except for one
thing; she is not married and does not have any children. So, to fix
that, the midrash explains that the meaning of the passage, "And it
came to pass, because the midwives feared God, that He built them
houses" (Exod 1.21), is that "they were founders of a royal family."
They show that Miriam founded a royal family, with David
descending from her. The genealogy is a bit complex but,
essentially, Miriam marries Caleb, who begets Hur, who has Uri
who begets Bezalel, leading ultimately to King David (*B. Sotah* 12a
and *Exod. Rabba* 1:17).

---

[94] *Deut. Rabba* 6:14.

Many problems are solved by this marriage: Amram's line is continued; Caleb, the faithful spy, is rewarded; and Moses' children (sons of a black woman) are written out of Jewish history. But, most importantly, Miriam is not an anomalous, unmarried, spinster anymore; rather, she is a happily married mother and wife whose offspring brings fame and glory to her. Were it not for the incident when Miriam asserts herself and attacks Moses (God's choice), Miriam would be one of the few women in the Bible about whom the Rabbis have nothing bad to say (*B. Ber.* 19a). That this is not the case we see in the examples of castigation concerning her punishment by leprosy.

EXAMPLES OF CASTIGATION

In Numbers 12, it is not clear who is the Cushite woman, and whether Miriam's case against Moses was just or not. Both she and Aaron claim that God speaks through them as well as through Moses. They both speak up against God's chosen leader. Yet, the popular interpretation is that Miriam was behind it. God, the father figure, reprimands them both, but punishes only Miriam with a skin disease. The fact that Miriam is punished and Aaron is untouched is a discriminatory decision against her, and has the effect of ending Miriam's "legitimate public aspirations."[95]

To see this we must look at the story's textual context, which deals with the people's discontent and their questions concerning authority. We see this in the texts both before and after chapter 12. Chapter 11 depicts the people's popular rebellion based on general dissatisfaction and, in particular, over the boring daily menu of manna. Moses has trouble handling the people and, right after this episode, God tells Moses to share the burden of his leadership with the 70 elders. During this period, when God's spirit has descended on the elders, Eldad and Medad also experience God's spirit and, unlike Aaron's sons (Nadav and Avihu, who were punished with death on a similar occasion), these latter-day prophets (possibly Moses' half-brothers according to one midrash)[96] are rewarded

---

[95] E. R. Zweiback Levenson, "Sexegesis: Miriam in the Desert," *Tikkun* 4/1 (1989): 96.

[96] Devorah Steinmetz, "A Portrait of Miriam in Rabbinic Midrash," *Prooftexts* 8 (1988): 35-65. Eldad and Medad prophesy in the camp in contrast to Moses, who prophesies in the Tent of Meeting.

with Moses' protection and the famous statement, "Would that all the Lord's people were prophets?"

In chapter 13, we read the story of the twelve spies or scouts who went out on a reconnaissance mission to study the Land of Canaan, ten of whom come back with slanderous comments about the Land. The midrash connects the two texts (chapters 12 and 13) in its exposition of the passage: "Send thou men, that they may spy out" (Num 13.2).

> First we read, *And Miriam and Aaron spoke against Moses* (ib. 12, 1) and after that, *Send thou men*. What reason had Scripture for saying, after the incident of Miriam, *Send thou men?* The fact is that the Holy One, blessed be He, foresaw that the spies would utter a slander about the Land. Said the Holy One, blessed be He: "They shall not say, 'We did not know the penalty for slander.'" The Holy One, blessed be He, therefore placed this section next to the other—for Miriam had spoken against her brother and had been smitten with leprosy—in order that all might know the penalty for slander, and that if people were tempted to speak slander they might reflect what had happened to Miriam. Nevertheless the spies did not want to learn (*Num. Rabba* 16:6-7).

It is actually possible to connect the three texts (on Miriam, Eldad, and the spies), since anyone who speaks badly of God or his chosen is guilty of slander. According to the midrash (*Sifre Zuta* 12:1), it is through casual gossip that Miriam finds out from Zipporah, Moses' wife, about the high price (Moses' failure to engage in marital relations) of being married to a public figure and, thus, there is a connection between slander and rebellion. At any rate, there are clearly others besides Miriam who prophesy together with Moses, or criticize him. Some of them are not punished but praised (like Eldad and Medad), while others, like the spies, are punished in that none of them (except for Caleb and Joshua) gets to the Promised Land. But this still does not explain why Miriam, and not Aaron, comes in for most of the criticism.

Let us recall the midrash where Miriam's father, Amram, is portrayed as a coward who stopped having intercourse with his wife, and divorced her after Pharoah's decree to kill all the baby boys born to the Israelites. As a result of Miriam's advice, Amram took his wife back, and his example was followed by all the

Israelites (*Exod. Rabba* 1:13). In this midrash, Miriam was praised for her assertiveness. Yet, in a midrash which has the same theme, and starts by portraying Miriam "as one who is concerned about the observance of the commandments and Jewish survival...,"[97] Miriam is punished for the same act of assertiveness. In this midrash, Zipporah complains to Miriam that, since her husband Moses was chosen by God, he no longer sleeps with her. Miriam consults with her brother, Aaron, and it turns out that although they, too, have received Divine revelations, they—unlike Moses— did not separate themselves from their mates. Furthermore, they claim that Moses abstains to show that he is better than they are and, in Miriam's view, Moses, rather than serving as a "model of the observance of the commandment concerning procreation,"[98] abstains from conjugal joys out of pride.

Why did the Rabbis go along with Miriam in the case of Amram her father, yet punish her here? The Rabbis themselves ask this question. The answer has to do with R. Judah b. Levi's saying:

> Anyone who is so arrogant as to speak against one greater than himself causes the plagues to attack him. And if you do not believe this, look to the pious Miriam as a warning to all slanderers (*Deut. Rabba* 6:9).

In other words, one can stand for procreation as long as one does not attack the leader for not procreating! The leader is different; there are other criteria by which he is to be judged. Devorah Steinmetz argues that the Rabbis excused Moses from the commandment of "be fruitful and multiply"; agreed that it was correct for him to dedicate himself totally to God; and that to be an effective leader he had to separate himself from the people.[99]

That is not Miriam's and Aaron's concept of what leadership should be, and, if one reads the Bible carefully, there are enough hints that Moses' distancing himself from the people may ultimately have been the cause of his downfall. However, the Rabbis do accept the justice of punishment by leprosy, for that is

---

[97] Norman J. Cohen, "Miriam's Song: A Modern Midrashic Reading," *Judaism* 33 (1984): 185.

[98] E. R. Zweiback Levenson, "Sexegesis: Miriam in the Desert," *Tikkun* 4/1 (Jan. Feb, 1989): 96.

[99] Devorah Steinmetz, "A Portrait of Miriam in Rabbinic Midrash," *Prooftexts* 8 (1988): 35-65.

what is ordained for those who speak ill of their neighbors. Presumably it would have been proper, or less objectionable, if Miriam had spoken about her concerns to Moses directly, rather than about him, behind his back.

According to the Rabbis, Aaron became leprous as well, but only for a moment, because his sin was not as great. Why was Aaron's sin not considered as great a sin as Miriam's? Because Miriam was behind it all. On that the Rabbis all seem to agree.[100] The Rabbis explicate the passage, "Miriam and Aaron spoke against Moses..." in such a way that Aaron is a passive accessory rather than an active co-agent. They reason that malicious gossip is to be associated with women, who have nothing better to do with their time, as we see in a very revealing midrash:

> R. Isaac said: It is like the snake that bites everyone who passes by and it is surprising that anyone is willing to associate with it. So Moses said: "Miriam spoke slander against me, that I can understand since women as a rule are talkative..."(Deut. Rabba 6:11).

Another example of this bias against women is the saying of R. Levi:

> Women possess the four following characteristics: they are greedy, inquisitive, envious and indolent... The Rabbis add two more characteristics; they are querulous and gossips. Whence do we know that they are gossips? For it is written, "And Miriam spoke" (Deut. Rabba 6:11).

The usual punishment associated with slander is leprosy because leprosy is also associated with quarantine, and lepers must be removed from the camp or city. One is in isolation—husband from wife, child from parent, friends from each other. This is also the effects of *lashon ha-ra'*, the evil tongue, which causes separation. *Lashon ha-ra'*, done often in secrecy, has the effect of isolating the

---

[100] This may remind the reader of the "temptation" of Adam by Eve. Aaron, like his "brother" Adam seems unable to say no. This is borne out by the text, since Aaron was the one who was "dragged" into the episode of the Golden Calf. In all fairness to the Rabbis, Miriam is depicted in some midrashim as refusing to give over the gold jewelry to Aaron for the creation of the calf, saving it for the creation of the Mishkan.

victim from the rest of society, often without her/him even knowing why.

This sin was so egregious that the Rabbis inserted two prayers about it into the daily silent recitation; one, at the conclusion ("Keep my tongue from evil and my lips from speaking guile") and one, a curse ("there shall be no hope for those who slander"). The Rabbis think of slander as worse than rape, and equivalent to murder: the rapist must pay 50 *selas* to the victim, whereas whoever slanders must pay 100 *selas* to the slandered person (*M. Arakin* 3.5).

One might think that here is a case of over-reaction: surely the punishment for slander is not to be more severe than for rape. However, in the eyes of the Rabbis, since the rapist also has to marry the victim and cannot ever divorce her, there is some kind of closure, whereas one never knows what the ripple effects of slander may be. The Rabbis recognized the power of the spoken word to build or ruin human relationships, and considered the tongue the "elixir of life" (*Lev. Rabba* 16:2) and the primary source of good and evil (*Lev. Rabba* 33:1).

The Rabbis tell us that the blame for *lashon ha-ra'* falls equally on those making their decisions on the basis of what they hear. And *lashon ha-ra'* is prohibited even when the remarks are true (Lev 19.16). It is written about those who utter slander: "they begin by speaking well of one and conclude by speaking ill" (*Num. Rabba* 16:17).

The effects of slander (or what we might want to call, today, character assassination) are deadly. They are like that of the "serpent who bites into one limb and whose poison travels to all the limbs. *Lashon ha-ra'* slays teller, listener and subject" (*Lev. Rabba* 26:2).

Character assassination of leaders or of God's chosen is, therefore, surely very serious—how serious can be seen in this final midrash, based on the passage: "Suffer not thy mouth to bring thy flesh into guilt" (Eccl. 5.5).

> R. Manni interpreted the verse as alluding to Miriam...
> Miriam spoke slander with her mouth, but all her limbs were punished. R. Joshua learnt: A word for a sela, but silence for two selas. Rabbi Judah Ha-Nasi said: Best of all is silence; as we have learnt in the Ethics of the Fathers: All my days I grew up among the Sages, and I have found nothing better for a person than silence (*Eccl. Rabba* 5:1).

Perhaps here lies the clue. Silence is a virtue; yet to women is attributed the gift of speech. It is said that of the ten measures of conversation that were given to the world, nine were given to women (*Kiddushin* 49b).[101] If silence is the supreme virtue, surely the nine measures of conversation are a dubious gift at best!

The punishment for *lashon ha-ra'* does not distinguish between men and women. However, the Rabbis stack the decks against women. They predict that 90 percent of the time women will be doing the talking. This, then, leads the Rabbis to expect the worst from women—even to assuming that when the Bible says that Miriam and Aaron spoke, it was principally Miriam who was at fault! Thus women's talk was viewed at best as worthless, at worse as dangerous. If women are naturally talkative, then silence, by contrast, will naturally be considered golden.

The Rabbis glorified Miriam when she asserted herself to defend the values of nurturance and motherhood, but disparaged her when she stepped out of line and spoke up to challenge Moses' authority.

Are rabbinic attitudes different today? Let us examine a fairly modern interpretation of the text, which glosses over the inequity of Miriam's punishment by minimizing it. In his commentary on the Torah, Rabbi Gunter Plaut writes that it was Aaron who was more severely disciplined than Miriam.[102] Though, to the ordinary reader of text, this goes against the grain of the *peshat* (the self-evident meaning), Plaut points out that Miriam is only punished corporally whereas Aaron is punished mentally, a suffering which is more intense. How so?

1) First, because Aaron suffers guilt when he sees Miriam disfigured hideously, while he is let off free. Plaut writes: "the hurt of seeing a dear one suffer is often far greater than one's own physical agony."[103]

2) Second, because Aaron has to humiliate himself before his younger brother by begging Moses' forgiveness, and by asking him to intercede with God on Miriam's behalf.

---

[101] The context in the Talmud makes clear that this is a negative association.

[102] Gunther Plaut, *The Torah: A Modern Commentary* (New York: Union of American Hebrew Congregations, 1981).

[103] Idem: 1101.

Plaut asserts that Miriam's pain is short-lived and, like most physical ailments, quickly forgotten once she is healed, whereas Aaron's punishment probably leaves deep scars. He agrees that Miriam's leprosy is a warning to the people that slander and rebellion are evil, but argues that the sight of Aaron, the High Priest, bowing down before Moses and begging his pardon is a warning which was equally potent and "surely more memorable."[104]

I am not arguing that Plaut's reading is wrong or even narrow-minded, but I hope it is clear that in emphasizing Aaron's pain it is minimizing Miriam's. Like all the jokes about the poor expectant father in the hospital waiting-room, who suffers so from the traumatic experience while his wife is calmly going through the process of childbirth, Plaut's reading takes the limelight away from Miriam.

This type of modern interpretation assaults our sense of the meaning of the text by smoothing over the injustice inherent in the original story to make an apologetic statement. Can men and women who experience a conflict with those who continue to interpret the biblical text in such a biased manner, do anything about it? I think, yes! We can insist that the partnership model be considered as the traditional Jewish midrashic approach to text. Its starting point is that the Bible is a "sacred" text, but there is no monopoly on its interpretation. New insights are welcome, and the more diverse they are, the more enrichment and understanding of God's purpose.

We must start imaginatively to re-engage with our sacred texts, by writing midrash.[105] Only in that way can all voices, not only a few, be part of the partnership. Then, we hope, different views will be voiced and will not be dismissed as just gossip or as *lashon ha-ra'*, but welcomed as the "beginning of moral inquiry... [and] self understanding."[106]

---

[104] Idem: 1102.

[105] See Naomi Graetz, *S/He Created Them: Feminist Retellings of Biblical Stories* (Piscataway, NJ: Gorgias Press, 2003).

[106] Phyllis Rose, *Parallel Lives: Five Victorian Marriages* (New York: Alfred A. Knopf Inc., 1983): 9.

Metaphors Count

Formation Of Metaphor

Myth (*aggadah*), narrative, and metaphor play a central role in forming the mindset of rabbis who create and apply Jewish law (*halakha*) or nomos to the life of the Jewish community.[107] The reciprocal relationship between *aggadah*/narrative/metaphor and *halakha*/Jewish law/*nomos* is a central issue in this book. Robert Cover, in his article "Nomos and Narrative" insisted that, "for every constitution there is a epic, for each decalogue a scripture."[108] Rules are embedded in the narrative and are equal partners in the evolution of law and custom. Law does not exist in a vacuum. It is given guidelines by the beliefs and metaphors that constitute our shared experiences; that is, our communal "script."[109]

Metaphor is not only words, and it is not only similarity. It is basic to how we think about all human concerns and a necessary tool that we use automatically to express our thoughts. Conceptual

---

[107] Robert Cover discusses the categories "nomos" and "narrative" in his seminal paper, "The Supreme Court, 1982 Term-Foreword: Nomos and Narrative," *Harvard Law Review* 97:1 (1983). Rachel Adler summarizes part of Cover's article in "Feminist Folktales of Justice: Robert Cover as a Resource for the Renewal of Halakha," *Conservative Judaism* XLV: 3 (1993): 41. "Law is not reducible only to formal lawmaking, Cover maintains, because it is generated by a nomos, a universe of meanings, values and rules, embedded in stories. A nomos is not a body of data to master and adapt, but a world to inhabit. Knowing how to live in a nomic world means being able to envision the possibilities implicit in its stories and norms and being willing to live some of them out in praxis."

[108] Robert Cover, as cited in Gordon Tucker, "The Sayings of the Wise are Like Goads: An Appreciation of the Works of Robert Cover," *Conservative Judaism* XLV: 3 (1993): 4.

[109] Gordon Tucker, "The Sayings of the Wise are Like Goads: An Appreciation of the Works of Robert Cover," *Conservative Judaism* XLV: 3 (1993): 24.

metaphors about life, love, death, and relationships are "part of the way members of a culture have of conceptualizing their experience."[110]

Prophets and law-makers, among others, as members of their cultures, use metaphors to communicate. Successful communication and the vitality of metaphor depend on "its reliance on shared moral assumptions, and its ability to convey to the reader or hearer the existence of some similarity between the metaphorical image and what it is meant to explain."[111] The success of the prophets and law-makers depends on their ability to extend their "moral revulsion from the primary realm of the metaphor to the realm it represents—that is, from the relations among human beings to the relations between them and God."[112] In the process, there is an intentional blurring of the "primary distinction that ostensibly exists between them and God [which] transforms God into a fellow human being."[113]

The beliefs of prophets and law-makers are part of the formulation of metaphor. Metaphor is a basic building block of the description of and the human conception of reality. Behavior is predicated on an understanding of reality. People do what they think is expected of them to live out their lives in accordance with their vision of "what should be." Behavior in relations between men and women are highly dependent on perceptions of the other as "male" or "female," and thus our basic metaphoric handling of these categories informs all behavior.

Why does a writer choose a particular metaphor? A metaphor is useful only if it expresses the author's perception of reality and human interaction. The right metaphor sharpens and organizes thoughts, which the author then uses to influence his audience so that they will adopt his perspective. The belief system is often

---

[110] George Lakoff and Mark Turner, *More than Cool Reason: A Field Guide to Poetic Metaphor* (Chicago: University of Chicago Press, 1989): 9.

[111] Moshe Halbertal and Avishai Margalit, "Idolatry and Betrayal," in Naomi Goldblum (tr.), *Idolatry* (Cambridge, MA: Harvard University Press, 1992): 10.

[112] Idem.

[113] Idem.

shared by the audience, otherwise the metaphor doesn't usually work.[114]

Once the metaphor has been composed, it is learned and gets to be used "automatically, effortlessly, and even unconsciously."[115] The metaphor becomes so much part of us that "we accept its validity. Consequently, when someone else uses it, we are predisposed to accept its validity. For this reason, conventionalized schemas and metaphors have persuasive power over us."[116] It is often impossible to distinguish between the metaphor and reality.

According to Lakoff and Turner, there are five sources of the power of metaphor: the power to structure; the power of options; the power of reason; the power of evaluation; and, the power of being there.[117] Because they are there, available as tools, they are hard to question. Once in the public domain, metaphor is out of control of its creator, and, according to Moran,

> will lead the mind in unanticipated directions. It is possible to get more out of it than one has explicitly put into it. The audience as well may engage in interpretation of the metaphor that is an exploratory elaboration of it, and which involves attention to the word rather than to the speaker.[118]

The sociologist Nisbet wrote of "the power and danger of metaphor when taken not as analogy but as attribute of reality,"[119] and Moran wrote that "part of the dangerous power of a strong metaphor is its control over one's thinking at a level beneath that of deliberation or volition."[120] Metaphor works by moving from the better-known concrete object to the lesser-known abstraction.

---

[114] Richard Moran, "Seeing and Believing: Metaphor, Image, and Force," *Critical Inquiry* 16:1 (1989): 107-109.

[115] George Lakoff and Mark Turner, *More than Cool Reason: A Field Guide to Poetic Metaphor* (Chicago: University of Chicago Press, 1989): 62.

[116] Idem: 63.

[117] Idem: 64-65.

[118] Richard Moran, "Seeing and Believing: Metaphor, Image, and Force," *Critical Inquiry* 16:1 (1989): 109.

[119] Nisbet (1969:6), quoted in Tom Craig Darrand and Anson Shupe, *Metaphors of Social Control in a Pentecostal Sect* (Lewiston, NY: Edwin Mellen Press, 1983): 20.

[120] Richard Moran, "Seeing and Believing: Metaphor, Image, and Force," *Critical Inquiry* 16:1 (1989): 90.

It is a process that compares and extends meaning to encompass the similarity of difference.[121] Yet, metaphor is doomed to fail in its attempt to describe the lesser-known (in our case, the divine), and ultimately highlights the disparity of the two realms being depicted.[122] According to Susan Niditch:

> ... metaphoric texts are rich indicators of their composers' mythology, of shared cultural values and aspects of world-view symbolically represented. Myths and metaphors if properly read may be the truest indicators of essential perceptions of existence.[123]

METAPHOR AND BATTERING

There are many examples of metaphoric abuse of women in the Jewish tradition. It does not matter that some of these texts do not deal with actual battering of women. Carol Newsom, in an article dealing with female imagery, writes that texts that use symbolic language referring to women influence the behavior of the group of people that reads these texts.[124] The institution of marriage is the context in which wifebeating takes place, and the history of

---

[121] "This semantic process involves the cooperation of two elements, a vehicle and a tenor. The vehicle is the base of metaphor, the better known element, while the tenor is its underlying (or overarching) subject, the lesser known element. The sense of the metaphor results from the interaction of vehicle and tenor, an interaction that varies with different metaphors. For instance, vehicle and tenor may call attention to each other equally, or one may highlight the other. Nevertheless, both are essential for the comparison; neither is an embellishment. Together they produce new meanings that are not available through the individual elements. Though clearly distinguishable, vehicle and tenor constitute the unit that is itself a metaphor." Phyllis Trible, *God and the Rhetoric of Sexuality* (Philadelphia: Fortress Press, 1978): 17. She uses I. A. Richards, *The Philosophy of Rhetoric* (London: Oxford University Press, 1936): 89-138 and Philip Wheelwright, *Metaphor and Reality* (Bloomington, IN: Indiana University Press, 1962): 70-91.

[122] See Phyllis Trible, *God and the Rhetoric of Sexuality* (Philadelphia: Fortress Press, 1978): 20 (using I. A. Richards, see note 121).

[123] Susan Niditch, *War in the Hebrew Bible* (New York: Oxford University Press, 1993): 37.

[124] Carol Newsom, "Woman and Patriarchal Wisdom," p. 155, as quoted by Mary E. Shields in "Circumcision of the Prostitute," *Biblical Interpretation* 3:1 (1995): 72. Shields does not list a journal for Newsom.

marriage allows for, and sanctions, a relationship between a submissive wife and a demanding husband. According to Nye, there is an "oppressive dynamic" at work in which a wife is expected to stay put until she cannot stand it any longer, and

> then is punished and then is forgiven because she cannot be allowed to leave but must be made to stand back out of the way, be there and not there at the same time, obedient to the will of her husband but at the same time a presence that reassures him that he is not alone as he attempts time after time to discipline her and break her will, but not destroy her or allow her to leave, because without her he could not live.[125]

In my reading of the biblical and midrashic texts I found that the values that are implicit in these texts reflect a climate of social conventions that accept or condone real battering. I also found that there was an ambiance of explicit and implicit family violence in seemingly unconnected episodes about Cain, Hagar, Lot's Daughters, the Concubine at Gibeah, and the law of the Sotah.[126] These five passages demonstrate how easy it is to perform violent acts against women in a patriarchal society in which women have little power and intrinsic value, as defined in terms of that society's needs. These very texts became the metaphors of Western society.

In previous works, I have shown how the prophets used the image of the helpless woman of no intrinsic worth in relationship to a male lord and master who becomes the image of the chosen people of Israel in relationship to an omnipotent god. Although this metaphor expressed the reality of the hierarchical relationship between a husband and his wife in patriarchal society, the prophets elevated that hierarchy to a description of how God meant the world to be. Northrop Frye writes that we should "consider the possibility that metaphor is not an incidental ornament of biblical language, but one of its controlling modes of thought."[127]

---

[125] Andrea Nye, *Words of Power: A Feminist Reading of the History of Logic* (London: Routledge, 1990): 150.

[126] The laws of *Sotah* are considered to be halakha, yet they have narrative or metaphoric nuances.

[127] Northrop Frye, *The Great Code: The Bible and Literature* (New York: Harcourt Brace Jovanovich, 1982): 23.

How is it that the same prophets who speak so persuasively of social justice are themselves responsible for some of the worst examples of misogynistic texts in the Bible? Part of any explanation will have to take into account that the prophets chose to use the marriage metaphor and female imagery to depict relationships that could be understood in the historical context of the patriarchal society in which they lived. At the same time, however, there were other conceptions and relationships in the social structures of their time[128] against which the prophets rebelled.

Similarly we need to explain the paradox of legal codes, which on the one hand assume that women are the chattels of their husbands or fathers, yet, on the other hand, are concerned with the protection of the poor, the orphans, widows, and strangers in their midst.

Beyond that, of course, is the fact that both the prophets and the rabbis used female sexual imagery, and the violence which often accompanies it, because of their lack of ease with female sexuality and their desire to control it.[129]

---

[128] See T. Drorah Setel, "Feminist Insights and the Question of Method," in Adela Yarbro Collins (ed.), *Feminist Perspectives of Biblical Scholarship* (Chico, CA: Scholars Press, 1985): 41.

[129] Katheryn Darr, "Ezekiel' s Justifications of God," *JSOT* 55 (1992): 97-117.

IS *KINYAN* ONLY A METAPHOR?

In the Mishnah it is stated that a woman is acquired (*nikneyt*) in three ways.[130] She is acquired through means of money; through a legal document (*shetar*, something in writing/*ketubah*), and through the act of intercourse (*biyah*). The word for acquisition in Hebrew (*kinyan*) is also a purchase although many rabbis try to distance themselves from this and speak of acquisition-*kinyan* as being different from purchase-*kinyan*. However, any way you look at it, acquiring a bride is a one-sided affair and the woman remains passive in this act. If women are possessions rather than agents, a dangerous environment can be created. Thus modern apologetic readers such as Yacov de Wolff cannot stomach this idea:

> "The idea of women being property is un-Jewish," he claims. "The fact that a women [sic] is 'acquired' (*Mishna Kiddushin* 1:1) doesn't mean that she's property! It should be stressed that a marriage...is the fusion of two people into one—a fusion in which the man traditionally plays the active role because he 'lost' the female part of himself in Creation (see *Gemara Kiddushin* 2b)."[131]

Kinyan is an act in which a person obtains rights of ownership or use in exchange for monetary (or other) payment. There are two major types of *kinyan*: original and derivative acquisition. Original acquisition is when the "property" being acquired is not owned by anyone else and derivative acquisition is when the property is acquired from a previous owner. It would seem that the "purchase"

---

[130] Much of the material in this chapter appears in chapters four and five of my book *Silence is Deadly: Judaism Confronts Wifebeating* (Northvale, NJ: Jason Aronson, 1998).

[131] J. F. de Wolff <jfdwolff@dds.nl> on the Bais-Medrash List, vol. 1, 58 (November 29 1998) in a subject entry entitled "Changing Gender Roles," (sent 18 Nov 1998).

of a bride is a form of derivative acquisition, since the bride "belongs" to her father until her marriage. The function of *kinyan* is to demonstrate that the acquirer and the object of his acquisition are performing a transaction in which mutual benefit is being derived. The act of *kinyan* indicates that the two parties have made up their minds to conclude the transaction and the person who acquires the bride has to indicate his intention in the contract by mentioning an agreed monetary price (*kinyan kesef*). According to the Talmud (B. *Kiddushin* 2a-b), the bride cannot be acquired if she does not voluntarily agree to the act of betrothal.[132]

Rachel Biale, in her discussion of the mishnah and gemara text, "A Woman is acquired in three ways" (B. *Kid.* 2a-b), points out that the acquisition of a woman by money is not purchase of property, since a man may not sell the woman he "acquires" and the amount of money is so small that it is not a "regular financial transaction." The amount of money is immaterial, because "the acquisition is symbolic," she states, and then asks, "If the exchange of money is not an actual purchase, what then is the 'real' meaning of acquiring a woman in marriage?"[133]

Although the bride was purchased in biblical times, "in the post-biblical era, the betrothal was realized by the performance of an act of acquisition (*kinyan*) and the making of a declaration by the bridegroom to the bride in the presence of two witnesses."[134]

According to Boaz Cohen, the understanding is that, although the word *kanah* (acquire) literally means to purchase, in the Mishnah it means "a symbolical form of acquisition."[135] The bride price in the Tannaitic era was symbolic and was given to the bride, or to her father if she were a minor.

---

[132] Although it is ideal that the bride agrees, it is possible that the bride be "purchased" through an agent, since it is better for a woman to be unhappily married than to be single (B. *Kiddushin* 41a-b). For more details, see the entry, "Acquisition," in the *Encyclopedia Judaica*, vol. 2 (Jerusalem: Keter, 1971): 216-21.

[133] Rachel Biale, *Women and Jewish Law* (New York: Schocken Books, 1984): 48.

[134] Boaz Cohen, "Betrothal in Jewish and Roman Law," *Proceedings of the American Academy for Jewish Research* XVIII (1948-49): 75.

[135] Idem: 75-76. See too David Halivni Weiss, "The use of KNH in Connection with Marriage," *Harvard Theological Review* (July 1964): 244-248.

Marriage in Tannaitic times was more than a business arrangement—it was a religious institution and the word for betrothal was called *kiddushin* (lit. sanctification), as opposed to the biblical term of *erusin*.[136] The new term "*kiddushin*" also reflects the transition of the marriage "acquisition" from a private deal between two adults or between two families to a social and religious institution administered by the community and under rabbinic supervision. This change gives rise to rabbinic controls over marriage and divorce, matters, which in the biblical period were purely familial.[137]

Although the Mishnah does speak of the woman who is purchased (i.e., acquired), according to Cohen, "the noun *kinyan* is not used as a term for betrothal."[138] Through marriage, however, the woman becomes "the sacrosanct possession, *res sacra*, of her husband, or, as the Talmud puts it—*de'asar la achula alma ke-hekdesh*"—that is, she is forbidden to others just as a sacred object is forbidden, or as Cheryl Beckerman puts it "*kiddushin* is an unambiguously one-sided monogamy clause, forbidding the wife to all other men."[139]

In the Gemara's discussion of this mishnah, it explains that the biblical "take" refers to money; however this money does not signify purchase but rather is the symbol of a legal transaction.

---

[136] In footnote 38 on p. 222 of *Chattel or Person? The Status of Women in the Mishnah* (New York: Oxford University Press, 1988), Wegner writes "Mishnaic marriage law employs three technical legal terms: *erusin*, here translated as 'betrothal'; *qiddushin*, here translated as 'espousal'; and *nissui'in*, here translated as 'consummation.' In post-Mishnaic usage (e.g., at B. *Kiddushin* 12b), *erusin* and *qiddushin* are used interchangeably. However, the Mishnah's use of three technical terms must reflect a time when the first two denoted separate stages in the process." Thus, according to Wegner, the betrothed girl is not permitted sexually to the bridegroom. Contrast this with the expression we will see in the next chapter that comes from Hosea "*ve-eyrastich li l'olam*," which is usually translated as espoused, since, in biblical times, the term *qiddushin* did not exist.

[137] See Avraham Freiman, *Seder Kiddushin ve Nissuin* (Jerusalem: Mosad Harav Kook, 1964) [Hebrew].

[138] Boaz Cohen, "Betrothal in Jewish and Roman Law," *Proceedings of the American Academy for Jewish Research* XVIII (1948-49): 77.

[139] Cheryl Beckerman, "Kiddushin and Kesharin: Toward an Egalitarian Wedding Ceremony," *Kerem* 5 (1997): 84-100.

(The money specified is so minimal as to eliminate any possibility of its constituting a real financial transaction; and unlike other acquisitions, a wife can not be resold or transferred.) Thus, it is clear that Jewish marriage is not just a sacrament nor is it just a legal transaction. It involves a contract, formal declaration, witnesses, signatures, and an exchange of monetary value.

Although Biale and Cohen dismiss the acquisition as a "symbolic" purchase, Judith Romney Wegner and Mordecai Friedman read the same text of the mishnah differently. Wegner writes that the mishnah prescribes the same modes of acquisition for wives as for Canaanite slaves and real property, and that marriage is a "formal sale and purchase of a woman's sexual function—a commercial transaction in which a man pays for the bride's virginity just as for any other object of value."[140] Wegner points out that the husband's purchase of his wife's biological function means that he has full legal claim on her sexuality; so much so that this claim overrides the woman's rights of personhood and makes her a form of chattel.

In a disclaimer to the popular concept of the sanctification of marriage, Mordechai A. Friedman believes that the specific religious significance of

> the prophetic image of marriage as a covenant between a man and women solemnized by an oath to which God Himself served as witness…failed to exert an influence in Talmudic and post-Talmudic literature… There, notwithstanding the rabbinic term qiddushin, believed by many to have originally denoted a type of "sanctification" and, despite the religious significance of the seven marriage benedictions, marriage is basically treated as a secular institution.[141]

Today the traditional wedding ceremony includes *kabbalat kinyan* (acquisition) in which the groom formally undertakes the obligations written in the *ketubah* and holds up a handkerchief

---

[140] Judith Romney Wegner, *Chattel or Person? The Status of Women in the Mishnah* (New York: Oxford University Press, 1988): 42. See also Rachel Adler, "I've Had Nothing Yet So I Can't Take More," *Moment* 8:8 (1983): 22-26, esp. 23.

[141] Mordechai A. Friedman, "The Ethics of Medieval Jewish Marriage," in S. D. Goitein (ed.), *Religion in a Religious Age* (New York: K'tav, 1973): 83.

given to him by the officiating rabbi who represents the bride. This action is witnessed by two Jews. Under the ḥuppah, the *mesader kiddushin* reads blessings and the groom places a ring (whose value has to be *shaveh perutah*—worth a cent) on her right index finger and "consecrates" her unto him. The ketubah is then read with the words: *Vekanina* and the groom and bride's names, and witnessed by the *aidim* as to the *kabalat kinyan* by the groom on the same day as the *ḥuppah*. (The translation of this is usually: "We have followed the legal formality of symbolic delivery (*kinyan*) between the bridegroom and bride, this virgin, and we have used a garment legally fit for the purpose, to strengthen all that is stated above.")

Symbolic or metaphoric acquisition continues to have a place in the marriage ceremony, and the bride's virginity is mentioned in the marriage contract (*ketubah*) as well as the symbolic sum of money which becomes hers if the marriage ends due to a fault of the husband's. Although the bride stands under the bridal canopy (*ḥuppah*), it is the husband who recites the formal declaration of espousal, not the woman. She does not say, "I do" or "I am espoused to you," since he formally acquires her. Although she has to agree, she does not give herself to him.

In her feminist-critical reading of a section of the ketubah text, Laura Levitt points out that "Jewish men's power over Jewish women through the institution of marriage is divinely sanctioned," and that the ketubah text advocates a particular type of relationship that was not necessarily normative. She does this by showing the repetition or restatement of the husband's obligations to the wife. She sees the references to virginity and conjugal needs as making clear the husband's sole access to his wife's body as part of his overall control over her life. Thus she sees male dominance as both "commanded and natural."[142]

Rachel Adler also shows how the metaphor of *kinyan* is linked to its literal sources and shows that even if the "purchase" of the bride was a mere formality, the language of acquisition reflects a relationship in which the woman is possessed. She shows clearly that *kiddushin* is "derived from property law and defined by layers of biblical and rabbinic precedent as a transaction in which a man

---

[142] Laura S. Levitt, "Reconfiguring Home: Jewish Feminist Identity/ies," in Tamar Rudavsky (ed.), *Gender and Judaism* (New York: NYU Press, 1993): 43-44. See too Rachel Adler's *Engendering Judaism: An Inclusive Theology and Ethics* (Philadelphia: Jewish Publication Society, 1998).

acquires rights over a woman."[143] There is no reciprocity in Jewish marriage—only the woman can be acquired, not the man.

METAPHOR/MIDRASH

We see a merge of legal literature with midrashic material in the Talmudic text which discusses Hosea's relationship to his wife and children (God to Israel) and God's relationship with the people of Israel as one of his possessions. Hosea complains to God that it is difficult for him to separate himself from his wife and divorce her. God asks: Why should it be a problem since she's a prostitute and his children are the fruit of prostitution? How do you know whether they are yours or not? And, I, God (in contrast to Hosea), know that the people of Israel are My children, one of four possessions (*kinyanim*) that I purchased in this world. The Torah is one possession (purchase), heaven and earth is another, the temple is another and Israel is another... (B. *Pesachim* 87b).

It is interesting that the marriage ceremony is likened to *kinyan*. Also, note the four categories of *kinyan* in this text—they are all instances of eternal possession and mastery over someone/thing else. These four cases (Israel being the fourth) are based on an inherent, not acquired "ownership." Despite protestations that *kinyan* in marriage does not give the husband possession of his wife, the metaphor suggests otherwise. Israel (the wife) is God's property to do with as He pleases. In a midrash in which God is likened to a heroic figure with great strength, we see an acceptance by the sages that Israel is God's possession, to do with her what he pleases.

> *I will bear the indignity of the Lord, because I have sinned against him* (Mic 7.9). This can be compared to a hero who strikes a man with one slap and one blow, and he immediately kills him. Then he enters his house and hits his wife with one slap and she stands firm. Her neighbors said to her: Are you stronger than all those athletes?! All the heroes die from one blow and from one slap, but you receive so many [blows] from him and still you can stand firm?! She said to them: When he hits those, he hits them with anger and with all his

---

[143] Cheryl Beckerman, "Kiddushin and Kesharin: Toward an Egalitarian Wedding Ceremony," *Kerem* 5 (1997): 90, quoting Adler.

strength, but when he hits me, he hits me according to
my strength, and therefore I can stand it.[144]

The wife (Israel) is justifying her husband's (God's) abuse of her.
The midrash continues and asks, "how do we comfort ourselves
and how is it that we can stand up against God's anger. Because
although He hits us, He repents and creates us anew."[145] Implicit in
this is that God owns Israel.

Although male God-language may seem innocuous,
metaphors do matter. Though we have become desensitized to
their implications on an individual and social level, through their
long and established usage, we should remember that religious
symbols are chosen carefully to communicate to society its values
and help the community to understand itself and its conception of
the world.[146] Thus if God is perceived as a father or a husband
ruling and controlling "his" people, then the "nature of things" and
the "divine plan," and even the "order of the universe," will be
understood to be male dominated as well.[147]

The Possession = Jealousy Equation (Knh = Kna)

Another disturbing metaphor has to do with the jealous God:
Adonai kana shemo is how God describes himself. *El kana hu*—HE
is a jealous god (Exod 34.14). The usage of *kana* is very often
combined with *nekamah*, vengeance. The jealous God seeks
vengeance. As you will note, the JPS version "impassioned"
sloughs over the problematics of the implication that God's name
or essence is jealousy, or that God seeks revenge.

In English it is very easy to move from the idea of a
possessive husband to a jealous husband. Possession, jealousy,
passion, and vengeance all go together. In Hebrew, one can free

[144] *Aggadat Bereshit* (Buber Version), Chapter 8:3. Solomon Buber,
Aggadat Bereshit (Krakow 1903=New York 1973): 21. L. M. Teugels (tr.),
Aggadat Bereshit. Translated from the Hebrew with an Introduction and Notes
(Leiden: Brill 2001): 29. For further discussion of this midrash, see
"Jerusalem the Widow," in this book.

[145] Solomon Buber, *Aggadat Bereshit* 8:4. [My translation].

[146] Judith Plaskow, *Standing Again at Sinai: Judaism from a Feminist
Perspective* (San Francisco: Harper & Row, 1990): 125.

[147] Mary Daly, *Beyond God the Father* (Boston: Beacon Press, 1973): 13,
as quoted in Judith Plaskow in *Standing Again at Sinai: Judaism from a
Feminist Perspective* (San Francisco: Harper & Row, 1990): 126.

associate because the words share the same two letters in reverse order. If we look at all these words in different contexts, we can see that these words take us from cradle to grave to redemption. Therefore, I have combined free association of biblical and midrashic texts to suggest that there is an inherent connection between such words as *ken* (nest) and *hanakah* (nursing). We see it in Cain's relationship with his mother, who named him because she gained (*kanah*) a male child—which can be connected to the jealous God. God creates (*koneh*) and is then jealous, possessive of what he has created. This is similar to the mother who brings a child in the world, sees him as a possession, and does not know when or how to let go, to allow the child autonomy.

In the worst case scenario, we have the vengeful God, who punishes his people—like the vengeful husband who goes after his wife, even after the divorce. Because once his, always his. In biblical texts we sometimes have *nikayon* (*nakeh*)—cleansing out of sin (and people) in the ultimate form of vengeance—total wiping out, annihilation, not to speak of the modern day cleaning up (mopping up) (*nikayon*) after the mess is made during warfare. And we do in euphemistic fashion speak of a "clean up" operation. Afterwards, because of the tragic toll, we lament, lamentations (*kinah*), because of our sorrow about what has been done to us. If we are not to end on this note, we must change, by engaging in *tikkun* (repair) and *takkana* (emendation) of our laws. I suggest in particular, that the repair should be connected with looking at the possessive aspect of the Jewish marriage contract.

I would hope that the "message" we take from this is that *kinyan* is more than just a metaphor and we should be re-thinking its use in the Jewish marriage ceremony. We should also note, as Judith Plaskow has, that "criticism is essential to transformation... Without it, the negative aspects of tradition are left to shape consciousness and affect our heart and minds... Acknowledging those aspects of tradition that need to be repudiated and exorcised is part of the process of creating something new."[148]

Both Rachel Adler and Cheryl Beckerman are examples of people who have addressed the structural inequities in the halakhic

---

[148] Judith Plaskow, "Decentering Sex: Rethinking Jewish Sexual Ethics," presented at the Jewish Feminist Research Group of Ma'Yan, The Jewish Women's Project (January 19, 1999): 7.

system and have proposed alternative *ketubot* (plural of *ketubah*). The Reconstructionist Movement has developed an egalitarian *get* and it is not difficult for those who wish to sidestep the traditional *ketubah* to find models for change and creativity. As Adler points out, *kinyan*, the acquisition of human beings implicit in *kiddushin*, "violates values conscientious people have come to regard as moral goods... We have just reached a point where it is possible to envision, and sometimes to realize, marriages in which two remain two, marriages that are not incorporations but covenants."[149] A piece of property cannot commit to a covenant. Thus she used a partnership model. Cheryl Beckerman[150] did something more interesting. She incorporated additional phrases into her wedding ceremony to make it clear that this is not a purchase. When putting the ring on her finger, her husband prefaced the traditional *harei at mekudeshet li* with *birshuteikh u-virtzoneikh* (with your consent and by your will). She responded by saying that she was consecrated to him and he responded by saying: call me *ishi* (my man) and not *ba'ali* (my master) from the Book of Hosea. He also vowed to be monogamous, which goes beyond the halakhic requirements of Judaism.

---

[149] See Rachel Adler, *Engendering Judaism: An Inclusive Theology and Ethics* (Philadelphia: Jewish Publication Society, 1998): 191-192.
[150] See footnote 139.

GOD IS TO ISRAEL AS HUSBAND IS TO WIFE: THE METAPHORIC BATTERING OF HOSEA'S WIFE

Reading a Haftara (an additional reading from the Prophets) after the weekly reading of the Torah (the Pentateuch) is a time-honored custom among Jews, although the origin of the custom is obscure. The rabbis who initiated the custom may have wanted to make a religious statement that the writings of the Prophets, not only the Torah, are also divinely inspired.[151] Perhaps it also fits the philosophy of the Pharisaic approach: seeing the Torah as an open, fluid text, subject to constant scrutiny and interpretation. At a time when the reading of the Five Books of Moses took between two and a half to three and a half years to complete, the Haftara simply consisted of several random verses, not necessarily related to the weekly portion.[152] Later, when the weekly portion became standardized, the Haftara also became fixed. It served, among other things, as a sort of internal commentary on, or an elucidation of, the Torah portion itself.

An example of this is the Haftara accompanying the first portion of the Book of Numbers. The opening chapter of Numbers *bammidbar* ("in the wilderness") is a census of the Israelites during the wilderness period. The Haftara, from the second chapter of the Book of Hosea, refers to "the multitudes of the people who are as the sands of the sea." Hosea's message is that the people no longer listen to God's word (*dabar*) and, if they

---

[151] See the blessings surrounding the Haftara reading.

[152] For detailed information on the Haftara tradition see Joseph Jacobs, "Triennial Cycle" in *The Jewish Encyclopedia* 12 (New York: Funk and Wagnalls, 1917): 254-257; Louis I. Rabinowitz, "Haftara" in the *Encyclopedia Judaica* 6 (Jerusalem: Keter, 1971): 1342-1345. Both entries have excellent bibliographies.

do not shape up, they will be in danger of entering a spiritual wilderness (*midbar*). However, when (and if) the people of Israel will again be faithful to Him (as they were during the period of the wilderness (*bammidbar*), He will renew His covenant with them. Hosea speaks for God and says:

> Assuredly, I will speak coaxingly to her
> And lead her through the wilderness (*midbar*)
> And speak (*dibbarti*) to her tenderly
> (Hos 2.16)

There is an integral connection between the associative wordplay of the root *dbr*, which has to do with God's word, and the wilderness. The wordplay echoes important themes and serves as a rhetorical device which unites and connects the Haftara from the Book of Hosea with the Torah portion from the Book of Numbers.

THE MARRIAGE METAPHOR

Hosea was an eighth century BCE prophet who, most commentators[153] believe, addressed himself to the Northern Kingdom of Israel. This kingdom, according to the Bible, was destined to be exiled because of its sins. Hosea describes God's relationship to Israel in metaphorical terms as a marriage. According to Gershon Cohen, such a marriage metaphor is not found in the literature of any other ancient religion beside Israel's. He writes, "The Hebrew God alone was spoken of as the lover and husband of His people, and only the house of Israel spoke of itself

---

[153] We know next to nothing of Hosea ben Beeri's background, lineage or locality—only the name of his father. Those who study the book have difficulties dating the work and identifying people, places and events. According to Peter Machinist, "Hosea and Ambivalence of Kingship in Biblical Israel" (Matilda Roeffer Lecture at Ben Gurion University, May 14, 2003) it was common practice among some scholars (see Ginzburg, note 174 below) to remove references to Judah in this book since the consensus among scholars is that Hosea's audience is Israel and not Judah. See the "Introduction" in Francis I. Andersen and David Noel Freedman, *Hosea: A New Translation* (The Anchor Bible: New York: Doubleday, 1980): 31-77 for a detailed background to this book.

as the bride of the Almighty."[154] Hosea's protagonist is the prophet himself—representing God—, the husband who casts out his wife for being unfaithful to him and then takes her back—with the understanding that "she" will behave herself.

According to Harold Fisch,

> Hosea more than any other book of the Bible...gives us God's side of the relationship. It is dominated by the first-person mode of address as God himself cries out, cajoles, reprimands, mourns and debates with himself... Hosea gives us fundamentally "the prophet's reflection of, or participation in, the divine pathos," as that pathos is directed toward man,[155]

who in this case is depicted as woman.

According to Benjamin Scolnic, who paraphrases Gershon Cohen,

> God, not Baal, is Israel's husband and lover... Since a wife's loyalty to her husband must be absolute and unwavering, it is a powerful analogy to the complete loyalty that God demands of the Israelites. The covenant between God and Israel made at Mount Sinai is a marriage; idolatry, which breaks the covenant, is adultery.[156]

God orders Hosea to marry Gomer daughter of Diblaim, a promiscuous woman (*eshet zenunim*)[157] who, metaphorically speaking, is Israel while Hosea is placed in the position of God.

---

[154] Gershon Cohen, "The Song of Songs and the Jewish Religious Mentality," *Studies in the Variety of Rabbinic Cultures* (Philadelphia: Jewish Publication Society, 1991): 6.

[155] Harold Fisch, "Hosea: A Poetics of Violence," *Poetry with a Purpose* (Bloomington, IN: Indiana University Press, 1990): 141; Fisch calls our attention to A. J. Heschel, *The Prophets* (Philadelphia: Jewish Publication Society, 1962): 27.

[156] Benjamin Scolnic, "Bible Battering," *Conservative Judaism* 45 (1992):43.

[157] See Phyllis Bird, "'To Play the Harlot': An Inquiry into An Old Testament Metaphor," in Peggy L. Day (ed.), *Gender and Difference in Ancient Israel* (Minneapolis: Fortress Press, 1989): 75-94. Bird writes, "Although the underlying metaphor is that of marriage, the use of *znh* rather than *n'p* serves to emphasize promiscuity rather than infidelity, 'wantonness' rather than violation of marriage contract or covenant" (80).

God/Hosea punishes Gomer/Israel for committing adultery/worshipping other Gods. However, because of "his" great love for "her," and "his" commitment to the covenant of marriage, "he" begs "her" to come back and restores "her" to "her" former state. Thus we have a male prophet, who represents a male God. Gershon Cohen writes,

> The Bible unquestionably affirmed the masculinity of God and spoke of Him graphically as the husband... By proclaiming His masculinity...Judaism affirmed His reality and...potency... To such a person one could proclaim fealty, submission and love.[158]

This God, however, threatens the people for not worshipping Him exclusively. Though presumably the entire community, male and female alike, sins against God, the prophet has chosen to describe the people of Israel exclusively in terms of imagery which is feminine.

The standard interpretations of Hosea sympathize with the husband who has put up with so much from this fickle woman, and who desperately promises his wife everything if only she will return to him. The midrash depicts the relationship between God and His people in a poignant manner.

> After [Hosea's wife] had borne him several children, God suddenly puts the question to him: "Why followest thou not the example of thy teacher Moses, who denied himself the joys of family life after his call to prophecy?" Hosea replied: "I can neither send my wife away nor divorce her, for she has borne me children." "If, now," said God to him, "thou who hast a wife of whose honesty thou art so uncertain that thou canst not even be sure that her children are thine, and yet thou canst not separate from her, how, then, can I separate Myself from Israel, from My children, the children of My elect, Abraham, Isaac, and Jacob!"[159]

---

[158] Gershon Cohen, "The Song of Songs and the Jewish Religious Mentality," in *Studies in the Variety of Rabbinic Cultures* (Philadelphia: Jewish Publication Society, 1991): 15.

[159] B. *Pesahim* 87a-87b as related by Louis Ginzberg, *The Legends of the Jews* (Philadelphia: Jewish Publication Society, 1968): vol. IV: 260-261.

God is seen here as all-forgiving, and the husband who cannot separate himself from his wife is the model after which Hosea is expected to pattern himself. In *Numbers Rabba* there are several parables which depict God as a king who is angry with his wife, or as a father who is angry with his son. In these stories there are "happy endings": the king buys his wife some jewelry and they presumably kiss and make up, despite his previous statements that he will divorce her; the father scolds his son for not going to school and then afterwards invites him to dine with him.[160]

If we disregard the sympathetic overtones in the midrash and read between the lines of Hosea, we see that in the biblical text the "poignant relationship" is achieved at a price. We see it well in a midrash from *Exodus Rabba* which compares God to a wife-beater. It is on the verse "If thou lend money to any of my people" (Exod 22.24). It describes how after Israel was driven from Jerusalem, their enemies said that God had no desire for His people. Jeremiah asked God if it was true that He had rejected His children:

> "Hast Thou Utterly rejected Judah? Hath Thy soul loathed Zion? Why hast Thou smitten us, and there is no healing for us?" (Jer. 14.19) It can be compared to a man who was beating his wife. Her best friend asked him: "How long will you go on beating her? If your desire is to drive her out [of life], then keep on beating her till she dies; but if you do not wish her [to die], then why do you keep on beating her?" His reply was: "I will not divorce my wife even if my entire palace becomes a ruin." This is what Jeremiah said to God: "If Thy desire be to drive us out [of this world], then smite us till we die." As it says, "Thou canst not have utterly rejected us, and be exceedingly wroth against us! [Lam 5.22], but if this is not [Thy desire], then "Why hast Thou smitten us, and there is no healing for us?" God replied: "I will not banish Israel, even if I destroy my world," as it says, "Thus saith the Lord: If heaven above can be

---

[160] *Num. Rabba* 2:15. All English translations are from H. Freedman and M. Simon (eds.), *Midrash Rabba* (London: Soncino Press, 1983): 51-52.

measured…then will I also cast off all the seed of
Israel, etc. [Jer. 31.37].[161]

This midrash depicts an emotional bond that has developed
between God and his people which has resulted in Israel being
gradually taken prisoner by a pathological courtship.

The psychiatrist Judith Herman, in her recent book, *Trauma
and Recovery*,[162] describes a woman who becomes involved with a
batterer. She interprets his attention as a sign of love. The woman
minimizes and excuses his behavior, because she cares for him. To
avoid staying in this relationship she will have to fight his
protestations that "just one more sacrifice, one more proof of her
love, will end the violence and save the relationship."[163] Herman
writes that most women are entrapped by the batterer because he
appeals to "her most cherished values. It is not surprising,
therefore, that battered women are often persuaded to return after
trying to flee from their abusers."[164] This is the relationship
expressed by Jeremiah according to the midrash.

Turning back to Hosea, we see that our text details very
explicitly a case of domestic abuse. We see this in the punitive
measures Hosea plans to take. In verse 5, God/Hosea threatens to

> strip her naked and leave her
> as on the day she was born;
> And I will make her like a wilderness,
> render her like desert land,
> and let her die of thirst
> (Hos 2.5).

In verse 8, God/Hosea threatens to

> hedge up her roads with thorns
> and raise walls against her.

In verse 11 God/Hosea says he will humiliate her by taking back

---

[161] *Exod. Rabba* on *Mishpatim* 31:10. H. Freedman and M. Simon (eds.),
Midrash Rabba (London: Soncino Press, 1983): 388-389. Thanks to
Howard Adelman for bringing this midrash to my attention.

[162] Judith Herman, *Trauma and Recovery: The Aftermath of Violence from
Domestic Abuse to Political Terror* (New York: Basic Books, 1992).

[163] Judith Herman, *Trauma and Recovery: The Aftermath of Violence from
Domestic Abuse to Political Terror* (New York: Basic Books, 1992): 83.

[164] Idem.

My new grain in its time
and My new wine in its season,
And I will snatch away My wool
and My linen that serve to cover her nakedness.

If this depicts the real state of Hosea/God's and Gomer/Israel's relationship we have here a very troubled marriage. Gale A. Yee, in the new *Women's Bible Commentary*, writes that:

> Chapter two pushes the marriage metaphor to dangerous limits, whereby [God's] legitimate punishment of Israel for breach of covenant is figuratively described as threats of violence against the wife.[165]

Hosea begins with the threats to strip her naked. These threats escalate with the children being abused by association with the mother's shamelessness (vv. 6-7). The next thing he does is to isolate his wife from her lovers by "building a wall against her," so that she is totally dependent on her husband. Then he withholds food from her and publicly humiliates her by uncovering her nakedness.[166]

Benjamin Scolnic's reaction to Hosea 2 is as follows:

> I don't mean to pretend that this isn't rough stuff. But we must remember that this really is a metaphor understood...by the Israelites *as a metaphor*... I will not hide behind the notion that since this is all "just a metaphor" or polemic against Baal-worship, we don't have to take the words themselves seriously. But there is never a chance that any of the things threatened here will be carried out.[167]

---

[165] In Carol A. Newsome and Sharon H. Ringe (eds.), *The Women's Bible Commentary* (Louisville, Kentucky: Westminster, 1992): 199.

[166] Ilana Pardes, *Countertraditions in the Bible* (Cambridge, MA: Harvard University Press, 1992) writes, "To further understand the sin and punishment, one needs to bear in mind that 'uncovering the nakedness' is a biblical expression designating illicit sexual relations (from incest to adultery). Conversely, 'covering the nakedness', as is evident in both Hosea 2:11 and Ezekiel 16:8 is a synonym for marriage" (134).

[167] Scolnic, Benjamin Edidin. "Bible Battering," *Conservative Judaism* 45 (Fall, 1992): 47-48. Scolnic's article was written as a response and companion piece to my article "The Haftorah Tradition and the

However, F. I. Andersen and D. N. Freedman, the commentators on Hosea in the Anchor Bible series, are not so sure that Hosea's threats are benign. They hint that God's threats of death in Hosea 2.5 (see above) might have been carried out when the people betrayed God in Hosea 6.5.[168]

> That is why I hacked them with my prophets; I killed them with the words of my mouth. My judgment goes forth like the sun (Hos 6.5).

Scolnic, however, minimizes these threats, viewing them as an act of prophetic desperation. These threats, he writes, are

> about love, not wife-battering. They are about forgiveness, not punishment… [The perspective is] of a man who has the right to…strip her, humiliate her, etc., but doesn't and, instead, seeks reconciliation.[169]

Is Scolnic correct in arguing that this is just some mild form of verbal abuse? Again, the commentators of the Anchor Bible disagree. They write,

> the passage expresses both an ardent will to reconciliation and an indignant determination to use coercive or punitive measures to correct or even to destroy her.[170]

One can argue that by using the marriage metaphor we are allowed to glimpse the compassionate side of God.[171] Because of the intimate relationship, God is more accessible to His people. Not only do we have descriptions of an intimate relationship with

---

Metaphoric Battering of Hosea's Wife," *Conservative Judaism* XLV (1992): 29-42, which is an earlier version of the article appearing in this volume.

[168] Francis I. Andersen and David Noel Freedman. *Hosea: A New Translation*, The Anchor Bible (New York: Doubleday, 1980): 129 write about Hosea 2.5 that "A fourth possible stage, death, threatened in v. 5, is apparently never reached (but see Hosea 6:5)."

[169] Scolnic, Benjamin Edidin. "Bible Battering," *Conservative Judaism* 45 (Fall, 1992): 48.

[170] Francis I. Andersen and David Noel Freedman. *Hosea: A New Translation*, The Anchor Bible (New York: Doubleday, 1980): 128.

[171] We can only guess what the marriage metaphor meant in Hosea's day. We, however, view the marriage metaphor through our eyes and see how it came to be used and abused in later generations.

God but, also, we have allusions to the idyllic, pre-expulsion relationship of equality between God and humanity.[172]

> In that day, I will make a covenant for them with the beasts of the field, the birds of the air, and the creeping things of the ground... And I will espouse you with faithfulness; then you shall know *yada'* God intimately (Hos 2.20-21).

However, unlike the relationship between Adam and Eve, the relationship between God and Israel is one-sided. God would like the uncomplicated pre-expulsion relationship, before the people "knew" (*yada'*) about choice. God promises the returning nation an intimate covenantal relationship with Him despite the fact that knowledge (*da'at*) was the reason Adam and Eve were punished.

Jeremiah, too, depicts a God who loved his young, eager, naïve Israel, yet turns on His people when "she" grows up and wants some independence. When God decides to espouse Israel forever with faithfulness, it is so that the people will "know" (*yada'*) only God. If Israel wants to know more than just God, if she wants to take fruit from the tree again, the implication is that she will again be expelled from the Garden of Eden, stripped naked and left as on the day "she" was created—with nothing (Hos 2.5). God is telling Israel/Gomer that she can either be intimate with Him (her husband) or with other Gods/lovers but not with both of them at the same time. She can have knowledge of good and evil from Him or from others. If she chooses others, He will destroy her. So despite the potential glimpse of a compassionate God, He is accessible to His people only on His own terms.[173]

---

[172] In Genesis 1.27 male and female are created in one act. I do not agree with Trible's "depatriarchalizing" of Genesis 2-3. See Phyllis Trible, "Depatriarchalizing in Biblical Interpretation," in Elizabeth Koltun (ed.), *The Jewish Woman: New Perspectives* (New York: Schocken Press, 1976): 217-240.

[173] It is worthwhile comparing the Book of Hosea to the Song of Songs which is probably the only completely non-sexist biblical account of a relationship between a man and a woman. There are echoes of this relationship in Hosea 2.9. Van Dijk-Hemmes argues that there is an intertextual relationship between the two texts and that if we "re-place the 'quotations' back into the love-songs from which they were borrowed, the vision of the woman in this text is restored." To see how she develops this idea see Fokkelien Van Dijk-Hemmes, "The Imagination of Power

Finally, one can argue as Scolnic does, that this "really is a metaphor," that is, that the marriage metaphor is "only a metaphor" and the motif of sexual violence is "only a theme of the metaphor." H. L. Ginsberg, in his articles on Hosea,[174] has pointed out that Hosea's important innovation is the "husband and wife allegory."

> The doctrine of God's jealousy and His insistence that His covenant partner Israel worship no other gods beside Him [is a] factor favorable to the birth of such an allegory... This, however, was heavily outweighed by a horror of associating sexuality with God, and only the need of the...hour overcame this inhibition to the extent of giving rise to the wife metaphor, or allegory...[175]

In his discussion of the commentators on Hosea, Ginsberg writes that the rabbis of the Talmud "accepted literally the divine command to Hosea to marry a prostitute,"[176] and that Rashi was still satisfied with such a view. But Ginsberg's sympathy is clearly with Ibn Ezra, Kimhi and Maimonides who maintained that the story was "but accounts of prophetic visions."[177] Even if we accept Ginsberg's view that the book of Hosea is not a real description of a husband/wife relationship but only a metaphorical, allegorical vision, that does not mean that such metaphoric imagery has no power, no force. As many have pointed out, it is no longer possible to argue that a metaphor is less for being a metaphor. On the contrary, metaphor has power over people's minds and hearts. As Lakoff and Turner write,

> Far from being merely a matter of words, metaphor is a matter of thought—all kinds of thought... [It] is part

---

and the Power of Imagination: An intertextual Analysis of Two Biblical Love Songs: The Song of Songs and Hosea 2," *Journal for the Study of the Old Testament* 44 (1990): 86.

[174] H. L. Ginsberg, "Studies in Hosea 1-3," in Menachem Haran (ed.), *Yehezkel Kaufmann Jubilee Volume* (Jerusalem: Magnes Press, 1960): 50-69 English Section; and *JBL* 80 (1961): 339-347; and "Hosea, Book of" in *Encyclopedia Judaica*, vol. 8:1010-1025.

[175] H. L. Ginsberg, "Hosea, Book of" in *Encyclopedia Judaica*, vol. 8:1016.

[176] Idem:1011.

[177] Idem:1012.

of the way members of a culture have of conceptualizing their experience... For the same reasons that schemas and metaphors give us power to conceptualize and reason, so they have power over us. Anything that we rely on constantly, unconsciously, and automatically is so much part of us that it cannot be easily resisted, in large measure because it is barely even noticed. To the extent that we use a conceptual schema or a conceptual metaphor, we accept its validity. Consequently, when someone else uses it, we are predisposed to accept its validity. For this reason, conventionalized schemas and metaphors have *persuasive* power over us.[178]

One of the side effects of thinking metaphorically is that we often disregard the differences between the two dissimilar objects being compared. One source of metaphor's power lies precisely in that we tend to lose sight of the fact that it is "just" a metaphor. What this means in our case, writes Renita J. Weems, is that "God is no longer like a husband; God is a husband." If "God's covenant with Israel is like a marriage...then a husband's physical punishment against his wife is as warranted as God's punishment of Israel."[179]

DANGEROUS ASSUMPTIONS

Let us turn to two rabbis who use similar metaphors in their midrashim: one classic and one contemporary. The first example appears in a midrash which connects the Torah portion of Numbers to the Haftara from the Book of Hosea.

R. Ḥanina said, "Only in ignorance could one think that what He meant by saying 'I will not be to you' was that He would not be to you for a God. That is certainly not so; what then does, 'and I will not be to you' mean? That even though you would not be My people and would seek to separate yourselves from Me,

---

[178] George Lakoff and Mark Turner, *More than Cool Reason: A Field Guide to Poetic Metaphor* (Chicago: University of Chicago Press, 1989): xi, 9, 63.

[179] Renita J. Weems, "Gomer: Victim of Violence or Victim of Metaphor?" *Semeia* 47 (1989): 100. She is quoting Sallie McFague, *Metaphorical Theology* (Philadelphia: Fortress, 1982).

yet 'I will not be to you'; My mind still will not be the same as yours, but in spite of yourselves you will be My people... *As I live, saith the Lord God, surely with a mighty hand, and with an outstretched arm, and with fury poured out, will I be king over you*" (Ezek 20.33).[180]

One can look at this extraordinary proclamation in two ways: 1) Positively: as a sign of God's devotion; no matter what the people does He still loves them. Or: 2) Negatively: as a sign of God's over-possessiveness. There is no mutual consent. This is all against "her" (the people's) will. There has been no discussion, no ending of mutual recriminations. "He" does not recognize the writing on the wall. "She" does not want "him," she has had it with "him"; sick of "his" mighty hand, outstretched arm and fury. She has decided to leave him, but he refuses to face facts. To him marriage means "I will espouse you to me forever," even if it does not work out. She feels she has no option, that she is trapped in the marriage.

Now let us turn to Rabbi Shlomo Riskin, who writes a weekly column for *The Jerusalem Post*.[181] His midrash is on The Song of Songs, generally considered to be an allegorical depiction of the mutual love of God and Israel:

> When God knocks in the middle of the night, He wants the Jewish people to let Him in and end their long exile... But the nation answers...that it is too difficult to dirty oneself by joining God in His Land, stepping into the "mud" of a struggling country... Rejected, God removes His hand from the latch... Only then does the nation grasp the significance of her hesitation and her innards begin to turn as she rises to open the door. Unfortunately, her actions, because she is *smothered in perfume*, are dull and heavy, her arms and fingers *dripping with cold cream* and *Chanel No. 5*. By the time the latch is opened, God is gone, and she goes on searching desperately everywhere for her beloved.[182]

---

[180] *Num. Rabba* 2:16 (53 in H. Freedman & Maurice Simon (eds.), *Midrash Rabba* (London: The Soncino Press, 1983)).

[181] *The Jerusalem Post* is a daily English newspaper in Israel. Riskin's weekly column "Shabbat Shalom" appears in the popular overseas edition as well.

[182] *The Jerusalem Post* (Friday, April 13, 1990). [italics mine]

Here Riskin, in his reading of the Song of Songs, has chosen to use the metaphor of a sinning woman to depict the entire nation (both men and women!) which does not heed God's call to settle in the Land of Israel. He does this without being in the least cognizant of the anti-female bias of the metaphor. The ancient metaphor—God as male and the sinning people as female—is alive and well in present day rabbinical thinking.

Harold Fisch, another contemporary writer, uses the prooftext of Hosea 11.7-8 to keep this bias alive:

> And my people are bent
> On turning away from me...
> But how can I give you up, O Ephraim?
> How shall I surrender thee, O Israel?

Writing as a literary critic, he states that:

> paradoxically we discover God's unconditional love only through the negating of it... Through the language of denial, God's *overmastering love* is manifested. It cannot be overcome, nor can the name *Ammi* (my people) be eradicated[183]

I find this imagery and way of thinking reminiscent of John Donne's famous Holy Sonnet 14.

> Batter my heart, three person'd God; for you
> As yet but knock, breathe, shine, and seek to mend.
> Take me to you, imprison me, for I,
> Except you enthrall me, never shall be free,
> Nor ever chaste, except you ravish me.

Both the prophet and Donne accept the assumption that God is an aggressive, domineering being who is master over His passive, female, adoring people. There is a need to eradicate the self through an intense sexual relationship. The implication is that in order to find God one must sacrifice one's sense of self-hood.[184]

But this type of thinking is dangerous both to women and to society in general. I argue, along with other feminist

---

[183] Harold Fisch, "Hosea: A Poetics of Violence," in *Poetry with a Purpose* (Bloomington, IN: Indiana University Press, 1990): 145. [emphasis mine]

[184] This message is familiar to women.

commentators,[185] that the language of Hosea and the other prophets and rabbis who use "objectified female sexuality as a symbol of evil"[186] has had damaging effects on women. Women who read of God's relationship with Israel through the prism of a misogynist male prophet or rabbinical commentator, and have religious sensibilities, are forced to identify against themselves.[187]

Fokkelien van Dijk-Hemmes asks the salient question:

> Why is Israel, first the land but then also the nation, represented in the image of a faithless wife, a harlot and not in the image of e.g. a rapist? This would have been more justified when we look at Israel's misdeeds which YHWH/Hosea points out in the following 4.1-5.7... And beyond that, it is the men who are held responsible for social and religious abuses; it is the

---

[185] See Mayer I. Gruber, "The Motherhood of God in Second Isaiah," *Revue Biblique* 3 (1983): 251-259.

[186] T. Drorah Setel, "Prophets and Pornography: Female Sexual Imagery in Hosea," in Letty Russell (ed.), *Feminist Interpretation of the Bible* (Philadelphia: Westminster, 1985): 86. Tikva Frymer-Kensky, *In the Wake of Goddesses* (New York: The Free Press, 1992): 150, recognizes the problematic nature of our text and the marriage metaphor but is not willing to accept that the negative portrayal of Israel-as-wife rises from misogyny. She writes that except for Ecclesiastes, "there are no overt anti-woman statements in the Hebrew Bible...[although] the depiction of the Wanton City-woman is the most truly negative portrayal of any female in the Bible" (150). But she stresses that the prophets' anger is directed against the people (city) and not the women. She admits, however, that "the intensity of these passages and their sexual fantasies of nymphomania and revenge seem to be fueled by unconscious fear and rage."

[187] Mayer I. Gruber, "The Motherhood of God in Second Isaiah," *Revue Biblique* 3 (1983): 358, writes that Jeremiah and Ezekiel "intimated that in the religion of Israel maleness is a positive value...while femaleness is a negative value with which divinity refuses to identify itself." Tikva Frymer-Kensky, *In the Wake of Goddesses* (New York: The Free Press, 1992): 152, writes that "the marital metaphor reveals the dramatic inner core of monotheism: the awesome solo mastery of God brings humans into direct unadulterated contact with supreme power...in this relationship, the people stand directly before and with God... There is only us and God." Clearly the relationship is awesome, but to the battered wife/people, there is something frightening about there being no buffer or intercessor between us and a God who is depicted as a vengeful husband.

priests who mislead the people (4.4-6) and the fathers who force their daughters to play the harlot (4.13-14).[188]

Why did it not occur to Riskin to say that "Israel was too busy fiddling with his computers or tinkering with his cars or watching football on the Sabbath to have time to pay attention to God?"

The problem is that the ancient metaphors of marriage, in order to emphasize God's love, take for granted the patriarchal view of women's subservient role. They represent God's punishment of Israel as justice. According to Ilana Pardes, God's severe response to Israel is "almost moderate, given her ingratitude. One is expected to take pity on God for having to play such a violent role, for having to suffer so for the sake of Law and Order."[189] Prophets and rabbis should not be enshrining the legal subordination of women in metaphor.[190] In my view, love, punishment, and subservience are not compatible concepts.

Why should this concern us at all, since presumably the metaphor only expresses the social reality of the biblical period? In fact one can argue that understanding "the historical setting of prophetic texts may provide a perspective of "moral realism" which allows them to be read as sacred writing."[191] However, the argument for a historical setting recedes if we realize that because of the sanctification of Hosea 2 in a fixed Haftara, it plays a role in perpetuating biblical patriarchalism into our own day. Because of its morally-flawed allegory, the message of the prophets can be understood as permitting husbands to abuse their wives psychologically and physically.[192]

---

[188] Fokkelien Van Dijk-Hemmes, "The Imagination of Power and the Power of Imagination: An Intertextual Analysis of Two Biblical Love Songs: The Song of Songs and Hosea 2," *Journal for the Study of the Old Testament* 44:6 (1990): 85.

[189] Pardes, Ilana. *Countertraditions in the Bible* (Cambridge, MA: Harvard University Press, 1992): 136.

[190] Judith Plaskow, *Standing Again at Sinai: Judaism from a Feminist Perspective* (San Francisco: Harper & Row, 1990): 6.

[191] T. Drorah Setel, "Prophets and Pornography: Female Sexual Imagery in Hosea," in Letty Russell (ed.), *Feminist Interpretation of the Bible* (Philadelphia: Westminster, 1985): 95.

[192] See Judith Plaskow, *Standing Again at Sinai: Judaism from a Feminist Perspective* (San Francisco: Harper & Row, 1990): 6. See also Mayer I.

An argument for the continuance of this fixed Haftara in the tradition might be that of its so-called "happy end." If we examine God's declaration of love to "his" people superficially, it appears to be a monogamous declaration by God to "his" formerly faithless people. Hosea 2.16-22 goes as follows:

> I will speak coaxingly to her
> and lead her through the wilderness
> and speak to her tenderly...
>
>> There she shall respond as in the days of her
>> youth, when she came up from the land of Egypt.
>
> And in that day—declares the Lord—
> you will call [Me] *Ishi* [husband],
> and no more will you call Me *Baali*.
>
>> For I will remove
>> the names of the *Baalim* from her mouth,
>> and they shall nevermore be mentioned by name.
>
> In that day, I will make a covenant for them
> with the beasts of the field, the birds of the air,
> and the creeping things of the ground;
> I will also banish bow, sword, and war from the land.
> Thus I will let them lie down in safety.
>
>> And I will espouse you forever:
>> I will espouse you with righteousness and justice,
>> and with goodness and mercy,
>
> and I will espouse you with faithfulness;
> Then you shall be devoted to [*yadat et*] the Lord.

One might claim that in a polytheistic society, the assumption of total faithfulness on God's part and the demand of faithfulness to a single God on the people's part was revolutionary. The prophet's use of the marriage metaphor "You will call [Me] *'ishi* [my man/husband]" is a new vision of a God who will not tolerate a polygamous association. "And no more will you call me *Ba'ali*

Gruber, "The Motherhood of God in Second Isaiah," *Revue Biblique* 3 (1983): 35, who concludes his article by saying: "...a religion which seeks to convey the Teaching of God who is above and beyond both sexes cannot succeed in conveying that Teaching if it seeks to do so in a manner which implies that a positive-divine value is attached only to one of the two sexes."

[my husband/lord/master]. For I will remove the names of the *Ba'alim* [pagan gods]…"[193] The monogamous aspect of marriage on the part of the husband is clearly unusual, but it still does not address the problematics involved in monogamy when one side controls the other.

Mary Joan Winn Leith argues that:

> The rejected form of address, Ba'al, implies not only a different deity, but also a different, more dominating relationship… God's new title, "husband" [*ishi*], signals a new beginning, a new betrothal, and a (re)new(ed) covenant, whose inauguration sounds strikingly like a (re)creation of the world.[194]

But there is a terrible assumption here in Leith's argument. Israel has to suffer in order to be entitled to this new betrothal. "She" has to be battered into submission in order to kiss and make up at the end. She has to agree to be on the receiving end of her husband's jealousy. The premise is that a woman has no other choice but to remain in such a marriage. True, God is very generous to Israel. He promises to espouse her forever with righteousness, justice, goodness, mercy and faithfulness. But despite the potential for a new model of a relationship between God and Israel, it is not a model of real reciprocity. It is based on suffering and the assumption that Israel will submit to God's will. Hosea, however, rejoices in this transformation and in the "ordeal [which] has fit the woman for a new, enhanced relationship with God."[195]

The reader who is caught up in this joyous new betrothal and renewed covenant overlooks the fact that this joyous reconciliation between God and Israel follows the exact pattern that battered wives know so well. Israel is physically and psychologically punished, abused, and then seduced into remaining in the covenant by tender words and caresses. The religious images may be as beautiful and profound as Leith has pointed out but, as Yee writes,

---

[193] There is a *double entendre* here since *ba'al* can also be understood to mean husband/owner.

[194] Mary Joan Winn Leith, "Verse and Reverse: The Transformation of the Woman, Israel, in Hosea 1-3," in Peggy L. Day (ed.), *Gender and Difference in Ancient Israel* (Minneapolis: Fortress Press, 1989): 101.

[195] Idem: 103.

studies have shown that many wives remain in abusive
relationships because periods of mistreatment are often
followed by intervals of kindness and generosity. This
ambivalent strategy reinforces the wife's dependence
on the husband. During periods of kindness, her fears
are temporarily eased so that she decides to remain in
the relationship; then the cycle of abuse begins again.[196]

God is not suggesting a full-fledged partnership, despite his
declarations. Hosea's portrayal of Israel as a sinning woman
returning abjectly to the open arms of her husband who graciously
accepts her—after her great suffering, and providing she repents
—has limited the potential of the relationship. Thus, the prophet's
marriage metaphor is problematic. It makes its theological point at
the expense of women and contracts rather than expands the
potential of partnership.

One might argue that Jewish tradition did try to expand the
potential. This can be seen in the assumption that Jewish males
gain sensitivity from their obligation to recite the concluding
phrases from the Haftara when they put on their *tefillin*
(phylacteries) every morning.

> And I will espouse you forever:
> I will espouse you with righteousness and justice,
> and with goodness and mercy,
> and I will espouse you with faithfulness;
> Then you shall be devoted to [*yadat et*] the Lord
> (Hos 2.21-2).

What does it mean to daily identify with a woman's position?
For that is what the male does. The male wraps the bands of the
tefillin around his middle finger—almost like a wedding ring. He
repeats the words God says to his bride. He affirms and re-affirms
his binding relationship with God. Clearly God is binding Himself
to Israel as a groom binds himself to his bride. The male who puts
on tefillin identifies with the bride. Since the male (identifying with
the female) is in a subservient relationship to God in this daily re-
run of the ritual of marriage, does he gain any insight from this
experience which forces him to subconsciously reverse roles? Can
this ritual act be a basis for re-interpreting Hosea?

---

[196] Gail A. Yee, "Hosea," in C. A. Newsom and S. H. Ringe (eds.), *The
Women's Bible Commentary* (Louisville, KY: Westminster, 1992): 200.

REINTERPRETING HOSEA

There are two midrashim which shed light on this question. One of them, a midrash on a verse from *Parashat Ekeb* (Deut 7.12), looks promising as a basis for reinterpretation. This midrash connects the covenant between God and Abraham with the marriage of a king and a noble lady who brings two valuable gems into the house. In this partnership type of relationship she brings gems and he also brings gems. When she loses the gems, he takes away his. When she finds them, he restores his and decrees that,

> a crown should be made of both sets of gems and that it should be placed on the head of the noble lady... God too set up corresponding to them two gems, namely, loving kindness and mercy... Israel lost theirs... God thereupon took away His... And after Israel have restored theirs and God has given back His, God will say, "Let both pairs be made into a crown and be placed on the head of Israel," as it is said, "And I will betroth thee unto Me, yea, I will betroth thee unto Me in righteousness and in justice, and in loving kindness, and in compassion. And I will betroth thee unto Me in faithfulness; and thou shalt know the Lord" (Hos 2.21).[197]

The greater context of this midrash is that of the book of Deuteronomy. In this book Israel is constantly being berated and threatened by God. If Israel behaves as God demands, Israel will be treated well. If Israel strays from the narrow path, Israel will be punished. However, the rabbis have made a tremendous conceptual leap forward by allowing us to imply from the relationship that God has with Abraham the potential relationship of partnership that a man can have with his wife.[198]

However, in another less promising midrash which connects the passage "For the Lord your God is a consuming fire, an impassioned God *'el qana'*" from Deuteronomy 4.24 with the passage "I will espouse you with faithfulness" (Hos 2.21), we have a different kind of relationship: God as a jealous husband. In

---

[197] *Deut. Rabba (Ekeb)* 3:7 (H. Freedman & Maurice Simon (eds.), *Midrash Rabba* (London: The Soncino Press, 1983): 75-76).

[198] Thanks to Michael Graetz for bringing the midrash to my attention and discussing its meaning with me.

contrast to those who merit *'olam habba'*—the next world—are those who are consumed by a great fire. The rabbis ask, How do we know that God is jealous? The answer is, Just as a husband is jealous of his wife, so is the God of Israel.[199]

Thus, the use of the *tefillin* ritual could become a means of reinterpreting the Haftara from Hosea only if it is accompanied by specific interpretation.

REFORMING THE HAFTARA READINGS

What can be done to address the problem of women's subordination, yet remain within the bounds of the tradition? The easiest approach is to simply disassociate ourselves from the text with a disclaimer such as, "This was the way women were seen in ancient times; this way of continuing to view women is dangerous and we of course do not view women as subordinate to men, as sexual objects to be vilified." We should not continue to honor this tradition. Today, there can never be extenuating circumstances that encourage violence in a marriage.

Another option is to take a second look at the tradition, with a view to reforming the present fixed cycle of Haftara portions, by choosing other prophetic passages in place of offensive ones.

When the sages introduced the additional readings and when the weekly Torah portion was fluid, any reading could suffice to fulfil the requirement of the blessing of reading from *nebi'ey ha'emet wasedeq* ("prophets of truth and righteousness"). Later when *haftarot* (the additional portions) were codified, that is, were associated with particular weekly portions, the *haftarot* also served the purpose of interpreting the Torah, of being a sort of first-line midrash on the portion. As with so much else, what started out as fluid is now fixed, virtually codified. Thus, although the custom of fixed *haftarot* exists, we have ample precedent to change the readings completely.

THEOLOGICAL IMPLICATIONS

It is almost a truism to speak of God as having the power and authority to control and possess. However, it is theologically debatable whether God wants to use this power to interfere in our lives. Unfortunately, the prophets persisted in representing God as having and wanting the same authority to control and possess that

---

[199] *Midrash Tanhuma* (Warsaw), *Parashat saw* 14.1 [Hebrew].

a husband has traditionally had over his wife. In an ideal marriage, in which there is a relationship of equality, a wife should not have to submit to her husband's authority.

The purpose of the metaphor is to enhance acceptance of God's relationship with Israel. But that can only be the case in a society in which the marriage metaphor is acceptable to men and women. When the marriage metaphor is *a priori* unacceptable to men and women of a particular society then it no longer serves as an acceptable mode of thought concerning God's relationship to Israel.

It is difficult, perhaps impossible, to sustain a metaphoric relationship that implies a double standard. We need new metaphors—perhaps to be inspired by the Song of Songs.[200] Scolnic objects to my thesis that we need alternative *haftarot*, arguing that "dropping a Haftarah is not the Jewish way...certainly [he says, it is] not the Conservative Jewish approach."[201] I disagree. Today, when the ideal of marriage has shifted to a more congenial ideal of partnership, the classic, ancient metaphors in the *haftarot* describing the relationship between God and "his" people have proved to be limited, misleading and repugnant.

---

[200] Ilana Pardes, *Countertraditions in the Bible* (Cambridge, MA: Harvard University Press, 1992). Pardes contrasts the patriarchal marital model in Hosea with the antipatriarchal model of love in the Song of Songs. She writes that the Songs of Songs could be made to function as a countervoice to the misogynist prophetic degradation of the nation. It could offer an inspiring consolation in its emphasis on reciprocity. For once the relationship of God and His bride relies on mutual courting, mutual attraction, and mutual admiration, there is more room for hope that redemption is within reach (127). She also takes issue with Phyllis Trible (see note 172 above). But here too all is not perfect, for rabbinic interpretation appropriated the Song of Songs for its own theological purposes. In the midrash on *Shir ha-Shirim* the sages co-opted the female beloved/male lover images by identifying her as male Israel and the beloved man as God.

[201] Benjamin Edidin Scolnic, "Bible Battering," *Conservative Judaism* 45 (Fall, 1992): 52-53.

WILL THE REAL HAGAR PLEASE STAND UP?

> Sarai, Abram's wife, had borne him no children. She had an Egyptian maidservant whose name was Hagar. ²And Sarai said to Abram, "Look, the LORD has kept me from bearing. Consort with my maid; perhaps I shall have a son through her." And Abram heeded Sarai's request. ³So Sarai, Abram's wife, took her maid, Hagar the Egyptian—after Abram had dwelt in the land of Canaan ten years—and gave her to her husband Abram as concubine. ⁴He cohabited with Hagar and she conceived; and when she saw that she had conceived, her mistress was lowered in her esteem. ⁵And Sarai said to Abram, "The wrong done me is your fault! I myself put my maid in your bosom; now that she sees that she is pregnant, I am lowered in her esteem. The LORD shall decide between you and me!" ⁶Abram said to Sarai, "Your maid is in your hands. Deal with her as you think right." Then Sarai treated her harshly, and she ran away from her. (Gen 16.1-6)

The story of Hagar is one of the most poignant and disturbing tales in the Bible. Throughout history, sensitive readers have been perturbed by the cynical exploitation of Hagar and her expulsion. The attitude toward the "other," which already began in biblical times, continues to plague us today; thus, it is important to study problematic texts, such as this one, in view of the fact that Sarai and Hagar's discord have reverberated until the present day.

Why this concern with the fate of Hagar? Why is her story important to us—especially since after the expulsion we do not hear of her again, at least in the biblical story? We do know that her son, Ishmael, attends Abraham's funeral where he meets up with Sarah's son, Isaac. These concerns can be read into the Bible, the Hadith, and various midrashim. Often the midrash and the Hadith tend to resist the story in the Bible by devising a different plot, with a happy ending, or by showing the evil consequences of a particular act.

The Bible does not tell us anything of Hagar's origins. In Genesis 12.16 it is mentioned that Abram acquired some maidservants when he was in Egypt. The Koran does not mention her at all. According to one of the Muslim traditions,[202] Pharaoh gave to Sarai, Hagar, a Coptic slave-girl of his, because he was impressed with Sarai's goodness and beauty. Rashi writes that Hagar was a daughter of Pharaoh (Rashi on Gen 16.1). The midrash also identifies Keturah (Abraham's new wife in Gen 25.1 after Sarah dies) as Hagar. If Abraham had really divorced her (cast her out), he could not then have taken her as a wife, according to halakha. Thus, rabbinic tradition, in its positive reception of her, takes pains to show that Abraham did not "cast" her out; rather she was "sent" out. This would also apply to Ishmael. In redeeming Hagar, the rabbis trace her nobility and emphasize her qualities to justify her conversing freely with the angels and her attributing a name to God (*el roi*, God sees me). Following this same type of reasoning, Muslim tradition redeems Ishmael by telling how his father Abraham established the Kaaba in Mecca for him.

Some feminists depict Hagar as an object that is given by Sarai to Abraham. Although Sarai sees Hagar purely in terms of her breeding potential—like the handmaidens in Margaret Atwood's utopian novel, *The Handmaid's Tale* (1985)[203]—the breeder rebels, in keeping with her status as Abraham's wife, not concubine. Other feminists see Hagar the bondmaid (*shifhah*) and/or slave (*amah*), as an exploited (second) wife, abused by those who are the first of our forefathers and foremothers. According to Phyllis Trible, Hagar is "one of the first females in scripture to experience use, abuse, and rejection."[204] She is a triple-fold alien: from her country, in her

---

[202] Al-Tabiri, "The History of al-Tabari," in William M. Brenner (tr.), *Prophets and Patriarchs* II (Albany: State University of New York Press, 1987): 62-63.

[203] Margaret Atwood, *The Handmaid's Tale* (Toronto, Canada: McClelland and Stewart, 1985).

[204] Phyllis Trible, *Texts of Terror: Literary-Feminist Readings of Biblical Narratives* (Philadelphia: Fortress Press, 1984): 9.

status, and in her sex.[205] She is an Egyptian maidservant living in Canaan; she is "single, poor and bonded."[206] She is a powerless object whose status is contingent on that of her mistress, Sarai, the wife of Abram.

> [7]An angel of the Lord found her by a spring of water in the wilderness, the spring on the road to Shur, [8]and said, "Hagar, slave of Sarai, where have you come from, and where are you going?" And she said, "I am running away from my mistress Sarai." [9]And the angel of the Lord said to her, "Go back to your mistress, and submit to her harsh treatment." [10]And the angel of the Lord said to her, "I will greatly increase your offspring, And they shall be too many to count" (Gen 16.7-10).

The Bible's attitude towards Hagar is very sympathetic. In a story such as this—where Sarah calls the shots, Abraham displays ambivalence, God decides and Hagar behaves passively—the focus would not normally be on Hagar after she is expelled. Instead, this silent woman becomes the center of the story, which turns into a story about her strength and feelings of pain and love for her child. Moreover, the angel clearly "cares" about her and talks to her, for she is a victim who is given an unequivocal message to remain a victim. It is as if he says to her, "Go back to this oppressive situation. Stay, don't run away. Your reward will be a son who will be a strong warrior." She is like a battered wife who runs away, yet doesn't know what to do with herself, thus returning to her original situation of learned helplessness.[207]

Despite this abusive situation, the angel of the Lord speaks to Hagar on two occasions. The first is when she is pregnant with Abram's seed and Sarai is threatened by Hagar's new position. Sarai was tacitly allowed by Abram to do with Hagar as she pleased. "Your maid is in your hands. Deal with her as you think right" (Gen 16.6).

---

[205] Bruce Rosenstock, "Inner-Biblical Exegesis in the Book of the Covenant," *Conservative Judaism* (Spring 1992): 45 points out that the name Hagar may be a pun on *ger* (alien).

[206] Phyllis Trible, *Texts of Terror: Literary-Feminist Readings of Biblical Narratives* (Philadelphia: Fortress Press, 1984): 10.

[207] Lenore Walker, a forensic psychologist, in *The Battered Woman* (Harper & Row, 1979) relied heavily on the concept of learned helplessness to support the view of battered women's syndrome.

The midrash, perhaps aware of the unfairness in this, reveals a shade of ambivalence on Abram's part:

> Said he: "I am constrained to do her neither good nor harm [since she is now my wife]. It is written, Thou shalt not deal with her as a slave, because thou hast humbled her (Deut xxi, 14): after we have vexed her, can we now enslave her again? I am constrained to do her neither good nor harm" (*Gen. Rabba* 45:6).

The midrash goes on to shift the blame to Sarai making her totally responsible for the physical and mental violence inflicted upon Hagar.

> R. Abbah said: She restrained her from cohabitation.
> R. Berekiah said: She slapped her face with a slipper.
> R. Berekiah said in R. Abbah's name: She bade her carry her water buckets and bath towels to the baths (*Gen. Rabba* 45:6).

In light of the fact that Hagar had the status of a wife, Sarah, in giving her menial work, both mistreated and humiliated her.

Hagar is not encouraged to fight for her freedom; rather it is assumed that she remain in her servant status. She is advised to stay where she is and suffer for the sake of her future child: Accept the abuse now, because your own life is of no intrinsic worth. You live for the sake of your son; you are the caretaker of his future.

When Hagar has her son, Ishmael, Sarah[208] is again incensed and this time tells Abraham to "cast out that slave-woman and her son..." (21.10). This time, as Trible points out, "Hagar has lost her name... Moreover; the absence of dialogue continues to separate the females. Inequality, opposition, and distance breed violence."[209]

Although the matter distressed Abraham greatly, not because of Hagar, but because it "concerned a son of his" (Gen 21.11) God tells him not to be

> ...distressed over the boy or your slave; whatever Sarah tells you, do as she says... As for the son of the slave-

---

[208] Sarai gets her name changed to Sarah in Gen 17.15 and Abram to Abraham in Gen 17.5.

[209] Phyllis Trible, *Texts of Terror: Literary-Feminist Readings of Biblical Narratives* (Philadelphia: Fortress Press, 1984): 13.

woman, I will make a nation of him, too, for he is your
seed (Gen 21.12-13).

Thus, the "son" becomes "a boy" and "Hagar" becomes a "slave."
As Trible puts it, "if Abraham neglected Hagar, God belittles
her."[210]

In these biblical texts, God identifies with the oppressor, not
with the oppressed. God and Abraham are accomplices in the
decision to cast out the object, the slave-woman of no account.
Abraham cares only about his seed, his son, not about the woman.
It is Sarah who cares about being supplanted and who initiates the
act. It would appear that the Bible also sympathizes with Sarah's
plight when it writes that it is a "loathsome" situation when "a
slave girl supplants her mistress" (Prov 30.23).

What does it mean that the Angel sees the suffering of the
despised woman, the Egyptian stranger (ha-ger)? What are the
parallels between his promises to her and to Abraham? Compare
the fact that the Angel of God speaks twice to Hagar and only once
to Sarah. The rabbis themselves wonder at the fact that God speaks
to Hagar and explain it by saying that "Abraham's household was
used to seeing angels up close because of his close relationship with
God." Is God's blessing of Ishmael a fair distribution of goods
between Abraham's two sons?

It is not only Hagar who is damaged; her child suffers as well,
both physically and spiritually. Hints of this can be read in the
blessing (or perhaps curse) given to Hagar by the divine messenger:

> Behold, you are with child
> And shall bear a son;
> You shall call him Ishmael,
> For the Lord has paid heed to your suffering.
> He shall be a wild ass of a man;
> His hand against everyone,
> And everyone's hand against him;
> He shall dwell alongside of all his kinsmen
> (Gen 16.11-12).

Ishmael has witnessed that God had not "paid heed to [her]
suffering" and that, in fact, she had been abused by all those close
to her. It is likely that he will grow up with a chip on his shoulder,
perceiving that "everyone's hand [is] against him" and that "his

---

[210] Idem: 22.

hand [will be] against everyone." He will also become an oppressor, when he gets the chance, even against the people of Israel.

What does biblical law have to say about the expulsion of Ishmael?

> The laws of the Torah do not permit parents, or even legal authorities, to expel a son or daughter from the home for any reason. According to the Torah, nobody can divest an offspring of his legal status in the household to which he belongs. This was not the practice among other peoples in the ancient Near East: Various codices and ancient legal documents, some even predating the time of Abraham, attest that expelling one's offspring from the parents' home, i.e., divesting a child of his legal status in his father's house, was a legitimate legal procedure in cases of offenses committed against the parents. While the Torah was not lenient about the punishment of a child who committed an offense against his parents—a child who struck or cursed his parents could be sentenced to death, if proven guilty—nevertheless he could not be banished for delinquent behavior.[211]

Hence, Abraham's casting out of Hagar and Ishmael is problematic. Ishmael is a legal son of Abraham's whom he circumcised at age thirteen. Sarah's words, "Cast out that slave-woman and her son, for the son of that slave shall not share in the inheritance with my son Isaac" (21.10), make it obvious that she thought he did have rights to Abraham's inheritance by virtue of being Abraham's son.

To make this illegality more palatable, traditional midrash demonizes Ishmael to illustrate how his action against Isaac was worthy of his being demoted as a legal heir and deserving of exile. The pretext that Sarah used to expel Ishmael was that he was making "sport" with (*metzahek*) Isaac. The midrash says that this refers to his immorality and Sarah's prophetic vision that he would ravish maidens and seduce married woman in the future (*Gen. Rabba* 53:11). Maimonides comments that God saw Hagar's affliction and gave her a son who was destined to be a lawless person. This contradicts the biblical text which states that Abraham

---

[211] Joseph Fleischman "*Parashat Vayera* 5760/1999, The Expulsion of Ishmael," (Bar Ilan University, Weekly Internet Sermons).

loved Ishmael too (Gen 17.18; 21.11, 26) and that Ishmael was
blessed in his ways (17.20) and God was with the lad (21.20). Surely
the bible would not have said this about someone who was
destined to be a lawless person.

There are those who identify the victimization of Hagar as a
prefiguration of Israel's enslavement in Egypt. According to Trible,
Hagar, unlike Israel,

> ... experiences exodus without liberation, revelation
> without salvation, wilderness without covenant,
> wanderings without land, promise without fulfillment,
> and unmerited exile without return. This Egyptian slave
> woman is stricken, smitten by God, and afflicted for
> the transgressions of Israel.[212]

Following Trible's insights one step further, I would argue
that Hagar, the suffering slave woman, serves as a prototype for the
metaphor of Israel as the suffering, mistreated wife of God.[213]

In the Islamic versions of the expulsion of Hagar and Ishmael
there are many expansions on the original biblical text to
emphasize Ishmael's mother's extraordinary stamina and dedication
as a mother. In one tradition, Abraham goes with them as far as
Mecca and then returns home. When she asks, "To whom are you
leaving us?" He replies "to Allah." When her water is used up she
goes down a mountain and runs back and forth seven times
between the mountains of Safa and Marwa, before she hears from
the angel Gabriel. He causes water to gush forth from the earth
(the sacred well of Zamzum) and this attracts first birds and then
people who join her and form a community. Muslim pilgrims
traditionally imitate Hagar's distress by encircling these sacred
spots. After Ishmael's mother dies, Abraham returns several times
to visit his son and the relationship continues. He checks to see if
Ishmael has married a suitable wife by testing them with riddles
(2.127 *Sahih Bukhari* 4.584). Abraham and Ishmael together build
the temple in Mecca and place in it the black stone.

---

[212] Phyllis Trible, *Texts of Terror: Literary-Feminist Readings of Biblical
Narratives* (Philadelphia: Fortress Press, 1984): 28.

[213] For an expansion of this point see the previous article in this book
"God is to Israel as Husband is to Wife" on page 69.

CONCLUSION

One father, two wives, two sons, and two different traditions emerge from this original biblical tale. Why was Abraham destined to have the two sons? Wouldn't it have been much simpler if there were only one? Every child with a brother or sister fantasizes about being an only child. What does it mean when our tradition tells us that one child is predestined to cause the other trouble? Moreover, why does God cause suffering to both their mothers? There are no real answers to these questions. Perhaps it is only an articulation of reality: this is the way of the world; very few of us are "lucky" enough to be an only child; most of us have to learn how to live with the other. The problem with this is that often we find "the other" too difficult to deal with and we end up demonizing him or her[214] to keep them at bay and justify our treatment of those who are different.

Issues such as these become even more complicated when God is introduced into the discussion, and we are taught that the Deity has commanded us to behave in such a fashion, that is, to cast out the one who is not the favorite son. Sarah and Hagar's enmity had repercussions that we, the heirs of Ishmael and Isaac, still suffer from. When one is asked, "where have we come from" and "where are we going to," I suggest being prepared with the following answer: Our mutual past history may have limited and enslaved us, but now it is time to move beyond the past.

---

[214] For instance there was Rabbi Ovadia Yosef's sermon which compared Arabs to snakes that should all be annihilated. In this utterance, Yosef, once known as a political dove, denounced Barak for "running after" the Palestinians. "Why are you bringing them close to us?" he asked. "You bring snakes next to us. How can you make peace with a snake?" Dismissing the Arabs as "Ishmaelites," he added for bad measure: "They are all accursed, wicked ones. They are all haters of Israel. It says in the Gemara that the Holy One, Blessed be He, is sorry he created these Ishmaelites" *The Jewish Journal of Greater Los Angeles* (August 11, 2000).

A MIDRASHIC LENS ON BIBLICAL WOMEN

Since the mid-70s feminists have begun reclaiming the canon and have engaged in the re-reading of texts which often omitted women's presence while at the same time prescribing our essence and behavior. Canonical texts, whether in literature, philosophy, or religion, delineated women's proper role, defining us as irrational, passionate human beings. Religious feminists began to liberate the canon when they discovered that the Bible was being used as a weapon to keep women in their place by legitimizing patriarchal power.

As early as the 70s Jewish women were re-engaging with our canonical texts and doing such things as liberating God, writing new rituals, critiquing *mikvah*, creating *rosh ḥodesh* observances, writing *Haggadot* for women—in short, de-patriarchalizing our tradition. In the first collection of works published in this period Mary Gendler restored Vashti to her rightful place and Linda Kuzmack in her article "Aggadic Approaches to Biblical Women," discussed three alternative "explanations of why the aggadah overwhelmingly presented women in relation to men, with relatively little freedom to act on their own initiative."[215] In the

---

[215] Elizabeth Koltun (ed.), *The Jewish Woman: New Perspectives* (New York: Schocken Books, 1976): 251. Although many of the articles in the book had been previously published, this article was written especially for the collection which started out as a special issue of *Response*. Other works which have paved the way for feminist Jewish writers are: Sharon Cohen, "Reclaiming the Hammer: Toward a Feminist Midrash," *Tikkun* 3, 2 (March/April 1988): 55-57; 94-95; Phyllis Trible, *Texts of Terror: Literary-Feminist Readings of Biblical Narratives* (Philadelphia: Fortress Press, 1984); Letty Russell (ed.), *Feminist Interpretation of the Bible* (Philadelphia: Westminster Press, 1985); David Stern, *Parables in Midrash: Narrative and Exegesis in Rabbinic Literature* (Cambridge, MA: Harvard University Press, 1991); Leila Leah Bronner, *From Eve to Esther: Rabbinic Reconstructions of Biblical Women* (Louisville: Westminster John Knox Press, 1995); Elyse

1980s Phyllis Trible's feminist interpretation of biblical texts influenced both those who were writing midrash and studying biblical criticism—there was clearly a non-patriarchal way of looking at text. Letty Russell's edited book, *Feminist Interpretation of the Bible*, was quoted by all later scholars who were working in the field. Sharon Cohen, a rabbinical student when she published her "state of the art" article about the need for feminists to reclaim midrash, quoted from Trible, Daly, Schussler Fiorenza, and Letty Russell to make the point that diversity of interpretation can only enhance the whole and that the rabbinic paradigm of partnership should be inclusive rather than exclusive.[216]

Goldstein, *Revisions: Seeing Torah Through a Feminist Lens* (Woodstock, VT: Jewish Lights, 1999); Atalyah Brenner's collections (see footnote 229, infra); Devorah Steinmetz (see footnote 233 infra); Marc Gellman's many books of midrashim for children; Naomi Graetz (see footnote 229, infra); David A. Katz and Peter Lovenheim (eds.), *Reading Between the Lines: New Stories from the Bible* (Northvale NJ: Jason Aronson, 1996); Jane Sprague Zones (ed.), *Taking the Fruit: Modern Women's Tales of the Bible* (San Diego: Women's Institute for Continuing Jewish Education, 1st edition, 1981, 2nd edition, 1989). I believe that women who are concerned about rewriting our Herstory should make an effort to mention our predecessors whenever possible and that we should not be afraid to admit that others have made similar points to ours, rather than writing: "I am part of a growing cadre of contemporary scholars who are taking a variety of approaches to the study of women and rabbinic dicta. What sets my work apart is its particular interest in aggadic texts. Much of the work in this field has dealt with women in Jewish legal writings. This volume differs in its emphasis on non-halakhic rabbinic exegesis…" (Judith Baskin, in the book under review in this essay.) To imply that this is what makes her book unique is disingenuous and damaging to the credibility of the book which otherwise rests on very sound scholarship. That Jill Hammer leaves out so many of her antecedents is equally grievous. However, she makes no claim to scholarship and thus her oversight can be more easily forgiven. The above list is not meant to be exhaustive, it was simply compiled by a look on my library shelf and basic works I regularly consult in my own research.

[216] Sharon Cohen, "Reclaiming the Hammer: Toward a Feminist Midrash," *Tikkun* 3, 2 (March/ April 1988): 55-57; 94-95; Phyllis Trible, *Texts of Terror: Literary-Feminist Readings of Biblical Narratives* (Philadelphia: Fortress Press, 1984); Letty Russell (editor), *Feminist Interpretation of the Bible* (Philadelphia: Westminster Press, 1985).

The contemporary resurgence in Jewish women writing midrash was sparked by our exposure to new interpretations exemplified by Reform Rabbi Marc Gellman's midrashim in *Moment* magazine. Although his work was not necessarily feminist, the fact that a committed Jew was re-interpreting the tradition with a contemporary voice legitimatized the religious creative act and freed us to relate to our concerns using a similar vehicle.

Judith Plaskow writes of the midrash's power to remember, to invent and receive the "hidden half of Torah, reshaping Jewish memory to let women speak."[217] Modern feminist midrash attempts to redress the misogynist tendencies of traditional mainstream midrash. The mainstream of rabbinic tradition depicts biblical women positively only if they are willing to assume the enabling roles of wife and/or mother.[218] Since most mainstream midrashim present biblical women as being of marginal importance or in a negative light there is a need for contemporary feminist midrash to change this image, to create role models for the next generation of women.

Not everyone agrees with Plaskow that Jewish women should be writing midrash. There are those women such as Jennifer Gubkin who critique the use of midrashim by women since it "holds marginal authority in the economy of rabbinic texts." Secondly it may possibly obscure the processes by which midrash is produced. Finally, "midrash as the appeal to women's voices, risks essentializing women…"[219] She writes that one should be careful to make explicit that our woman's voice is not necessarily all women's voice. Gubkin writes that the usual

> interconnection of voice and partnership that [the feminist midrash writer] presents deserves closer examination because it makes explicit the theoretical presuppositions which undergird many feminist

---

[217] Judith Plaskow, "Standing Again at Sinai," *Tikkun* I: 2 (1986):32.

[218] Linda Kuzmack, "Aggadic Approaches to Biblical Women," in E. Koltun (ed.), *The Jewish Woman: New Perspectives* (New York: Schocken Books, 1976).

[219] Jennifer Gubkin, "If Miriam Never Danced… A Question for Feminist Midrash," *Shofar* 14:1 (Fall 1995): 59. She is referring to Miriam Peskowitz's, "Engendering Religious History," in the same volume. This article was not included in Miriam Peskowitz and Laura Levitt, *Judaism Since Gender* (New York and London: Routledge, 1997).

midrashim. The 'demand for the women's voice' when heeded has led to new interpretations of the biblical text. Often feminists offer new readings by creating voices for the silent women in the Bible... By speaking in the voice of biblical women the contemporary writer places her own needs and concerns onto the biblical text without explicitly claiming them as her own.[220]

Gubkin calls into question the use of midrash as a tool. Since women are marginalized then we cannot simply add women's voices and stir. Secondly "the authority of midrash within the traditional economy of rabbinic texts was marginal, as these texts were accorded lesser status than halakhic forms."[221] Thus there is no liberatory power, no gaining of partnership if women, who are marginal to begin with, latch on to a marginal activity that has no authority in the patriarchal community. She feels that by devoting our energies to this activity we are solidifying our position as the "other" within Judaism. Gubkin would prefer to deal with the meta-text rather than the content itself. Rather than empower the historical biblical women through imaginative creations, she would prefer to ask how silencing of a particular woman functions in the text.

Feminist interpretation begins with a "hermeneutics of suspicion"[222] which is applied to both the biblical text and the

---

[220] Jennifer Gubkin, "If Miriam Never Danced... A Question for Feminist Midrash," *Shofar* 14:1 (Fall 1995): 61.

[221] Gubkin quoting Peskowitz, Jennifer Gubkin, "If Miriam Never Danced... A Question for Feminist Midrash," *Shofar* 14:1 (Fall 1995): 62.

[222] The term was first used by the French philosopher Paul Ricoeur in *Freud and Philosophy: An Essay on Interpretation* (New Haven: Yale University Press, 1970): 32, 33. He wrote: "Three masters, seemingly mutually exclusive, dominate the school of suspicion: Marx, Nietzsche, and Freud.... All three clear the horizon for a more authentic word, for a new reign of Truth, not only by means of a 'destructive' critique, but by the invention of an art of interpreting." The influence of Ricoeur's hermeneutic of suspicion can be seen in feminist liberation theology which exposes the unquestioning attitude toward ideologically entrenched ideas about women typical of the hegemony. For more about this hermeneutics of suspicion see Miriam Peskowitz, "Engendering Jewish Religious History," in Miriam Peskowitz and Laura Levitt, *Judaism Since Gender* (New York and London: Routledge, 1997).

traditional interpretations, or midrash. Westphal defines the hermeneutics of suspicion as

> the deliberate attempt to expose the self-deceptions involved in hiding our actual operative motives from ourselves, individually or collectively, in order not to notice how and how much our behavior and our beliefs are shaped by values we profess to disown.[223]

The very influential Christian theologian, Elisabeth Schussler Fiorenza, writing in the mid-80s, suggested that feminists move beyond suspicion (whose origins are often anti-religious) to reclaim or liberate the canon, arguing that intellectuals cannot remain neutral and must adopt an advocacy stance.[224]

Judith Baskin's *Midrashic Women* and Jill Hammer's *Sisters at Sinai* represent both stances: suspicion and liberation although neither define these terms in their introductions. [225] Baskin, a well-known academic, has edited many important books. She is now a Professor of Religious Studies and the Director of the Harold Schnitzer Family Program in Judaic Studies at the University of Oregon. Her book is part of the Brandeis Series on Jewish Women, sponsored by the Hadassah International Research Institute on Jewish Women. It is an exemplar of a writer influenced by the hermeneutics of suspicion.

Hammer, a creative writer, has had previous work published in many journals and anthologies. She is a licensed clinical psychologist and an ordained Conservative rabbi. She works at Ma'yan: The Jewish Women's Project of the Upper West Side, in Manhattan. Prior to this she was the editor of *Living Text: The Journal of Contemporary Midrash*. Her book provides a redemptive fix and a chance for the reader to recuperate from the gloomy picture provided by someone steeped in the stage of suspicion.

---

[223] Merold Westphal, *Suspicion and Faith: The Religious Uses of Modern Atheism* (New York: Fordham University Press, 1998): 13.

[224] Elisabeth Schussler Fiorenza, *Bread Not Stone: The Challenge of Feminist Biblical Interpretation* (Boston: Beacon Press, 1984): 137.

[225] Judith R. Baskin, *Midrashic Women: Formations of the Feminine in Rabbinic Literature* (Hanover, NH: Brandeis University Press, 2002). Jill Hammer, *Sisters at Sinai: New Tales of Biblical Women* (Philadelphia: The Jewish Publication Society, 2001).

Baskin's *Midrashic Women* examines the construction of women in aggadic midrash, with a focus on the following topics: The Otherness of Women in Rabbinic Judaism, Midrashic Revisions of Human (especially Female) Creation, Female Disadvantages and their Justifications by Rabbis, Women as Wives in Rabbinic Literature, Resolving the Anomaly of Female Infertility, and Rabbinic Delineations of the Worlds of Women, both in groups and as individuals. The book is scholarly and well aware of research trends in both biblical and midrashic scholarship.

In her introduction she sets the stage for the thesis of her book by quoting from the Bible, midrash and Simone de Beauvoir, "Biology is not enough to give an answer to the question that is before us: why is woman the Other?"[226] It is telling that *Le Deuxième Sexe*, written in 1949, traced the development of male oppression through historical, literary, and mythical sources, attributing its contemporary effects on women to a systematic objectification of the male as a positive norm. De Beauvoir was among the first to identify the female as Other, which involved a loss of social and personal identity. Following in her footsteps, Baskin focuses on women's essential alterity from men. She is man's companion, but different from him, since her function in life is to be a vessel for the nurturing of life. Her thesis, as stated in the introduction to her book is that "rabbinic sages deliberately constructed women as ancillary beings, shaped on the rib of the primordial man to fulfill essential social and sexual functions in an androcentric society."

Kuzmack allowed for the fact that different approaches to women in rabbinical texts may have reflected their different life experiences as well as their differing theologies. Thus her first alternative was that rabbis chose to depict women as subjugated to men and as having relatively little freedom out of an automatic choice conditioned by an ongoing tradition, thus: "the Rabbis really could not conceive of any other alternatives for women."[227] Kuzmack's Second Alternative was that "the Rabbis deliberately chose to make an already existent role the only role for Jewish

---

[226] Simone de Beauvoir, *The Second Sex*, H. M. Parshley (ed. and tr.) (New York: Vintage Books, 1989): 37.

[227] Linda Kuzmack, "Aggadic Approaches to Biblical Women," in Elizabeth Koltun (ed.), *The Jewish Woman: New Perspectives* (New York: Schocken Books, 1976): 251.

women, because they felt that the physical and spiritual survival of the Jewish people was being threatened to the point of extinction."[228] Baskin seems fixed on the Second Alternative, but she denies the 'rationalization' for the rabbi's choice. She, thus, turns rabbinic misogyny into a deliberate part of their worldview. In addition, she does not allow for an alternative view—whenever it seems possible she uses qualifying words to make it clear that it was a deliberate choice and not an "automatic" choice conditioned by a thousand years of tradition. It is unfortunate that Baskin does not engage in dialogue with Kuzmack, whose article may be outdated and somewhat conciliatory, but is multi-vocal and open-ended concerning rabbinic motivations. Thus, Baskin's book sets out to demonstrate that the rabbis were aware of the implications of denominating the feminine as having less value than the masculine and therefore had to "rationalize woman's less desirable place in their society as divinely intended."

She chose to focus on aggadic literature rather than halakhic discourse because, "the aggadah seems more reflective of the complexities of actual human relationships as they are lived, while the halakha appears to point toward an ideal, but not yet achieved, condition of order."

Her stated methodology is interesting and in itself is a critique of unnamed others who have used aggadah to "jump from statement to statement and text to text." What she does instead is to focus in each chapter on one or two lengthy and contextualized aggadic passages mostly from the Babylonian Talmud, occasionally from a midrash collection, in which the particular themes mentioned above are addressed. Despite her recognition that rabbinic literature is not monolithic, since it preserves both majority and minority points of view, she makes a convincing argument that "female alterity and women's innate inferiority to men emerge as primary."

Her goal in the book is focused: "my goal in this book is to recover from selected passages found in rabbinic literature those attitudes toward women which became authoritative in informing subsequent Jewish values and practices." Since she does not refer to medieval exegetes such as Rashi or the Tosafists she allows for the fact that others might argue that the strands she chose are not

---

[228] Idem: 252.

as central as she claims. While not arguing with her that rabbinic texts are misogynist, having myself written so,[229] I find problematic her unrelenting repetition that rabbinic texts could not rid themselves of these prejudices. Indeed, one could argue from her case that the rabbis, in their commitment to them, were obsessed and thus not "guilty" of intentional misogyny.

She does of course not make this claim; she says that they were totally aware of what they were doing and that it was part of their theological plan. Her argument in the first three chapters is that it all goes back to the privileging of the second account of creation and disregarding the challenging implications of the first. Even though she recognizes that there were some rabbinic references to a first Eve, they are few and obscure. The majority of rabbis agreed that the first woman was created from Adam's rib and this secondary origin accounts for the female inferiority which rabbinic writers took for granted. She finds it significant that rabbinic voices rationalized women's separate status and were unwilling to allow any woman entrance into their circles no matter how talented she was.

In chapter four "Fruitful Vines and Silent Partners: Women as Wives in Rabbinic Literature" she discusses good and bad wives. The good wife is one who enables her husband and male children to study Torah, while waiting patiently at home for him to return. The bad wife is one who goes outside the house, makes noise and brings attention to herself. Yet the rabbis are willing to put up with her as long as she continues to bring babies into the world. This section also introduces the idea of marriage as metaphor between the male community and God in order to point out that women get totally erased from the equation when God is the male lover and his beloved is female Israel which is comprised only of males as far

---

[229] "Dinah the Daughter," in Athalya Brenner (ed.), *A Feminist Companion to Genesis* (Sheffield UK: Sheffield Academic Press, 1993): 306-317; "Did Miriam Talk Too Much?" in Athalya Brenner (ed.), *A Feminist Companion to Exodus to Deuteronomy* (Sheffield UK: Sheffield Academic Press, 1994): 231-242; "God is to Israel as Husband is to Wife," in Athalya Brenner (ed.), *A Feminist Companion to the Latter Prophets* (Sheffield UK: Sheffield Academic Press, 1995): 126-145; "Response to Popular Fiction and the Limits of Modern Midrash," *Conservative Judaism* 54:3 (Spring 2002): 106-110; "Jerusalem the Widow," *Shofar* 17:2 (Winter 1999): 16-24. All of these articles appear in this book.

as rabbinic literature is concerned.[230] When Israel behaves and perfects herself, then God will intervene and save her. Women are always subordinate (or out of the picture) when the male community is busying itself with trying to please God. Despite the necessity of having wives, rabbinic society was ambivalent about them since "a hermeneutics of suspicion informed all rabbinic ruminations on their other halves; the supposed sexual unreliability of women was never forgotten."

Chapters 5 and 6 of the book about the barren matriarchs and rabbinic delineations of women's worlds are based on previous articles that Baskin wrote in the late-70s and 80s and have a different texture to them. They are less negative than the rest of the book. Although chapter 5 repeats some of the same themes from chapter 1-3 about man's mastery over women and that the mitzvah of procreation is men's alone, Baskin makes clear in the second half of this chapter that when it comes to the barren matriarchs, the rabbis were compassionate and well aware of their grief. One rabbinic answer to the question as to why the matriarchs were childless was that God likes to hear the prayers and supplications of the matriarchs. Prayer and suffering leads to purification and brings people closer to God. Alternate answers are that barren matriarchs can retain their beauty so that their husbands continue to derive pleasure from them and that infertility humbles the matriarchs who might otherwise be vain about their great beauty. Thus infertility is both a curse and a blessing.

The barrenness of the seven wives (Sarah, Rebecca, Rachel, Leah, Manoah's wife, Hannah, and Zion!) takes on metaphoric significance, for Zion is a barren woman who will ultimately be consoled and fulfilled by God when the Land of Israel is restored to its former glory. Men who have barren wives can still be fulfilled by having disciples when students are constructed as offspring: "the student fills the place of the natural child, allowing the childless scholar, too, to become a father in Israel." Baskin claims that when this happens men no longer need women for reproductive purposes since "insemination of Torah knowledge and the production of disciples takes precedence even over the

---

[230] An excellent example of this are the rabbinic interpretations of the Song of Songs.

legal obligation to beget biological offspring." This dictum was soundly challenged in Talmudic literature.

It is in chapter six that we finally have some real women who present a counter discourse to all the negativist views of rabbinic midrash that we have seen in the book until this point. We meet the daughters of Zelophehad who are represented as canny and competent women, the loyal sisters Rachel and Leah who put aside their biblical rivalry to present a united front. Though even here Baskin detracts from the poignancy of the midrash to ask "whether this midrash depicting Rachel's generosity in preserving her sister from humiliation is a tribute to the possibilities of admirable female behavior and self-sacrifice or a warning to men about the ultimate unreliability of women." It is interesting that the rabbis had an overly positive view of Rachel while looking upon Leah as a deceiver and usurper: "All hated her: sea travelers abused her...even the women behind the beams abused her, saying: 'This Leah leads a double life; she pretends to be righteous, yet [she] is not so, for if she were righteous, would she have deceived her sister?'..." (*Gen. Rabba* 71:2).

The book ends with the story of Raḥab, whose story is one of conversion as domestication, or the fallen woman redeemed. For the rabbis, Raḥab was

> the model of the righteous proselyte, one who went beyond all others in her recognition of God's great powers... [B]y imagining her as a repentant fallen woman who found the true God and emerged as a mother in Israel, the rabbis transformed Rahab into an exemplar of the efficacy of Judaism and its traditions in taming the disordering powers of female sexuality.

Baskin divides rabbinic musings on Raḥab into three groups: those who emphasize her sincerity as a convert; those who detail her descendants and how honored she was by Israel; and those who sanitize her from a prostitute to an innkeeper who was thus able to marry Joshua. Despite Baskin's very positive take about rabbinic attitudes toward Raḥab, she chooses once again to end her book on a negative tone by pointing out that Raḥab's conversion is a form of domestication—that the woman who epitomizes all the dangers of the gentile temptress is now turned into an unassuming compliant Jewish wife and mother.

Rabbi Elana Kanter anecdotically relates her disappointment with a course she took in the 1980s on Emerging Feminist Theologies.

> What I found, to my great disappointment, were regular conversations on competitive victimology, or who was the greater victim of white male oppression.[231]

She claims that this acknowledgement of oppression is a luxury available only to those in academia and that in the outside world (the real world) Jewish women want more than a critique, more than a rehash of patriarchy and the silencing and oppression of women. What they do want are "honest readings of texts, and when patriarchy rears its head, or when there are screaming silences, they need to be acknowledged and critiqued."

This, however, is not enough for Kanter. What she wants after honest critique is a positive expression of Judaism that allows us to remain hopeful: "A Judaism that addresses the human spirit, that speaks to our souls…" Baskin, the academic, is giving both critique and honest readings of texts. But her agenda (as she states clearly in her introduction) is not to speak to our souls. And thus she remains in the critique mode.

Hammer's agenda is different. She manages to strike the anvil of our mind and heart in contrast to Baskin's depiction of the rabbinic views of Rahab. Hammer has a different tale to tell about Rachav[232] the harlot in "And the Walls Came Tumbling Down." She too bases her tale on rabbinic text. Rachav and Joshua have been married a long time and fight all the time about "contemporary" issues such as who has the right to the land and whether it was right for Israel to displace Canaanite villages. They are involved in a dialogue. The fact that they have only daughters and no sons is ultimately seen by Joshua as blessing and not punishment. It is a very moving tale with a strong, non-compliant, and not necessarily converted woman. In Hammer's notes she

---

[231] Responses to Pamela S. Nadell, "An Angle of Vision: Jewish Women's Studies in the Seminaries," *Conservative Judaism* 55:1 (Fall 2002): 12.

[232] The inconsistent spelling of Rahab and Rachav (same woman) is due to Hammer's preference to use the Hebrew (Rachav) and Baskin's the English (Rahab). I have kept their spelling.

points out that "rabbinic midrash develops Rachav's character so that she is even more complex than she first appears to be." Her answer to the question of why the rabbis converted her is that it is to "keep Israel honest, as she keeps Joshua honest. She forces us to remember the people who we have pushed aside to become what we are…[since] the Rabbis tell us he woke up every morning beside the one woman who could intimately remind him of…" the act of destroying Jericho and its inhabitants.

This is a feminist interpretation of a biblical tale, but one, which has a more redemptive take, a more forgiving view of what rabbinic texts are saying. Perhaps this is because the rabbi and the clinical psychologist are very much in the consciousness of this creative writer as opposed to the more objectifying view of the academic. In contrast to Baskin, who states at the beginning of her book that "I approach rabbinic texts with no commitment to the special status with which they have been invested in traditional Judaism," Hammer is very committed. Although Baskin acknowledges the richness and genius of rabbinic literature she writes, "I have no stake…in affirming its divine origins or in justifying its prescriptive imperatives." This is clearly not the case with Hammer who has a different agenda. Perhaps this is why Baskin has chosen to ignore the very positive midrashim about Miriam,[233] whereas Hammer writes two very different midrashim about her, one of which builds on the tradition that she comes from a family of midwives.

In her collection of 23 original tales of biblical women, *Sisters at Sinai*, Jill Hammer has included not only original midrashim, but also commentary on her sources of information, the process of inventing midrash as well as painstaking details about the sources of her midrashim.

In her introduction and extensive notes to the reader she discusses the legitimacy of and need for midrash. Most of her

---

[233] Perhaps including Miriam would have caused Baskin to rethink her thesis. In contrast see Naomi Graetz, "Did Miriam Talk too Much," in Athalya Brenner (ed.), (see footnote 229); Devorah Steinmetz, "A Portrait of Miriam in Rabbinic Midrash," *Prooftexts* 8 (1988): 35-65; Phyllis Trible, "Bringing Miriam out of the Shadows," *Bible Review* 5/1 (1989): 170-190; E. R. Zweiback Levenson, "Sexegesis: Miriam in the Desert," *Tikkun* 4/1 (1989): 44-46, 94-96; Norman Cohen, "Miriam's Song: A Modern Midrashic Reading," *Judaism* 33 (1984): 179-190.

stories contain biblical material, her own ideas and snippets of rabbinic midrashim. Often she rejects rabbinic interpretation entirely if it is not to her liking. For instance, she writes: "When the Rabbis blame Dinah for her rape or demonize Vashti for her rebellion, I cannot include their perspective, except as a foil."

Like Baskin, she acknowledges that biblical and midrashic sources are both "skimpy and/or patronizing" in their attitudes toward women. But since she is writing midrash, she has more freedom to deal with the androcentric nature of these texts, rather than just recording and deconstructing them. Her strategy is first to look for positive texts; if she cannot find them, she often will reverse rabbinic misogyny, or she will read other modern midrashim and modern poetry. Finally, she will use her feelings of anger or sadness about the traditional texts as inspiration to tell a better story.

In her midrashim, her characters have much inner strength. Most of them can be role models for us. There is much sisterhood, many mysterious elements, an abundance of angels, and hints of portents and unknowable elements. She writes that unlike "much modern midrash, which is highly realistic in nature…I prefer to set my characters in a world of myth and mystery."

This I found personally interesting, and in contrast to the midrashim that I wrote in the mid-80s which were consciously realistic, so much so that I avoided reference to any supernatural elements—including God.[234] I found myself comparing some of my own work to Hammer's, especially when we look at the same character, Elisheva, Aaron's wife. We were both on the same wavelength as to the choice of midrash on which to base our tales. However she makes Elisheva a midwife (based on Sotah 11b) whereas my Elisheva is a scribe, intent on influencing Aaron and possibly involved with Moses, her brother-in-law. My Elisheva despises Pinhas for his narrow-mindedness and sees his zealousness and intolerance as a curse. In contrast, Hammer rewards her Elisheva for her humanity in going out during the tenth plague to deliver a child with the *yichus* of being the grandmother of Pinhas (the woman she saves is Putiel an

---

[234] Naomi Graetz, *S/He Created Them: Feminist Retellings of Biblical Stories* (Piscataway, NJ: Gorgias Press, 2003).

ancestress of Pinḥas). Hammer does not editorialize (as I do) about their mutual descendant, her grandson, Pinḥas.

Sisters at Sinai does not try to be representative of the entire Bible. It does not follow a chronological order. It is a book that can be read out of sequence—as the mood takes you. Some stories resonate more than others. Some stories read better than others and have more texture. She includes many familiar biblical women, but also other women who are less known like Mahalat, Esau's wife and Ishmael's daughter; Asenat, Joseph's wife; Bosmat, Achinadav's wife; and Solomon's daughter. Some of these women's names are known from lists in the Bible, others from rabbinic midrash and some are creations of the author. I don't really have any favorites, since I enjoyed all of the midrashim. However, worthy of mention is the "Song of Devorah" with its lesbian overtones, and "Lot's Wife," which is cute and modern and must have been fun to write. The Switch of Angels is an interesting twist on the akedah. I found the "Second Blessing about Esau" to be confusing but certainly politically correct. "Mitosis," with the four faces of Israel as revealed to Leah, is a virtuoso display of Hammer's creativity and force as a writer. Her story of Havdalah is a wonderful retelling of Eve and Lilith's story, which was influenced by Lurianic theology as stated by Hammer in her notes.

The book is very user friendly. When she introduces her sources, she makes statements like "Rashi is a great friend of mine." Her characters are very grounded. She sees Sinai as "a mountain of seeds of Torah, some lying on the surface, some deep with the earth." This particular reader took as much pleasure in reaping the plentiful harvest as the author did in planting it.

As someone who herself has been passionately engaged in midrash writing and study I find this book both an excellent introduction to modern feminist midrash and complementary to the many other fine works which have already been published. Rabbi Hammer generously acknowledges many but not all of her predecessors and mentors. My only problem with her book was that I read it before Baskin's. Her methodology to seek out the positive and downplay the negative struck me as being an apologetic approach which I was prepared to criticize. But after Baskin's book, which was like a glass of ice-cold water poured over me in the winter, I found myself, dipping into Hammer's book to get some warmth and sun.

One would think that Baskin might have focused on the many flavors of the midrash rather than focusing just on the vanilla and chocolate, and it is indeed remarkable that Hammer's name evokes what should epitomize midrash: the anvil and the hammer that evoke many sparks. That is why both books should be read: one for its reality take and the other for an uplifting experience. Baskin points to the problem; Hammer shows us a way out.

JERUSALEM THE WIDOW

On the ninth day of the month of Av (Tisha b'Av), the Jewish people commemorates the destruction by the Babylonians of the first temple (586 BCE) and the destruction of the second temple by the Romans (70 CE) by fasting, reading the Book of Lamentations, and special prayers of lament. In commemorating these destructions, some of us also remember the Holocaust and other tragedies that have befallen the Jewish people. Some observant Jews remember this date, and the three weeks preceding it, by abstaining from eating meat, not listening to music and by not participating in any joyous event. In Lamentations, which describes the pillage of the First Temple, Jerusalem is described as a widow after the destruction of the Temple:

> Lonely sits the city once great with people! She that was great among nations is become like a widow... Bitterly she weeps in the night... There is none to comfort her of all her lovers..." (Lam 1.1-2).

Jewish theology tends to be self-blaming for what has happened: *"u-mipnei hata'einu..."*—"on account of our sins, we have been exiled from our land [Israel]" goes the refrain in prayers Jews recite on the Sabbath celebrating Rosh Ḥodesh—the new month—the three major festivals of Succoth, Passover, and Pentecost, and the High Holidays of Rosh Hashanah and Yom Kippur.

The theological intent of chapter one of Lamentations is to justify God's destruction of the Temple in Jerusalem as punishment for sin. The disaster that befell the community is because of the sin and infidelity of the people, not God's failure.[235] The widow accepts the blame and says, "The Lord is in the right,

---

[235] Kathleen M. O'Connor, "Lamentations," in C. A. Newsom and Sharon Ringe (eds.), *The Women's Bible Commentary* (Louisville, KY: Westminster, 1992).

for I rebelled against His word" (Lam 1.18). But is a "widow" guilty of sin? If the City of Jerusalem is "as a widow," the modern reader would view the metaphorical widow, not as a sinner but as a "victim" of God's anger—who herself has not sinned? Should we be blaming ourselves for being the subject of God's aggression? Our modern sensibility suggests that perhaps we should be blaming the Angry God who has caused the destruction.[236] For a believing Jew, this is not a blasphemous stance, for in our tradition there is a heritage of doubt and protest.[237]

In this article, I wish to examine the implications of Jerusalem the downtrodden victim being described in feminine terms and specifically the implications of her being a widow. Then I will introduce the concept of a theology of protest. Finally, I will suggest several ways in which we can use our knowledge of the past to repair the present.

In chapter one of Lamentations, the city of Jerusalem is described in uncomplimentary female metaphoric terms. The metaphors that are used to describe women in this chapter include the menstruant, the rape victim,[238] and the battered woman. These female symbols are used to blame the people of Israel for their sins. Women are symbolically blamed for the destruction of the city. The abandonment theme is often described in ancient texts as a rape or spoliation. Thus in a Sumerian text we find the following: "That enemy entered my dwelling-place wearing (his) shoes...laid his unwashed hands on me...tore my garments off me...cut off my lapis-lazuli..."[239] The depiction of Jerusalem as an unprotected widow (usually lumped together with the stranger and the orphan), abandoned by her husband/God, destroyed by her supposed protector can be seen as a metaphorical justification of abuse of women by men. The difference between the Sumerian text and the

---

[236] On the other hand, if Jerusalem/Israel is a widow, then God is dead. This is the reason for the explanation of "like" a widow. See below.

[237] Anson Laytner, *Arguing With God: A Jewish Tradition* (Northvale, NJ: Jason Aronson, 1990): v.

[238] J. Cheryl Exum, "The Ethics of Biblical Violence Against Women," in John W. Rogerson, et al (eds.), *The Bible in Ethics*, JSOT Supplement Series 207 (Sheffield UK: Sheffield Academic Press, 1995): 256-257.

[239] F. W. Dobbs-Allsopp, *Weep, O Daughter of Zion: A Study of the City-Lament Genre in the Hebrew Bible*, Biblica et Orientalia 44 (Editrice Pontificio Istituto Biblico: Rome, 1993): 48.

text of Lamentations seems to be in the assignment of blame. Both cities are abandoned by their God—but only Israel is considered responsible for her own downfall—and therefore deserving of punishment.

The word *almana* (widow in the feminine) appears 43 times in the Bible, versus the word *alman* (widow in the masculine) which appears only twice.[240] What is the root of the word? Perhaps it is the same root as "silence, muteness" (*elem*) or "violence, strength" (*alimut*) or "not having a portion" (*al-maneh*).[241] Most often we have negative associations with widowhood, for instance there is the Black Widow, the spider who eats her mate!

Widowhood could be constructed positively; it could mean freedom from an abusive marriage. Yet widowhood has been constructed by most societies as a tragedy—except in the case of the opera of the Merry Widow (and even here, the happy end is that she gets married!). However, today more women are single by choice and widowhood has becomes a normative, not a deviant, status. Yet there are many who still think they (or others) are missing something when they are not married. Widowhood, therefore, is naturally constructed as loss (of more than just the husband) and not gain.

This was certainly true in rabbinic times when the Talmud had to legislate the rights of widows in order that they be protected from rapacious children (see *Ketuvot* 103a). The marriage of a widow was not a blessed event unless the husband himself was a widower (see *Ketuvot* 7a). In the Bible and midrash, the widow is always paired with the orphan and stranger. In the Talmud she is paired with the divorcee. Why? Because all of them are miserable. They lack something—a husband, a father, a protector.

> And who are these orphans, they are Israel...and who are these widows, they are Zion and Jerusalem, as it is said: *How the great city has become like a widow.* (Lam 1.1)[242]

---

[240] Isa 47.8, which the JPS translates as "widowhood" , since it applies to a woman; and Jer 51.5, which the JPS translates as "bereft" (widowed) of their God.

[241] *al* = negative prefix; *manah* (see the talmudic tractate *Ketuvot* 10b, where the widow gets half the portion of a virgin).

[242] Solomon Buber (ed.), *The Midrash on Psalms*, Psalm 146.9 [Bar Ilan Responsa Project CD-Rom]. My translation.

The rabbis sense that it is unjust to blame the widow as a sinner, so they say she is not a real widow. She is in the situation of a woman whose husband has gone off for a while—leaving her as a "grass widow." It could not be that Jerusalem, or the people of Israel, can be likened to a real widow. Were that to be the case it would imply that God is dead! Thus in the midrash, the letter "kaf" (which means "like") is emphasized. She is not a real widow, just like one whose father or husband has gone abroad and who intends to return to her, for it is said that Israel and Judah are not widowed from their God (Jer 51.5).[243]

Another implication of being a "grass widow" or "*like* a widow" is that her widowhood is qualified: she cannot marry another man, nor can she live off of her husband's earnings.[244] So what is her actual status? It would seem that she is a classic case of the *agunah*, the chained or anchored woman: One whose husband is unaccounted for, yet who is not free to marry again. This is developed in a midrash—one of many[245]—which draws an analogy (*mashal*) between God and a King who was angry at his wife and wrote her a bill of divorce.

The rabbis use this divorce scene as a "significant site for the discussion of the covenantal relationship" between God and the people.[246] The king/God reneges and snatches back the writ, saying as long as you wish to remarry another; you cannot, since you don't have your divorce decree. On the other hand, he also says whenever she requests monetary support that it's too bad, since I've already divorced you. The analogy with God is that when the people wish to worship other gods, God says that "you are mine"

---

[243] Solomon Buber (ed.), *The Midrash on Psalms*, Psalm 68:3 [Bar Ilan Responsa Project CD-Rom]. My translation.

[244] *Midrash Zuta* on Lamentations, chapter 1.5, Buber version.

[245] There are many *meshalim* (analogies) in *Lamentations Rabba* which include women, either as object or subject. In most of them, God is depicted as a king and Israel as his wife. Hasan-Rokem (see footnote 260 below) sees these midrashim as an inversion of the idyllic relationship depicted in the Songs of Songs.

[246] Aryeh Cohen, "Framing Women/Constructing Exile," *The Postmodern Jewish Philosophy Bitnetwork* 3,1 (May, 1994). [bitnet address: pochs@drew.drew.edu]

and when they ask God for a miracle to save them, God says, "But I've already divorced you." [247]

According to Aryeh Cohen, by:

> stressing the indefiniteness of the 'as a widow' and not a widow, the midrash articulates the existential fears of the exilic situation. Is the covenant broken and irreparable ('divorce') or is there still hope?[248]

David Stern, in his discussion of this *mashal*, senses that the king and, by extension, God is:

> not fully in control, that his emotions have gotten the better of him…[that the] people of Israel…tend to be the main victims of His unease and ambivalence.[249]

Stern shows that what the king is doing is illegal. In a real divorce situation, once the *get*, the bill of divorce is given, it cannot be retracted.[250] The *get* serves both as a "performative" function, that is, it serves the purpose of making the divorce, and as proof of divorce—in order to remarry, the wife must have the legal document in her hand to prove she is no longer married. Thus, the king is lying when he denies divorcing her; he "is immorally exploit[ing] her helpless position." Stern writes that the function of this *mashal* is to criticize God's treatment of Israel and that this critique may have

> served an apologetic end, if only by demonstrating that God refuses to release the Jews from the covenantal bond even *after* He has divorced them, and even though *they* are willing to dissolve their union with Him… [Therefore] this *mashal* attributes Israel's unhappy

---

[247] *Lamentations Rabba* (Vilna and Buber versions) Chapter 1.

[248] Aryeh Cohen, "Framing Women/Constructing Exile," *The Postmodern Jewish Philosophy Bitnetwork* 3,1 (May, 1994). [bitnet address: pochs@drew.drew.edu].

[249] David Stern, *Parables in Midrash* (Cambridge, MA: Harvard University Press, 1991): 99.

[250] According to Maimonides (*hilchot gerushim* 84) this should be the case; however, the modern tendency is often to retract a *get* if some scribal error is found or if the authority of the rabbis is doubted or if the husband is considered to have been coerced into giving the *get*.

existence to God and to the conflicts of his
personality![251]

There are no clear explanations for God/the King's behavior.
It is clear, according to Stern's understanding of the midrash, that
God is both alienated from and bound to Israel. God is
unpredictable, yet Stern hesitates to make theological assertions. By
choosing to anthropomorphize God, the Rabbis are able to portray
God's full complexity.[252] It is interesting that Stern does not
introduce the value laden term "*aguna*" in describing the people and
the wife of the *mashal* for it is clear that they both are in the classic
no win situation: damned if they do, damned if they don't. They are
in limbo, having the legal status of an *aguna*, the chained woman.
Stern does ask, however, "Must his indecision, his ambivalence
ruin her life? Or does the king possibly intend something crueler?
Not content with divorcing her, does he steal the *get* precisely in
order to make her situation more unbearable? Is this his idea of
punishment?"[253]

The use of negative feminine metaphors to depict God's
relationship with Jerusalem is both dangerous and powerful. There
is a midrash in which God is likened to a heroic figure with great
strength. He hits another man and the man immediately dies from
the blow. This hero then goes into his house and hits his wife and
she withstands the blow. Her neighbors say to her, "all the great
athletes have been killed from one of the hero's blows—but you
are able to survive more than one blow." She answers them that
"he hits *them* with all his might, out of anger, but to *me*, he gives
what I am able to take" (presumably out of love).[254] In a
continuation of this same midrash, the rabbis ask why it is that the
people of Israel can stand up to God's anger? The answer is:
because God hits us and then returns immediately and re-creates
us. This is the comfort that Israel can take in their unique
relationship to God.

---

[251] David Stern, *Parables in Midrash* (Cambridge, MA: Harvard
University Press, 1991): 100.

[252] Idem: 101.

[253] Idem.

[254] My translation of *Aggadat Bereshit* (Buber Version) Chapter 8:3 from
the Bar Ilan Responsa Project CD-Rom. cf. L. M. Teugels, *Aggadat
Bereshit. Translated from the Hebrew with an Introduction and Notes* (Leiden: Brill,
2001): 29.

Why do the prophets and rabbis need such myths and metaphors to depict their relationships with God? What is gained by blaming the people for their "female" weaknesses? Is the blame even full-hearted? According to Dobbs-Allsopp, "one could even gain the impression that the sin motif is almost perfunctory in nature. There is never any great specificity as to the nature of the sin involved… Moreover, the poem implicitly and explicitly questions the appropriateness and degree of Yahweh's punishment."[255]

What is whole-hearted is the depiction of the sinning city as female. The prophets condemn men and use female sexuality to represent male sin, which humiliates them, by placing them in the inferior female position. That may be the function of these metaphors. But what are we, the people, blaming ourselves for, besides the sins that came before? Isn't the punishment of being a widow enough? Should we be punished for being menstruants as well? Why should the victim have to atone for her sins in feminine terms? It is not the people who need to revictimize themselves, it is God who must atone for what he has done to his people and who must assure his people that he will not do it again.

In an article Kathryn Darr wrote an article about how to teach troubling texts. Using Ezekiel as her springboard, she writes that "in a world where holocausts happen, we dare not follow Ezekiel when he insists that suffering, alienation and exile are God's just punishments for sin."[256] She also points to the choice of deprecating female imagery which runs like a red thread throughout the Bible (cf. Hosea, Isaiah, Jeremiah).

> I become uneasy when Ezekiel employs female sexual imagery to depict the ostensible wickedness of sixth century Judeans…because imagery, especially biblical imagery, that details the degradation and public humiliation of women,…that displays women being battered and murdered, and that suggests such violence is a means toward *healing a broken relationship*, can have serious repercussions.

---

[255] F. W. Dobbs-Allsopp, "Weep, O Daughter of Zion: A Study of the City-Lament Genre in the Hebrew Bible," *Biblica et Orientalia* 44 (Editrice Pontificio Istituto Biblico: Rome, 1993): 54-55.

[256] Kathryn P. Darr, "Ezekiel's Justifications of God: Teaching Troubling Texts," *JSOT* 55 (1992): 114.

What, if any, are the redeeming possibilities of studying such texts? I will mention three other suggestions, before referring to my own.

David Blumenthal suggests a theology of protest in response to the possibility that abusiveness is an attribute of God. He writes that the definition of abuse is when the punishment is out of proportion to the sin. In his mind, God is sometimes abusive, and in wrestling with this truth, one must acknowledge and react to it. He uses Elie Wiesel's oratorio, *Ani Maamin* (I Believe), which is a modern rereading of a midrash on Lamentations that ends with the patriarchs reproaching God and God crying. Wiesel also discusses God's responsibility for the Holocaust in *The Trial of God*, a modern rereading of the Book of Job.[257] The hero, Berish

> insists to the very end that he will hold God responsible and yet stay loyal to his Jewish identity and to God... 'If He insists upon going on with His methods, let Him—but I won't say Amen. Let Him crush me, I won't say Kaddish.... And because the end is near, I shall shout louder... I'll tell Him that He's more guilty than ever!'[258]

Blumenthal raises the question of how God does *teshuva* (repentance, returning to God). The acknowledgment of abuse by the abuser is not enough. There must be a commitment, never to abuse again. Obviously the abused person has to accept the commitment, and accept reconciliation; but even with it, it is difficult to maintain a relationship of mutual trust with the abusing God. This is part of a theology of protest and sustained suspicions which are a proper response to God's abuse. The Book of Lamentations is clearly understood as a possible response and reaction to God's specific abuse of the Jewish people during the First Temple period. Brueggemann perceives lament as a "genuine covenant interaction" between us and God. He points out that when lament is absent, a cover-up and a practice of denial and pretense characterizes our relationship with God. When lament is allowed we can "take initiative with God" and criticize God for not functioning properly. "Lament occurs when the dysfunction [of

---

[257] David R. Blumenthal, "Who is Battering Whom?" *Conservative Judaism* (Spring 1993): 81.

[258] *The Trial of God*, 133-134, 156, quoted by David Blumenthal.

God] reaches an unacceptable level, when the injustice is intolerable and change is insisted upon."[259] In lamenting, we are recognizing the abusiveness of God, and we are also rejecting that aspect of Him/Her.

The Israeli folklorist, Galit Hasan-Rokem suggests "rescuing" from the midrashic texts a possible message to express today's female voice, and in particular to release the female aspect of God.[260] She sees this in a midrash which refers to Rachel[261] as the mother of the Messiah. One can argue that Jeremiah makes clear that all of Rachel's machinations are her part of God's promise to the "ancestors" of Eretz Yisroel (the land of Israel) and moveover, that her contribution is the crucial one![262] While I do not deny the importance of searching out symbols of women and building on them, it is important to point out that Rachel achieves this distinction through suffering; through sacrifice. It is only after she is dead that "she" (i.e., her sons, the children of Israel) are redeemed and can return to the Land of Israel.

It is possible to use Hasan-Rokem's reading of Jeremiah's Rachel to ask some hard questions about the role of suffering in Judaism, and in particular the role of women's suffering, since the suffering of the Jewish people is so often depicted through feminine images. I find the model of Rachel's weeping and altruism to be unsatisfactory. Jeremiah distorts the multi-dimensional Rachel of Genesis—who suffers silently while her sister Leah becomes Jacob's first wife, who envies her sister's fertility, who is punished

[259] Walter Brueggemann, "The Costly Loss of Lament," *JSOT* 36 (1986): 60-62. I would like to thank Rachel Adler for bringing this article to my attention. Although Brueggemann's texts are from the Book of Psalms, much of what he writes can be applied to the Book of Lamentations as well.

[260] Galit Hasan-Rokem, "The Voice is the Voice of My Sister: Feminine Images and Feminine Symbols in Lamentations Rabba," in Yael Azmon (ed.), *A View into the Lives of Women in Jewish Societies: Collected Essays* (Jerusalem: The Zalman Shazar Center for Jewish History 1995): 95; 105-108 [Hebrew]. See also her footnote (#3) referring us to Dov Noy, "The Daughters of Ztelophad and the Daughters of Jerusalem," *Machanayim* 48 (1970): 20-25.

[261] See also S. N. Kramer, "The Weeping Goddess: Sumerian Prototypes of the Mater Dolorosa," *BA* 46: 69-80.

[262] Michael Graetz, in a High Holiday sermon in Kehillat Magen Avraham.

for the boldness she displays in stealing the house idols of her
father. The various midrashim which link the Rachel of Genesis
with Jeremiah's Rachel depict the complexity of her character.[263]
Jeremiah, however, depicts her as a stick character, the weeping
mother, who is deified through the sacrifice of her life. This is the
prophet's "happy end." But the redemption is costly—Rachel has
been dead all these years.

J. Cheryl Exum has recently proposed three ways of dealing
with gender-biased prophetic rhetoric. One strategy is to pay
attention to the differing claims these texts make on their male and
female readers. The second is to recognize the violent
representations of God's sexual abuse of a nation personified as a
woman and to expose this prophetic pornography[264] for what it is.
Finally, she suggests looking for competing discourse to uncover
evidence of the woman's suppressed point of view in biblical
texts.[265]

Exum uses an article by A. R. Pete Diamond and Kathleen M.
O'Connor as an exemplar of competing discourse. While studying
Jeremiah 2-3 they ask "What would happen if female Israel told the
story?" Their answer is in the form of further questions:

> Would she tell of her husband's verbal abuse...? Would
> she recount how loving he had been and tell how he
> had become more and more controlling and
> demanding? We cannot know, of course, because in
> this case the husband is God, and not such a nice god,
> even if broken-hearted. What we do know about this
> metaphorical woman, though, is that she makes a moral

---

[263] See the following commentators: Rashi on Genesis 48; Rashi on
Jeremiah 31; Ramban on Genesis 48.7; Radak on Jeremiah 31; Metzudat
David on Jeremiah 31. See too the Midrashim in *Eicha Rabba* (Vilna)
Petichtot beginning with 24, R. Yochanan and *Pesikta deRav Kahanna*
(Mandelbaum) 20.

[264] See Athalya Brenner, "Pornoprophetics Revisited: Some Additional
Reflections," *JSOT* 70 (1996): 63-86.

[265] "The Ethics of Biblical Violence Against Women," in John W.
Rogerson et al (eds.), *The Bible in Ethics*, JSOT Supplement Series 207
(Sheffield UK: Sheffield Academic Press, 1995): 248-271.

and religious choice… She accepts the price of her autonomy.[266]

In my own work on midrash, I try to recreate a world in which women had a place. I find this a legitimate and necessary enterprise. It is a way of contributing new insights and/or perspectives to our Bible. Midrash flourishes today largely thanks to feminism. Books such as Alicia Suskin Ostriker, *The Nakedness of the Fathers: Biblical Visions and Revisions* (1994), Ellen Frankel, *The Five Books of Miriam: A Women's Commentary on the Torah* (1996), Norma Rosen, *Biblical Women Unbound* (1996) retell the stories of both male and female biblical figures and have paved the way for other modern feminist retellings. Modern feminist midrash attempts to redress the misogynist tendencies of traditional mainstream midrash. The consequences of a patriarchal world view for us are clear. Conventional attitudes toward women are still being transmitted to us as part of our heritage and too often we respond unquestioningly to these views as if they were absolute truths. Women should not have to identify against ourselves. On the one hand, we must seek out old texts where women appear and bring them to the surface, on the other hand, as part of our theology of protest against previous and present abuse, we must be revisers and revisionists. With new vision we bring new perspectives to the old text and in doing so, we contribute to the on-going work of revelation.

---

[266] A. R. Pete Diamond and Kathleen M. O'Connor, "Unfaithful Passions: Coding Women, Coding Men in Jeremiah 2-3," *Biblical Interpretation* 4 (1996): 288-310 [referred to by Exum on 169].

THE BARRENNESS OF MIRIAM: A MIDRASH ON THE *HAFTARA* OF *KI TETZEH* (ISAIAH 54)

> Buried within Scripture are bits and pieces of a story awaiting discovery. It highlights the woman Miriam. To unearth the fragments, assemble them, ponder the gaps and then construct a text requires the play of many methods but the dogmatism of none.[267]

> Individual things are for me such as they appear to me, and for you in turn as they appear to you.[268]

Every summer while I sit in the synagogue during the Torah reading of *Ki Tetzeh* (Deut 21.10-25.19)—sometimes I am the reader—I wait for the uplifting *haftara* for the week's portion, the fifth *haftara* of reconciliation, to be chanted. It begins with the words *roni akara* (Shout O barren one) and for about ten years I have associated the barren one with Miriam for reasons which will soon become apparent. The logic for my reasoning is textually based on both biblical and midrashic sources.

There are seven *haftarot* of Reconciliation following Tisha b'Av.[269] These special *haftarot* are an ancient custom associated with the Land of Israel and did not originate in the Babylonian diaspora. Normally a *haftara*, or additional reading, has a thematic connection with something in the Torah reading of that week. It can be a word association or it may lean on a sentence or it can be related to a

---

[267] Phyllis Trible, "Bringing Miriam Out of the Shadow," *Bible Review* 5/1 (1989): 170-190.

[268] Protagoras argues this in Plato's dialogue *Theaetetus*. G. P. Goold (ed.), *Theaetetus*: Plato, H. North Fowler (tr.) (Cambridge, MA: Harvard University Press, 1921): 152a.

[269] For the original source of this tradition see the Tosafot on B. Megillah 31b which gives the listing of the seven.

broader theme. Often the rabbis, both ancient and modern, connected the week's portion with the *haftara* in their writings of midrash.[270] In the case of these seven *haftarot*, the normal connections are suspended, since the focus is on reconciliation. Yet one can still ask the question why the rabbis chose a particular passage from all the choices available to them and one can say that certain items in the portion may lend themselves to this choice. So it is legitimate to ask why did they *davka* decide to choose this particular reading from Isaiah especially since the order of the seven *haftarot* of reconciliation is not the order in which they appear in Isaiah.

In three typical modern commentaries on the connection between the portions, we read the following. The first is from the Reform commentary, edited by Gunter Plaut:

> The end of the *sidra* with its message of hope is reflected in the Isaianic message of consolation, the fifth *Haftara* of comfort after Tisha b'Av. Whatever may have happened, God's love for Israel is unshakable: "The mountains may move...my loyalty shall never move from you." This message was chosen also as part of the Haftara for *sidra* Noach.[271]

The second is from the widely used Orthodox commentary, edited by J. H. Hertz:

> The fifth Haftora of Consolation. Its message is the everlasting mercy of God. "For the mountains may depart, and the hills be removed; but My kindness shall not depart from thee." This entails for the Israelites the sacred duty of imitating God's ways of loving kindness,

---

[270] An example of an ancient collection of midrashim which does exactly that is *Pesikta de Rav Kahana*, which has midrashim on the seven readings before and after Tisha b'Av. *Leviticus Rabba* is also considered to be a classical example of homiletical midrash, as opposed to the more popular and accessible works known as exegetical midrash. For a discussion of types of midrash, see Barry W. Holtz (ed.), *Back to the Sources: Reading the Classic Jewish Texts* (New York: Summit Books, 1984): 186-204.

[271] *The Torah: A Modern Commentary* (New York: The Union of American Hebrew Congregations, 1981): 1612.

by loyal observance of the precepts of humanity and pity proclaimed in the *Sidra*.[272]

In his very informative commentary on the fifth Haftara of consolation in the recent commentary put out by the Conservative Movement, Michael Fishbane makes no attempt to connect the Haftara with the portion of the week (*sidra* or *parsha*). He does, however, have several insightful comments to make concerning the promises made to Zion and its inhabitants whose "time of shame and desolation has passed" and should therefore rejoice. God gives assurance of reconciliation with the people which is comparable to God's pact with Noah after the flood. God is referred to as taking Israel back in love and with everlasting kindness. Fishbane refers to the stylistic strategy in this Haftara by using comparisons of exilic loss and restoration with the changes in a marriage.

> The marriage motif allows the prophet to focus on the dynamics of love and rejection, and of anger and its assuagement. God is presented as a faithful bridegroom who is able to overcome betrayal and anger.[273]

He writes that the "transfer of a primordial covenantal guarantee" to the sphere of the present is striking.

> Through the analogy of the Flood, we sense how deeply the Exile was felt to be a rupture in the divine order; and through the analogy of nature, we learn how disconsolate and without hope the people of Zion had been.[274]

In these three modern commentaries there is no linking of the Haftara with the proof texts from the Parasha.

In contrast to these commentators, Yehuda Shaviv suggests that some of the seven *Haftarot* of reconciliation might have connections to the parasha and he suggests that our Haftara, in particular Isaiah 54.1 and 54.6 may be connected to the beginning of Deuteronomy 24:

---

[272] J. H. Hertz, *The Pentateuch and Haftorahs* (London: Soncino Press, 1962): 857

[273] *Etz Hayim: Torah and Commentary* (New York: The Rabbinical Assembly, 2001): 1137.

[274] Idem.

A man takes a wife and possesses her. She fails to please him because he finds something obnoxious about her, and he writes her a bill of divorcement, hands it to her, and sends her away from his house; [2]she leaves his household and becomes the wife of another man; [3]then this latter man rejects her, writes her a bill of divorcement, hands it to her, and sends her away from his house; or the man who married her last dies. [4]Then the first husband who divorced her shall not take her to wife again, since she has been defiled— for that would be abhorrent to the LORD.

Shaviv connects the passage with the beloved wife versus the hated wife and the leaving of the bride of one's youth and then sending her away as depicted in the *haftara*.[275] He makes this suggestion, but does not bring any midrashim as prooftexts to support his assertion. I have my own associations which I will make clear to the patient reader. I would like to think that the reason the rabbis chose this particular *haftara* was its (to me) explicit connections to the rejected Miriam.[276] The two texts which I found relevant are:

Remember what the LORD your God did to Miriam on the journey after you left Egypt (Deut 24.9)

and

When brothers dwell together and one of them dies and leaves no son, the wife of the deceased shall not be married to a stranger…his brother's widow shall go up to him…*spit in his face*… Thus shall be done to the man who will not build up his brother's house! (Deut 25.5-9).

---

[275] Yehuda Shaviv, *Beyn Haftara le-Parasha* (Jerusalem: Reuven Mass, 2000): 200.

[276] For more about the connections between this Haftara of consolation and the weekly portion of *ki tetzeh* see the following: Tzvi Goldberg, *Sefer Ateret Tzvi: Midrashim ve-Maamarei Hazal al ha-Haftarot* (Jerusalem: *Merkaz Torani ha-Ketav ve-Hamichtav*, 1994): vol 2: 242-246; Michael Fishbane, *The JPS Biblical Commentary: Haftarot* (Philadelphia: Jewish Publication Society, 2002): 30-304. See also *Pesikta de-Rav Kahana* (ed. Mandelbaum): 20 on "*Roni Akara*."

It is the woman who is willing to take a chance of a future, whereas the brother-in-law is not willing to continue the family line.

Over the years I had become convinced that the rabbis had chosen this particular *haftara* because of its connection with Miriam and I set out to prove it. The context of Deuteronomy 24.9 and Deuteronomy 25.5-9 is very negative. Both refer to Numbers 12. The implication of Deuteronomy 24.9 is that God punished Miriam with scales for her speaking out against Moses because of the Cushite woman (Num 12.1) and what happened to her should serve as a lesson to the people of Israel. Rabbinic midrash associates this speaking out as the sin of gossip.[277] In Numbers 12.4 God says to Moses (in reference to Miriam):

> If her father *spat in her face*, would she not bear her shame for seven days? Let her be shut out of camp for seven days, and then let her be readmitted.

If we look at the Haftara and then at a well known midrash, found in various sources, whose genealogy is based on The Book of Chronicles, I hope it will be as obvious to the reader as it is to me that there is justification for my assumption that these biblical verses were the prooftexts behind the rabbinic choosing of the haftara. I am working with about six intertexts, that is. texts which interact and thus serve as internal commentary on each other. Most of the intertexts are biblical verses and some are midrashic commentary.

The first intertext is the rabbinic midrash from the Talmud B. Sotah 11b-12a:

> **"And the king of Egypt spoke to the Hebrew midwives…"** (Exod 1.15). Rav and Samuel disagree. One said they were a mother and her daughter, and the other said they were daughter-in-law and mother-in-law. According to him who declared they were mother and daughter, they were Jochebed and Miriam; and according to him who declared they were daughter-in-law and mother-in-law, they were Jochebed and Elisheba. There is a teaching (a *beraita*) in agreement with him who said they were mother and daughter; for it has been taught: 'Shiphra' is Jochebed; and why was she called *Shiphra*? Because she beautifies [*meshappereth*]

---

[277] See my article "Did Miriam Talk too Much?" in this book.

the newborn babe. Another explanation of Shiphra is that the Israelites were fruitful [*sheparu*] and multiplied in her days. 'Pu'a' is Miriam; and why was she called *Pua*? Because she cried out [*po'a*] to the child as she brought it forth. Another explanation of Pu'a is that she used to declaim with divine inspiration and say: 'In the future my mother will bear a son who will redeem Israel'...

"And it came to pass, because the midwives feared God, that He made them houses." (Exod 5.21) Rav and Samuel [differ in their interpretation]; one said they are the priestly and Levitical houses, and the other said they are the royal houses. According to the one who says they are the priestly and Levitical houses: this refers to Aaron and Moses; and according to the one who says they are the royal houses: **for also David descended from Miriam**, as it is written: "And **Azuva** died, and Caleb took Ephrath, who bore him Hur" (I Chron 2.19). And it is written: "Now David was the son of that Ephrathite..." (I Sam 17.12).

"Caleb the son of Hezron begat children by his wife Azuva and by Yeriot;[278] these were her sons: Jesher, Shobab, and Ardon" (1 Chron 2.18)... Conclude, therefore, that **Azuva is identical with Miriam**; and why was her name called *Azuva*? Because everyone left her ['*azabuha*] at the beginning. 'Begat!' But wasn't he married to her?[279] R. Johanan said: Whoever marries a woman for a higher purpose, the text considers it as if he begot her. She was named **'Yeriot'** because her face was like curtains. "And these were her sons"—read not *baneha* [her sons] but *boneha* [her builders]...

And Ashhur the father of Tekoa had two wives, **Hela and Naara** (II Chron 4.5). Ashhur is identical with Caleb. And why was his name called Ashhur? Because his face was turned black from fasting. "The father of"—because he became a father to her. "Tekoa"— because he dedicated [*taka*] his heart to his Father in heaven. "Had two wives"—[this means] **Miriam**

---

[278] The Hebrew reads וכלב בן חצרון הוליד את עזובה אשה ואת יריעות ואלה בניה... , but it has been translated by JPS as above; otherwise the text makes no sense.

[279] See the previous note.

became like two women. "Hela and Naara"—she was not both Hela and Naara at the same time, since first she was sickly [*hela*] and then afterward she was youthful, like a young girl [*naara*]...

This midrash is continued in *Midrash Rabba* on Exodus 1:17.

"And the families of Aharhel the son of Harum." **Aharhel is Miriam**: and why was she thus called? Because: "And all the women went out after her [*ahar-eha*] with timbrels and with dances" (Exod 15.20). What families was he privileged to raise from her? "The son of **Harum**": i.e. she was privileged to have among her descendants David whose kingdom God exalted (*rimam*) as it is said: "And He will give strength unto His King" (1 Sam 2.10).

The second prooftext is that of Numbers 12.9-15.

Miriam and Aaron spoke against Moses because of the Cushite woman he had married: "He married a Cushite woman!"... **Incensed with them**, the LORD departed. [10]As **the cloud withdrew from the Tent**, there was Miriam stricken with snow-white scales! When Aaron turned toward Miriam, he saw that she was stricken with scales. [11]And Aaron said to Moses, "O my lord, account not to us the sin which we committed in our folly. [12]**Let her not be as one dead**, who emerges from his mother's womb with half his flesh eaten away." [13]So Moses cried out to the LORD, saying, "O God, pray heal her!" [14]But the LORD said to Moses, "If her father **spat in her face**, would she not bear her shame for seven days? Let her be shut out of camp for seven days, and then let her be readmitted." [15]So **Miriam was shut out of camp** seven days; and the people did not march on until Miriam was readmitted.

In this text Miriam speaks against Moses. What interests me in this text is that God was incensed with Miriam. He withdrew his presence from her. She is cursed and shut out of the camp. For a relatively short moment He left her as the cloud withdrew from the tent and she was left with scales. When she is allowed back in the camp, after she is cured, God returns to her and she to Him. She is once more in favor.

I have written about how the rabbis liked Miriam because she was a forceful spokeswoman for marriage and procreation. She was also responsible for nurturing Moses, the savior of Israel. But the rabbis relate to the Miriam of Numbers 12 in a totally negative manner. Thus we have an angry God and rabbis who have seemingly forgotten their previous positive views of Miriam. We do not know what becomes of her after this episode except that a few chapters later she dies. In the biblical text, Miriam is unmarried and childless. A major problem for the rabbis is that there is no closure for Miriam in the Bible. This is the background of their midrash and for my reading of the Haftara: Yes, God was angry at Miriam, but He takes her back.

How did the rabbis arrive at the peculiar genealogy of the midrash above? Our answer comes from the third text in I Chronicles 2.1-51 and 4.1-17 which served as the source of the midrash in B. Sota and *Exodus Rabba*.

> I Chronicles 2:
>
> These are the sons of Israel... But Er, **Judah's** first-born, was displeasing to the LORD, and He took his life. [4]His daughter-in-law Tamar also bore him **Perez** ... [5]The sons of Perez: **Hezron** and Hamul. [9]The sons of Hezron that were born to him: Jerahmeel, Ram, and **Chelubai**... [18]**Caleb son of Hezron** had children by his wife **Azuva,** and by **Yeriot;** these were her sons: **Jesher,** Shobab, and Ardon. [19]**When Azuva died, Caleb married Ephrath, who bore him Hur.** [20]**Hur begot Uri, and Uri begot Bezalel**... [24]After the death of Hezron, in Caleb-Ephratha, Abija, wife of Hezron, bore **Ashhur,** the father of **Tekoa**..... [50]These were the descendants of Caleb. The sons of Hur the first-born of Ephratha: Shobal father of Kiriath-jearim, [51]Salma father of Bethlehem, Hareph father of Beth-gader.
>
> I Chronicles 4:
>
> The sons of Judah: Perez, Hezron, Carmi, Hur, and Shobal. ... [5]Ashhur the father of Tekoa had two wives, **Hela and Naara;** [6]**Naara** bore him Ahuzam, Hepher, Temeni, and Ahashtari. These were the sons of Naara. [7]The sons of Hela: Zereth, Zohar, and Ethnan. [8]Koz was the father of Anub, Zobeba, and the families of **Aharhel son of Harum**.... [17]The sons of Ezra: Jether, Mered, Epher, and Jalon. She conceived and bore **Miriam,** Shammai, and Ishba father of Eshtemoa.

In I Chronicles we have someone called Azuva (who may be conflated with Yeriot) who died. Then Caleb married several women and has children by them. This genealogy was of great interest to the rabbis who used it to show that houses were built for the midwives (which include Miriam). If we recall the houses of kings came from Miriam since Miriam was the progenitor of David. She is identified as *azuva* in this midrash.

Azuva is someone who is abandoned. By whom? The people? God? Moses and Aaron? It is God who abandoned her. God left her and returned to her. The rabbis built a fantasy: "Caleb begot Azuva his wife and these were her sons. Azuva is Miriam: and why was she so called? Because all had forsaken her." She is also called Ephrat, because Israel was fruitful thanks to her. She marries Caleb, but one could also say that she metaphorically marries God (just as Israel marries God—or is in relation with God). All the names in the genealogy end up being Miriam who was cured by God and was returned to her youth by God. She then had children from which we have the source of the rabbinic proof that David came from Miriam.

The fourth prooftext is from our Torah reading:

> Remember what the LORD your God did to Miriam
> on the journey after you left Egypt (Deut 24.9).

In a commentary on this verse in *Deuteronomy Rabba* 6:12, God is likened to a king who returned in triumph from war, and whose praises are sung by a noble lady (Miriam?). She was declared Mother of the Senate. But later when she began to cause disorder the king said she should be sent away to the mines.

> So, when God waged war at the Red Sea, Miriam
> chanted a song, and she was named prophetess...
> When, however, she slandered her brother, God
> commanded that she should be sent to the mines, as it
> is said, And Miriam was shut up.

Clearly the rabbis had an agenda—one of them which was to silence (shut up!) women's voices when they challenged God's chosen leaders. The fifth text is also from the Torah reading.

> When brothers dwell together and one of them dies
> and leaves no son, the wife of the deceased shall not be
> married to a stranger...his brother's widow shall go up
> to him...**spit in his face**... **Thus shall be done to**

the man who will not build up his brother's house!
(Deut 25.5-9).

I connect this text with Numbers 12. I conflate the spitting of the wife of the deceased in the treacherous brother's face with God who spits in Miriam's face. Also, the wife wants to build up a house, that is, to procreate, to have children. The brother does not, he lacks faith in the process, or has bad-mouthed her, or has heard negative things about her and doesn't want to marry her. Perhaps, spitting in someone's face is connected with *lashon ha-ra.'* When there is *lashon ha-ra'*, you cannot have a child—until the *lashon ha-ra'* ends, you cannot have children. Perhaps that is why she (her womb) is locked up, waiting to be released.

The connections I make are similar to the connections that the rabbis made. Some of their word plays and associations are even more tenuous than mine. There has been much discussion about the difference between exegesis (reading out from the text) and eisegesis (reading in to the text). The former is text-based, that is, it starts from the text and then interprets, whereas the latter starts with a point of view and then reads into the text for proof. I do not make these distinctions in this piece since I am doing both.[280] This will become clear with my reading of the haftara, which follows now.

Isaiah 54, the *Haftara* of *Ki tetzeh*, is our sixth text:

> Shout, O barren one, you who bore no child! Shout aloud for joy, you who did not travail! For the children of the wife forlorn shall outnumber those of the espoused—said the Lord. [2]Enlarge the site of your tent, Extend the size of your dwelling, do not stint! Lengthen the ropes, and drive the pegs firm. [3]For you shall spread out to the right and the left; your offspring shall dispossess nations and shall people the desolate towns. [4]Fear not, you shall not be shamed; do not cringe, you shall not be disgraced. For you shall forget the reproach of your youth, and remember no more the shame of your widowhood. [5]For He who made you will espouse you—His name is "Lord of Hosts." The Holy

---

[280] See Fernando F. Segovia, who writes "All exegesis is ultimately eisegesis" in "Cultural Studies and Contemporary Biblical Criticism," in Fernando F. Segovia and Mary Ann Tolbert (eds.) *Reading from this Place* (Minneapolis: Fortress, 1995): vol 2: 16.

One of Israel will redeem you—He is called "God of all the Earth." [6]The Lord has called you back as a wife forlorn and forsaken. Can one cast off the wife of his youth? said your God. [7]For a little while[281] I forsook you, but with vast love I will bring you back. [8]In slight anger, for a moment, I hid My face from you; But with kindness everlasting I will take you back in love—said the Lord your Redeemer. [9]For this to Me is like the waters of Noah: As I swore that the waters of Noah would never flood the earth anymore, So I swear that I will not Be angry with you or rebuke you. [10]For the mountains may move and the hills be shaken, but my loyalty shall never move from you, nor My covenant of friendship be shaken—said the LORD, who takes you back in love.

In my reading of this Haftara, it is Miriam who is the barren one, who until now had no children. She is told to be joyous, for in the future she shall have many children. The site (*yeriyot*) of her tent will be enlarged. Her progeny will be enlarged and strong. She will overcome the previous shame when God disgraced her in front of the people, and the additional shame of her not being married (like a widow without a husband or a portion of her own).

Who will bring about this great change? God! The same person who created her, who forsook her temporarily, is back now bringing his vast love. The same God who in anger hid His face from her/the female people (yet wasn't it only to Moses that He revealed his face) in Numbers 12, is now taking her back and redeeming her. Miriam, who is associated with water, is united with the symbol of the people of Israel, when God promises her (and Israel) that the waters of Noah (or any catastrophe for that matter) will never destroy the earth again. God swears on this and creates a covenant of friendship with the people/Miriam—by giving her/them the promise of children, that is, a secure future. Thus in this new scenario, God's loyalty (*hesed*) to Miriam will no longer be in doubt. To prove this He takes her back with love and compassion (*rahamim*) which may also hint at the connection of opening of wombs (*rehem*). Procreation and the Davidic dynasty

---

[281] Fishbane suggests that the Hebrew *be-rega katon* (for a little while) should be read *be-roga katon* (with a little anger) so that it is parallel to v. 8 (p. 303).

thus assure Miriam's/Israel's happiness and continuity. I also wanted to link the midrash I wrote with the people's waiting for her after she was struck by white scales, her being healed by Moses, the reconciliation with God and Moses.

It was clear to me that one could extrapolate the *azuva* (the forlorn and forsaken woman) of the midrash to the Haftara and say that the barren one (before she has children) is Miriam. Clear as this connection was to me, I was unable to find any rabbinical texts which made this connection or even hinted at it. I still believe that there was some rabbi out there who has made the connection. However, after searching over a period of five years, I grew impatient and had a click moment. I decided to take the bold move of writing my own midrash to prove that this is why the rabbis chose the haftara. I wrote the midrash, originally in Hebrew, in the traditional rabbinic, archaic form. I later translated it into English in order to reach a wider audience. My purpose was to create the missing midrash, that is, the one I am convinced exists. My midrash, based on biblical and midrashic takes, does not detract from the themes of reconciliation or from the allegory of marriage between God and his people. If anything it strengthens these themes by adding an additional dimension, another level to the allegory.

The genre of the midrash I composed is homiletic in style. It has the classic rabbinic *petiḥta* (or opening). It starts with the author literally opening (*pataḥ*) with the verse from Deuteronomy. This is immediately followed by another opening verse (or proem) from Isaiah. I then ask a question which should make the reader wonder why these texts are connected. Thereafter I treat the prophetic verses in the same order that they appear in the Bible. The end is in the form of a messianic peroration (*siyum*) which completes the homily, finally returning to the pericope verse from Deuteronomy.[282] Unlike the classical midrash, I openly refer to,

---

[282] I would like to thank my editor, Lieve Teugels for her suggestions in re-arranging this midrash so that it follows the form of the traditional homiletical midrash. Thanks to her, the pericope is clear and the text is organized according to the order of the *Haftara* rather than thematically (which was its original form). The other readers who read this midrash and/or commentary and made critical suggestions were Avram Holtz, Yael Levine Katz, Tamar Elad Appelbaum, David Segal. I was particularly fortunate in having Avigdor Shinan's sharp eyes for the final stylization in

quote from, utilize and build on prooftexts from previous midrash.
I have not invented this strange genealogy connecting Miriam and
the birth of the Davidic dynasty.

MIDRASH ON THE PARASHA OF 'KI TETZEH'

> Naomi Tova bat Sara and Yehezkel opened:
> "Remember what the LORD your God did to Miriam
> on the journey after you left Egypt" (Deut 24.9). Shout,
> O barren one, You who bore no child! Shout aloud for
> joy, You who did not travail!" (Isa 54.1). The barren
> one is Miriam. And why was Miriam referred to as
> barren? Didn't we study [in the midrash] that "the
> house of the Kingdom is descended from Miriam,
> because David was descended from Miriam?" (*Exod.
> Rabba* 1:17). Furthermore, does it not say: "Enlarge the
> site of your tent, Extend the size of your dwelling?"
> (Isa 54.2). Site (*yeriot*) is Miriam, for [according to the
> midrash] her face resembled *yeriot* (*Exod. Rabba* 1:17).
>
> "Shout aloud for joy." And Miriam was "jubilant and
> happy" (Esth 8.15), for her agony and desolation was
> changed to happiness and song. "May the barren one
> greatly rejoice and exult when her children will be
> gathered in her midst in joy.... You shall [in the
> marriage ceremony] create joy for the beloved
> companions as you used to gladden the hearts of your
> creatures in the Garden of Eden... Who has created
> joy and gladness, bridegroom and bride, rejoicing, song,
> mirth, delight, love and brotherhood, peace and
> friendship" (B. *Ketubot* 8a).
>
> And her creator [*ba'al*] swore to comfort [*rahem*] her,
> because He opened up [*patoah patah*] Miriam's womb.
> Therefore it is said "you shall not be called the forsaken
> [*azuva*] one anymore" for it is God who wants you and
> espouses [*ba'al*] you (Isa 62.4).

Hebrew. Although I tried to use rabbinic phraseology, I take full
responsibility for slipping into biblical usage when content takes
precedent over form. I presented the core ideas of this midrash at the
Rabbinical Assembly in Baltimore (1999) and received useful feedback
from those present at the session. For more about style see Barry W.
Holtz.

"You did not travail [*hala*]," that is Miriam. Why is Miriam referred to as did not travail? Is it not written "there was Miriam stricken with snow-white scales" (Num 12.10)? Aharon the priest, brother of Miriam, came and cried: "Don't be like a dead person" and Moses the Levite, brother of Miriam the prophetess, also cried: "O God, please heal her" (Num 12.12-12). This teaches us that Miriam took sick (travailed) and they treated her like they customarily do with the dead and even God deserted her. Miriam thought to herself: Don't call me Miriam (Mir-yam), call me Mar-Yam (bitter waters) for the nation has spat in my face, as it is written, "she spat in his face" (Deut 25.9). "But the Lord said to Moses, 'If her father spat twice [*yarok yarak*] in her face, would she not bear her shame/be locked up [*KLM*=root] for seven days'" (Num 12.14)? But the Holy One blessed be he, had mercy [*RHM*=root] on Miriam, for it is said "Fear not, you shall not be shamed, Do not cringe, you shall not be disgraced [*KLM*]. For you shall…not remember the shame of your widowhood anymore… For He who made you [*ba'al*] will espouse you—His name is "LORD of Hosts" (Isa 54.4-5). And how did Miriam become a widow? "Lonely she sat, like a widow" (Lam 1.1); not a real widow; just abandoned [*azuva*]: a woman whose husband deserted her, yet planned to return to her.

"For you shall forget the Reproach of your youth" (Isa 54.4), for it is written, "And Caleb took her" (1 Chron 2.19). What does "he took her" mean? After she was cured, he did an act of taking her to be his wife [*lakah*] because he was so overjoyed with her. "Instead of being neglected and hated…I made her an object of joy for generations" (Isa 60.15) as we studied in the midrash, "the houses of kings from Miriam, for David descended from Miriam" (*Exod. Rabba* 1:17).

"As a wife forlorn and forsaken" (Isa 54.6). Forsaken, that is Miriam. "For a little while I forsook you" (Isa 54.7) "as the cloud withdrew from the tent" (Num 12.10). And why is Miriam described as abandoned? For is it not written that "Miriam was shut out of camp…and the people did not march on until Miriam was readmitted?" (Num 12.15).

Don't call me Miriam (*Mir-yam*), call me *Mey-rim* (I will raise you up). How did the Holy One lift (*hey-rim*) Miriam up? Didn't our mother, the barren Hannah say in her prayer: "The Lord…humiliates and raises high (*meromem*). He raises the poor from the dust, lifts up (*yarim*) the needy from the garbage heap, placing them with the nobility and granting their descendants a seat of honor" (I Sam 2.7-8)? For "from the depths, I called you…and God listened to my voice…" and his ears "were attentive to my plea for mercy (Psalms 130.1-2). And with an upraised (*ramah*) hand, God took Miriam out of the depths [of her misery] for she had found favor with Him in the wilderness and He went to soothe her. God revealed Himself to her from afar and promised her "eternal love" and a continuance of His grace. Thus it is written "I will build you up again, O Maiden Israel! You shall take up your timbrels once again and go forth to the rhythm of the dancers" (Jer 31.2-4). And you shall be praised "with timbrel and dance" (Psalms 150.4).

"The Wife of his youth" (Isa 54.6). The wife of his youth, that is Miriam. And why is she referred to as youthful (*na'ara*)? For she was sick and her illness was shaken off (*nin'ara*) her and God restored her to her youth (*na-arutah*), and "a girl was born to her" (1 Chron 4.6) and after she recovered she had sons.

In my great anger, I momentarily hid My face from you" (Isa 54.7-8). "In great anger" for it is written, "God was incensed with them" (Num 12.9). "I hid my face from you momentarily"—"from you," that is, from Miriam. As it is written, "the cloud withdrew from the Tent" (Num 12.10). When the minute was over, the cloud returned to the tent, and God remembered (*pakad*) Miriam. *Pekida* (remembrance) is synonymous with *zekhira* (remembrance), as it is written "I remembered (*zakharti*) favorably the days when you were young and devoted to me (*hesed*)" (Jer 2.2).

"For this to Me is like the waters of Noah: As I swore that the waters of Noah would never again flood the earth, So I swear that I will not Be angry with you or rebuke you" (Isa 54.9). "The waters of Noah" refers to Miriam's well, one of the "ten things created on the eve of Sabbath during twilight (*beyn ha-shemashot*): the well...the rainbow..." (*Mishnah Avot* 5:6). "But with everlasting kindness (*hesed*) I will take you back (*rechem*)...and my loyalty (*hesed*) shall never waver from you" (Isa 54.8-10).

Kindness/Loyalty (*hesed*) is the "last act of loyalty" (Ruth 3.10) of Ruth the Moabite to Boaz. For we studied (in the midrash) that "from Boaz descended Oved...Yishai...David" (Ruth 4.21-22). And how do we know that David is also descended from Miriam? In the midrash it says, "*Achar*-chel is Miriam, and why is her name called thus? Because it is written 'and all the women went out after (*achar*) her with timbrels and dances'" (Exod 15) (see *Exod. Rabba* 1:17). And what last act of kindness did God do for Miriam? His act of kindness was "the kindness of youth" (Jer 2.2), for He restored Miriam to her former status of youthful wife and opened up her womb for it is written "while the barren woman bears seven" (I Sam 2.5) "who restored the childless one (*akara*) to her place in the household (*akeret ha-bayit*) as a happy mother of children, halleluja" (Psalms 113.9).

"Shout, O Barren One, You who bore no Child, Shout Aloud for Joy, You who did not travail!" And thus did God remember Miriam when she left Egypt. "Shout for joy, Fair Zion! For lo, I come; and I will dwell in your midst" (Zech 2.14); "Rejoice greatly, Fair Zion; Raise a shout, Fair Jerusalem! Lo, your king is coming to you" (Zech 9.9).[283]

How did God remember Miriam? Wasn't Miriam barren? And there are no texts associated with Miriam which say "And God remembered Miriam...and opened up her womb" as it is written about our mother Rachel (Gen 30.22).

However, it is written "'He restores the childless woman among her household as a happy mother of

---

[283] According to Buchler, who has traced prophetic portions for the triennial cycle in Israel, these two passages from Zechariah 2.14ff. and 9.9ff. were read in addition to Isaiah 54.1ff. See Joseph Jacobs, "Triennial Cycle of Readings," *Jewish Encyclopedia*, vol. 12 (New York: Funk and Wagnalls, 1906).

children' (Psalms 113.9). There were seven barren women who were restored: Sarai, Rebecca, Leah, Rachel, Manoach's wife, Hannah, and Zion. "Restoring the childless woman"—that is Zion, for it is said, "Rejoice Oh Barren Woman" (*Pesikta de Rav Kahana* 20:1). And why does Miriam fit into this picture? To restore the childless woman is like restoring barren Zion to her rightful place, giving her a House of Torah... And then Zion rejoiced in her children, and her children shared in her happiness, as is written, "O children of Zion, be glad, Rejoice in the Lord your God...and you shall know that I am in the midst of Israel...and my people shall be shamed no more" (Joel 2.23-27).[284] And thus Miriam was granted the crown of wisdom and royalty in that she gave birth to Bezalel who was the ancestor of David (*Exod. Rabba* 48:4).

Therefore: "Remember what the LORD your God did to Miriam on the journey after you left Egypt" (Deut 24.9). Don't read *zakhor* (remember in the future). Instead read *zakhar* (remembered in the past).

EXPLANATION OF THE MIDRASH

I would like to make some explanatory remarks—midrashic comments on my midrash. The words, *boshet alumaich* (the shame of your youth) resonates with echoes to *lo tevoshi ve-lo tikalmi* (Don't be embarrassed or shamed) in Lecha Dodi (Welcoming the Sabbath Bride prayer recited during the Kabbalat Shabbat service). One could possibly argue that the bride in Lecha Dodi is also Miriam following my reasoning (but that is the subject of another article). *Herpat almenutayikh* (the shame of your widowhood) also has echoes if we look at the Scroll of Lamentations in which exiled Israel is likened to a widow (*almana*). The *almana* is portion-less (*al maneh*) or rather she gets less of a portion when she remarries in comparison with the untouched virgin that is more valued on the market. A widow can also be considered to be abandoned (*azuva*) by her husband, or in Israel's case, by God.

---

[284] These verses from Joel are recited on Shabbat Shuva, the Shabbat between Rosh Hashana and Yom Kippur. During this time we are expected to repent and return to God. For the implications of this see the last paragraph of this article.

What does *tikalem* mean? Its root includes both "shut up" and "embarrassed." First God locked her up, by forcing her to go into quarantine with her skin disease; then He told her not to be embarrassed by anything that had happened to her. Metaphorically speaking, Miriam's husband is God. She was abandoned by Him, likened to an *almana*. He is also the one who opens the wombs of barren women (namely Sarah, Rebecca, Rachel, Hannah, etc.) or punishes them by keeping them closed.[285] I consider all texts that refer to Israel as a woman, to refer to Miriam as well.

In my midrash we move back and forth from sadness to joy. *Pitzchi Rina vetzahali!* (Sing out and rejoice). To accentuate this, I included the traditional blessing delivered at weddings (from the Talmud).

We have moved from a state of barrenness (*akara*) to weddings and motherhood! Rachel and Hannah are mentioned to demonstrate contiguity within the community of other barren women. From the Book of Genesis through the Book of Kings, there are a slew of women who are *akarot* and who get seed through divine intervention. I use the words *zakhor* and *pakad* interchangeably. They go together for it is God who remembers (*zakhor*) women by opening their wombs and depositing (*pakad*) seed in them. When god opens wombs (*patoah patah*) there is a play on words reminiscent of *atzor atzar* (closing the wombs of Avimelech's family in Genesis 20.18 ever so tightly). When God opens wombs, there is a future. That is the covenant! This is what we refer to today as the burning issue of Jewish continuity. If we have children, it follows that the world will not end. What we have here is cosmic happiness; not just Miriam's micro-happiness.

One might add that water is the flowing source that keeps it all going. Water has healing and restorative powers. We can even add the spittle that ends up on Miriam's face. Spit can clean, cure, and save you from evil influences (if you spit three times). Miriam is associated with wells and water and one can argue that God's expectorant (although from anger) ends up curing and restoring Miriam to herself. Spit is God's water. So when God seems to leave Miriam (his people) He doesn't leave them completely, even if they

---

[285] See 2 Samuel 6.16-23 for the story of Michal, daughter of Saul the King and David's rejected wife who did not have children, possibly as punishment for disobedience, or speaking badly of her husband (*lashon ha-ra*).

deserve to be punished or are unfaithful to Him or question His choices. God doesn't desert his people, He just rebukes them.

When the water breaks, women give birth. From the depths of our birth pains, we are saved (*mi-mamakim*). One can go no deeper than the womb. Women in their depths cry out to God—and when the water breaks they are healed, restored to their former state with an assurance of a future.

There is one last issue that must be addressed. I have made it clear that the treatment of Miriam in rabbinic text is unfair. She gets a slap in the face from the rabbis (when they associate her with gossip),[286] not only from God. One might argue that there are suppressed texts about her which account for her neglect in the Bible. My solution was to conflate the 6 intertexts to show that Miriam ends up happy with children. Since there is usually a relationship between barren women and God, I wanted to show that God opens Miriam's womb, together with the wombs of our other foremothers, Sarah, Rebecca, Rachel, and Leah.

Am I guilty of reducing Miriam to her biological function, of de-emphasizing her prophetic and leadership abilities in favor of essentializing her? Without being apologetic about it, we must recognize that in the context of biblical times, to be unmarried and childless means you have no status. By awarding Miriam a child (and the Messiah no less) we are fulfilling her in the biblical context. She does not only gain a child, she is also the recipient of wisdom (*ḥokhma*).

To counter any accusations of essentialism, I decided to add another layer to my midrash. I was influenced by Trible who found an allusion to Miriam tucked away in Jeremiah which "forecasts her restoration. Returned to her rightful place, she along with other females, will again lead with timbrels and dancing. She participates in the eschatological vision of Hebrew prophecy."[287] Trible has restored Miriam to her rightful place by weaving biblical texts together. She has not, however, dealt with rabbinic midrash which gives Miriam a place in the pantheon by making her the ancestress of the Messiah.

---

[286] See article in this book.

[287] Phyllis Trible, "Bringing Miriam Out of the Shadow," *Bible Review* 5/1 (1989):178.

To formulate my thoughts I found the writings of Charlotte Elisheva Fonrobert and Devora Steinmetz very helpful since they both look at the midrashic texts surrounding Miriam. Fonrobert argues that Miriam is a channel for patriarchal genealogy. "The very precondition for any kind of messianic future in rabbinic eyes is the commitment to giving birth, projected onto the women. They are confined and reduced to birthing roles, to the role as mother of the messianic leader or king." Her assessment is not totally negative of women's birthing roles as she makes a distinction between men and women. She sees that the message of the midrashim is that men are enslaved to the present, whereas women are committed "to the promise of the future and the change or redemption it may bring."[288]

Steinmetz points to the fact that the midrashic stories told about Miriam all have the same theme, namely the desertion of women by men (Zipporah, Yocheved, Miriam). The fact that the midrash goes to great pains to show that Miriam is taken back and that God establishes through her the institution of kingship is very relevant. The midrash wants to prove that Miriam was the progenitress of David. It is a fitting reward for Miriam who is a midwife according to the midrash and who saved the baby Moses. Miriam thus stands for both continuity and leadership. Her "ability at last to bear children guarantees her a destiny." The midrash makes a statement about her character. "(S)he, like the midwife who saves the newborn and the Azuva who establishes kingship, understands the importance of childbearing... It is this type of concern...which is the prerequisite for leadership, whether for the head of a tribe, the redeemer of a people, or the king of a nation."[289]

Trible points to a higher role for Miriam and ignores her birthing role, since she does not seem to be interested in the midrashic layers.[290] Fonrobert and Steinmetz who take into account

---

[288] Charlotte Elisheva Fonrobert, "The Handmaid, The Trickster and the Birth of the Messiah: A Feminist Reading of Midrash," at http://www.bet-debora.de/2001/jewish-family/fanrobert.htm.

[289] Devora Steinmetz, "A Portrait of Miriam in Rabbinic Midrash," *Prooftexts* 8 (1988): 35-65.

[290] Trible tends to be very midrashic herself in most of her interpretations of biblical text, but does not refer to rabbinic midrash in her books.

the birthing role of Miriam don't agree on its use. I find myself somewhere in the middle of this debate. As feminist Jews in the twenty-first century we must find a way to use Miriam as a model for both leadership and continuity. It has been a truism to point to the diminishing birth rate of highly educated Jewish women. Seeing the importance of children and grandchildren to my own continuity, I think I can safely argue that one can be pro-natal, while not necessarily accepting that women be confined to their essentialist role.

I would like to end by going back to my midrash. I included verses from the prophet Joel (2.23-27) which are recited on Shabbat Shuva, the Shabbat between Rosh Hashana and Yom Kippur. During this time the people of Israel are expected to repent and return to God. In my midrash God is returning to his people via Miriam. Miriam does not demand that God account for His actions towards her. God is doing *teshuva* (return or repentance) on his own by giving her a husband and by taking responsibility for her previous state of barrenness. He comes toward her of His own free will and grants her a son who will be the messianic figure of the future. In this way Miriam is restored to her people and granted immortality.

A MIDRASH ON KI TETZEH

מדרש הפטרת כי תצא (ישעיהו נד)

פתחה נעמי טובה בת שרה בת שרה ויחזקאל, **"זְכוֹר אֵת אֲשֶׁר־עָשָׂה ה' אֱל הֶיךָ לְמִרְיָם"** (דברים כד:ט). **"רני עקרה לא ילדה פצחי רנה וצהלי לא חלה"** (ישעיהו נד:א). עקרה זו מרים. ולמה נקרא שמה עקרה? והרי שנינו "בתי מלכות ממרים, לפי שדוד בא ממרים" (שמות רבה א:יז)? ועוד כתיב "הַרְחִיבִי מְקוֹם אָהֳלֵךְ וִירִיעוֹת מִשְׁכְּנוֹתַיִךְ" (ישעיהו נד:ב)? יריעות זו מרים, "שהיו פניה דומין ליריעות" (שמות רבה א:יז).

"פצחי רנה וצהלי" ומרים "צהלה ושמחה" (אסתר ח:טו), כי נהפך לה מיגון ועזבון לשמחה ורינה. **"שוש תשיש ותגל העקרה**, בקבוץ בניה לתוכה בשמחה... שמח תשמח ריעים האהובים, כשמחך יצירך בגן עדן מקדם... אשר ברא ששון ושמחה, חתן וכלה, גילה, רינה, דיצה, חדוה, אהבה, ואחוה ושלום וריעות" (כתובות ח עמ' א).

וישבע בועלה לרחמה, כי פתח פתח יהוה רחם למרים, על כן "לא יאמר לך עוד עזובה" כי יהוה חפץ בך ותבעל (ישעיהו סב:ד).

"לֹא חָלָה" זו מרים. ולמה נקראת מרים "לא חלה", הלא כתוב "והנה מצרעת" (במדבר יב:י)? בא אהרון הכהן, אחי מרים, וצעק "אל נא תהי כמת" וצעק אף משה הלוי, אחי מרים הנביאה, "אל נא רפא נא לה" (במדבר יב: יב-יג). מלמד שמרים נחלית ונהגו בה מנהג מתה וגם אלהים עזבה. אמרה מרים בלבה אל תקרו לי "מִרְיָם" אלה "מָרִים"; הלא ירק ירק העם בפני, דכתיב "וירקה בפניו" (דברים כה:ט)? "ויאמר יהוה אל משה ואביה ירק ירק בפניה הלא תכלם שבעת ימים..." (במדבר יב:יד)? אבל הקב"ה רחם על מרים דכתיב: "אל תיראי כי לא תבושי ואל תכלמי... וחרפת אלמנותיך לא תזכרי עוד... כי בעליך עשיך יהוה צבאות" (ישעיהו נד:ד-ה). וכיצד הגיעה מרים להיות אלמנה? "ישבה בדד... היתה כְּאַלְמָנָה" (איכה א:א) לא אלמנה ממש אלא עזובה, שעזבה בעלה ובדעתו לשוב אליה.

"**כִּי בֹשֶׁת עֲלוּמַיִךְ תִּשְׁכָּחִי**" (ישעיהו נד:ד), כדכתיב, "ויקח לו כלב" (דברי הימים א' ב:יט). מהו ויקח לו? שאחר שנתרפאת עשה בה מעשה ליקוחין ברוב שמחתו בה. "תחת היותך עזובה ושנואה... שמתיך למשוש דור ודור" (ישעיהו ס:טו), שנאמר "בתי מלכות ממרים, לפי שדוד בא ממרים" (שמות רבה א:יז).

"**כִּי כְאִשָּׁה עֲזוּבָה וַעֲצוּבַת רוּחַ**" (ישעיהו נד:ו). עֲזוּבָה זו מרים. "בְּרֶגַע קָטֹן עֲזַבְתִּיךְ" (ישעיהו נד:ז) והענן "סר מעל האהל" (במדבר יב:י). ולמה נקראת מרים עזובה? הלא כתוב "ותסגר מרים מחוץ למחנה... והעם לא נסע עד האסף מרים" (במדבר יב:טו)?

אל תקרה "מִרְיָם" אלה "מֵרִים". במה הרים הקב"ה את מרים? הלא אמרנו חנה העקרה אמרה בתפילתה: "יהוה... מַשְׁפִּיל אַף מְרוֹמֵם: מֵקִים מֵעָפָר דָּל מֵאַשְׁפֹּת יָרִים אֶבְיוֹן לְהוֹשִׁיב עִם נְדִיבִים וְכִסֵּא כָבוֹד יַנְחִלֵם..." (שמואל א' פרק ב:ז-ח)? כי "מִמַּעֲמַקִּים קְרָאתִיךָ... וַאֲדֹנָי שְׁמְעָה בְקוֹלִי... וְאָזְנֶיךָ קַשֻּׁבוֹת לְקוֹל תַּחֲנוּנָי" (תהלים פרק קל:א-ב). וביד **רָמָה** הוציא אדני את מרים ממעמקים. הלא מָצָאה חֵן בַּמִּדְבָּר וּהָלַךְ לְהַרְגִּיעָהּ? כי מֵרָחוֹק יהוה נִרְאָה לה והבטיחה "אַהֲבַת עוֹלָם". הלא כתיב: "אֲהַבְתִּיךְ, עַל כֵּן מְשַׁכְתִּיךְ חָסֶד"? ולכן: "**עוֹד אֶבְנֵךְ וְנִבְנֵית בְּתוּלַת יִשְׂרָאֵל עוֹד תַּעְדִּי תֻפַּיִךְ וְיָצָאת בִּמְחוֹל** מְשַׂחֲקִים" (ירמיהו לא: א-ד). ויהללו אותך "בתף ומחול" (תהלים קנ:ד).

"**וְאֵשֶׁת נְעוּרִים**" (ישעיהו נד: ו). אשת נעורים זו מרים. ולמה נקראה אשת נעורים? שחלתה ונערה מחלייה והחזירה הקדוש ב"ה לנערותה "ותלד לו נערה" (דברי הימים א' ד:ו) ולאחר שנתרפאה, ילדה לו בנים.

"**בְּשֶׁצֶף קֶצֶף הִסְתַּרְתִּי פָנַי רֶגַע מִמֵּךְ**" (ישעיהו נד:ז-ח). שצף קצף דכתיב "ויחר אף יהוה בם" (במדבר יב:ט). הסתרתי פני רגע ממך, "מִמֵּךְ" זה ממרים. דכתיב "והענן סר מעל האהל" (במדבר יב:י). בעבור הרגע, והענן שב אל האהל ויהוה פקד את מרים. אין פקידה אלא זכירה, כדכתיב "זכרתי לך חסד נעוריך" (ירמיהו ב:ב).

"**כִּי מֵי נֹחַ זֹאת לִי אֲשֶׁר נִשְׁבַּעְתִּי** מֵעֲבֹר מֵי נֹחַ עוֹד עַל הָאָרֶץ כֵּן נִשְׁבַּעְתִּי מִקְּצֹף עָלַיִךְ וּמִגְּעָר בָּךְ" (ישעיהו נד:ט). מי נח זה באר מרים, אחד מעשרה דברים שנבראו בערב שבת בין השמשות: "פי הבאר... והקשת" (משנה אבות פרק ה:ו). "**וּבְחֶסֶד עוֹלָם רִחַמְתִּיךְ**... וְחַסְדִּי מֵאִתֵּךְ לֹא יָמוּשׁ" (ישעיהו נד: ח-י).

חסד זה "חסדך האחרון" (רות ג:י) של רות המואביה לבועז. והרי שנינו
"בעז הוליד את עובד... את ישי... את דוד (רות ד:כא-כב). ומנין שדוד
בא גם ממרים? דכתיב "אחרחל זו מרים, ולמה נקרא שמה כן? ע"ש
"ותצאן כל הנשים אחריה בתפים ובמחלות" (שמות רבה א: יז). ומה
החסד האחרון שעשה יהוה למרים? חסדו זה "חסד נעוריך" (ירמיהו
ב:ב), שהחזירה לנעוריה ופתח את רחמה, "עד עקרה ילדה שבעה"
(שמואל א ב:ה). שהושיב עקרה ל"עקרת הבית אם הבנים שמחה
הלליה" (תהילים קיג:ט).

"רני עקרה לא ילדה פצחי רנה וצהלי לא חלה", ובכך זכר יהוה את
מרים בצאתה ממצרים. "רני ושמחי, בת-ציון, כי הנני בא ושכנתי
בתוכך... " (זכריה ב: יד). "גילי מאד, בת-ציון, הריעי, בת-ירושלים, הנה
מלכך יבוא לך..." (זכריה ט:ט).

במה זכר הקב"ה את מרים? הלא מרים עקרה? והלא אצל מרים לא כתוב
"ויפתח את רחמה" כדכתיב אצל רחל אמנו (בראשית ל:כב)?

אלא שכתוב "מושיבי עקרת הבית אם הבנים שמחה" (תהילים קיג:ט).
"שבע עקרות הן, שרה רבקה רחל ולאה ואשתו של מנוח וחנה וציון...
מושיבי עקרת הבית, זו ציון, רני עקרה לא ילדה" (פסיקתא דרב כהנא
[מנדלבוים] כ:א). ולמה מרים דומה? "מושיבי עקרת הבית" להושיב את
ציון עקרה ליתן לה בית תורה... ואז ציון שמחה בבניה ובניה באמם,
שנאמר, "וּבְנֵי צִיּוֹן גִּילוּ וְשִׂמְחוּ בַּ ה' אֱלֹ הֵיכֶם... וִידַעְתֶּם כִּי בְקֶרֶב
יִשְׂרָאֵל אָנִי וַאֲנִי ה' אֱלֹ הֵיכֶם וְאֵין עוֹד וְלֹ**א יֵבֹשׁוּ עַמִּי לְעוֹלָם**" (יואל
ב:כג-כז). "ומרים נטלה חכמה שהעמידה בצלאל ויצא ממנו דוד" (שמות
רבה [וילנא] פרשה מח:ד).

ולכן: **"זָכוֹר אֵת אֲשֶׁר עָשָׂה ה' אֱלֹ הֶיךָ לְמִרְיָם"** (דברים כד:ט). אל
תקרא "זכור" אלא "זכר".

FEMINIST JEWISH RECONSTRUCTION OF PRAYER

When we think of the monotheistic God as he/she/it appears in Jewish sources, we have many images associated with masculinity and strength. There is God the husband and father; the rescuer and protector of Israel; the owner of the strong arm who took us out of Egypt. There is the God who rewards us and punishes us, who forgives our unfaithfulness, who expresses his great passion for us with love and vengeance when betrayed. Most ominously there is the violent God who is depicted as a wifebeater.[291] Many of these masculine images are used to portray God, the object of prayer, in Jewish liturgy.

Today there is a groundswell of prayers, poetry, and readings being composed to meet the needs of women who are unhappy with the liturgy of male monotheism in its present form. Feminist theologians have argued that we should use female God language to complement the image of the male God in Jewish prayers. Writers of feminist prayers have substituted She for He, have added women's names to the litany of men's, and have created special prayers which address women's issues. But these changes, suggested and/or implemented by theologians such as Judith Plaskow, Rita Gross, and Lynn Gottlieb, among others, are merely cosmetic according to an article in *Tikkun* by Marcia Falk.[292]

Falk asserts that the problem is "not just that monotheism has been perverted throughout Jewish history to mean male monotheism," nor is the problem the obvious gender bias in liturgy

---

[291] Naomi Graetz, "The Haftara Tradition and the Metaphoric Battering of Hosea's Wife," in *Conservative Judaism* (Fall 1992): 29-42 and David R. Blumenthal, "Who is Battering Whom?" in *Conservative Judaism* (Spring, 1993): 72-89.

[292] M. Falk, "Toward a Feminist Jewish Reconstruction of Monotheism," *Tikkun* 4, 4 (1989): 53-56.

but rather the finding of adequate non-sexist metaphors about God to convey the truths of monotheism.

Because Falk views any transcendental Godhead—be it female or male—as being idolatrous and ultimately responsible for sexism, racism, and "specieism," it does no good to soften God's image by introducing compassion, giving God a womb or a sex change. For Falk the problem is that a "single-image God" is a Being who dwells "out there."

Falk distinguishes between a transcendent God and an immanent God. Transcendence incorporates the idea that God is beyond the world, "be it concerned or apathetic, personal or impersonal, powerful or impotent."[293] The concept of immanence—the idea that God is in the world—is harder for people to accept than is the concept of transcendence. God is within us, yet as Falk points out, even when we talk of God within ourselves, our prayers still relate to someone/thing other than ourselves that "we can localize and isolate, petition and address."[294] Her criticism of the transcendent God is based upon the fact that this view too assumes total a distinction between us and God.

"AUTHENTIC MONOTHEISM"

Falk states that the distinction between us and God does not only lead to a sense of difference but also to a sense of hierarchy and domination. She labels the form of monotheism which includes this hierarchy as a main component of its belief "inauthentic monotheism."

Falk describes her own vision as "authentic" monotheism, to contrast it with "single-image monotheism," for it embraces "a multiplicity of images…[which] celebrate pluralism and diversity." Her definition of authentic monotheism is "the affirmation of unity in the world… Monotheism means that, for all our differences— differences that [we] celebrate and honor—I am more like you than I am unlike you. It means that a single standard of justice applies to us equally. It means that we—with all of creation—participate in a single source and flow of life."[295]

---

[293] Idem: 53.

[294] Idem.

[295] Idem: 55.

I question Falk's use of the term "inauthentic monotheism."
On what grounds does she claim her reconstruction to be the
"authentic" one? Surely a feminist vision should reject all claims of
authenticity. The feminists' goal is one of extension of relationship,
rather than limitation. By ruling out one form of monotheism and
labeling it "inauthentic," Falk contracts rather than expands the
possibilities for understanding God. And why does she use the
term "monotheism" at all to describe her theology since her radical
proposal is a theology of immanence which will "shatter the
idolatrous reign of the lord/God/King."

AN IMMANENT GOD

To affirm the principle of unity in the world, Falk has introduced
the phrase *eyn ha-chaim* (source or well of life) to replace the
formulaic blessing which regards God as king of the world.
"Source," "Well of Life," and "Life-Force" are images used to
describe the deity in the ḥasidic and mystical movements. Falk
moves in the direction of pantheism when she extends her image
of deity to include "the basic elements of creation—earth, water,
wind and fire." She takes an ecological approach to religion when
she writes, "we—with all of creation—participate in a single source
and flow of life."

Arthur Waskow in his book *These Holy Sparks*,[296] describes an
emergent group of American theologians who are focusing on the
aspect of God that is immanent, fully present within the world,
rather than the aspect that is transcendent, wholly outside the
world. He writes that many Jewish feminist women are moving in
the direction of a fusion of secularist (ecological) and mystical
(ḥasidic, kabbalistic) thought.

When Falk describes the transcendent as the "idolatrous reign
of the lord/God/King," she identifies herself as one of these
renewers. But by focusing on immanence alone, Falk is in danger
of encouraging worship of the self. In my opinion it is equally
idolatrous and inauthentic to put the ME on a pedestal as she
suggests. The problem of ME-ism is that it is relative and
subjective. Relativism can lead to making distinctions that are not
moral. The murderer can claim his god condones the type of

---

[296] Arthur Waskow, *These Holy Sparks: the Rebirth of the Jewish People*
(San Francisco: Harper & Row, 1983).

murder he proposes; his subjective standard has the same weight as any other. Hierarchy, the result of transcendence, can also claim that murder approved by the transcendent is justified. Thus, when either the immanent or the transcendent stands alone, the dangers of abuse of theology become limitless. It should not have to be an either-or choice. We need both views: a transcendent and an immanent God. And both of these views need to be in dialogue rather than at odds with each other. The tension between the transcendent and the immanent must be maintained. The best way for this is the partnership model, which incorporates both.

AN ANCIENT PARTNERSHIP

In rabbinic thought, the Other, the Ruler, and the King are metaphors used to describe a transcendent God. Yet the assumption of a partnership between humanity and God was so basic to rabbinic thought that even though the liturgy was written in the form of "God does this and God does that" it is assumed that man's following this divine will is absolutely necessary for God to "do" anything.

Michael Graetz writes that the verbs used to describe God's actions in most prayers are verbs of process. More important, they are in the present continuous tense. It is not God up there in the past and we down here in the present. It is an ongoing process of cooperation. God alone does not perform these acts. Man's actions are necessary for God's "deeds" to be actualized. For example, when a prayer says "God makes salvation grow up" (*matzmiach yeshua*—using the continuous tense), one can understand it to mean that God and God's partners make salvation grow up. No one had to spell this out for the rabbis. The words of the prayers were understood in the context of a pervasive world-view which assumed this interpretation of the words automatically.[297]

The feminist argument with theological explanations such as these is that what counts are the actual words we use and repeat in

---

[297] I would like to thank Michael Graetz for sharing his as yet unpublished article on the *Amidah* (1976). See also Max Kadushin, *Worship and Ethics: A Study in Rabbinic Judaism* (Evanston, IL: Northwestern University Press, 1964) and Reuven Kimelman, "The *Amidah*: Its Literary Structure and Its Rhetoric of Redemption." cf. http://www2.bc.edu/~cunninph/kimelman_amidah.htm

our daily prayers; and that these words and images reflect our (and the world's) unequal relationship to God. Falk rejects the God whom she perceives as being apart from the world, to whom we are in a relationship of abject supplicants. To make this point she explicates the High Holiday prayer (*piyyut*) *anu amecha* (we are your people) from the Yom Kippur *Makhzor* to interpret *atta* (you—the second person singular) differently than do most people.

In modern day usage, *atta* (you—second person singular) implies a sense of closeness and even familiarity. There is also the Buberian I-Thou sense of the word, that denotes an ongoing dialogue between friends: God is close to me and thus is addressed as *atta*, Thou. Since Falk sees *atta* as being purely transcendent, she sticks us with a transcendent model and a perpetual state of inequality. However her argument is that we should be accepted for what we are in equal and reciprocal relationships with God, and thus she proposes using the construct *nevarech* (let us bless) to get around the masculine gender of *baruch atta* (blessed are you). But in doing so she loses the implied meaning of *atta*, which can convey the mystical consciousness of God's presence, addressing God as if God is standing before us.

The rabbis connected the habit of beginning a blessing with "*baruch atta adonai...*" (Blessed are you, Lord), with the verse "I am ever mindful of being in the Lord's Presence" (Psa 16.8). The very incantatory structure built on the repetition of *anu/atta* (we/you) that Falk objects to, can be understood as giving richer and deeper consciousness each time it is repeated. The climax in the last verse of the *piyyut* she quotes is the mutual pledging of covenant and closeness between God and man: "We are pledged to You and You are pledged to us." If one eliminates the idea of *atta* in order to achieve an equal relationship, one loses this sense of reciprocity.

Moreover, as some modern Jewish theologians have pointed out, it is precisely the *atta* which expresses God's immanence. Though God is transcendent, our worship makes God immanent. God's immanence depends on us. If there is no God to be addressed in the *atta* form, prayer will not make sense. Rather than choosing the dialectic model of God, one that points to the reciprocity of God and Man, Falk chooses to see the relationship of humanity and Divinity as one "related through opposition."

In Judaism, God is both transcendent and immanent. If God were only transcendent, we would indeed have no relationship with

God except as God's subjects. If God were only immanent we might as well worship Nature. It is the tension and constant give and take of the two which account for the moving nature of the classical Hebrew liturgy. This liturgy must be emended, however, to give women the same status as men, to express women's concerns, and to express different ways in which women may view the issues and events that prayer deals with.

LOOKING AT THE COVENANT ANEW

Falk's radical ideas are one possibility for an alternative liturgy. But, as I have pointed out, there are several disquieting elements in her theology:

1) She wants to be pluralistic and all-inclusive; yet, by rejecting the classical liturgy's tension between transcendent and immanent and by using the term "authentic monotheism," is she not substituting one orthodoxy for another?

2) Why is there no mention of holiness anywhere in Falk's text? If there is only immanence are we the source of holiness? Such a doctrine can lead to narcissistic self-worship.

Another approach for an alternative liturgy would be similar to the ideas proposed by Martin Buber. According to Buber, God can only be known through his relationship with us and cannot be described adequately if God is outside the relationship. The problem of the traditional covenantal relationship is that God is usually the superior being. Such a relationship can easily lead to the abuse of the inferior human beings. The covenantal relationship is often depicted as one of a master/slave or male/female relationship.

I propose a model of partnership in which there is mutual responsiveness and toleration of each other's right to growth. God must be willing to take into account that people should not be coerced into a relationship and that the relationship between God and people must be one of mutual respect. It is not enough for God to "espouse" the people (Hosea 2); the people must also say "we will espouse you"—the equivalent of a double-ring ceremony. If God respects the individual's right to independence then there should be no problem with a transcendent God. It is as important for God to be depicted as a being outside us as it is important for us to retain our identities. But we also need to incorporate God inside us—to feel God's immanence. God is both separate from us and in us.

The marriage metaphor is often used to describe this unique relationship between God and His people. But, until now marriage itself reflected an unequal partnership based on coercion, male power, and female servitude. New attempts to redefine marriage as equal partnership, mutual respect, and closeness, can lead to a revival of prayer based on this new understanding. We must feel comfortable reversing the persona—that is, God and Her people. I think the old marriage metaphor is problematic for feminists who will not accept God's relationship to the people of Israel in the patriarchal form of husband to wife. The new marriage metaphor—in which women take on what has been formerly perceived as male roles, and vice-versa—can have profound theological implications.

MODERN MIDRASH UNBOUND: WHO'S NOT AFRAID OF GODDESS WORSHIP?

Simone Lotven Sofian has taken upon herself the position of defender of the faith in her review essay of Anita Diamant's midrashic novel *The Red Tent* in *Conservative Judaism*.[298] I agree with her that Diamant has written a subversive book by taking biblical women's stories from behind the scenes, bringing them forward to center stage and in the process implying that Goddess worship is better for women than the cold rules of the Jewish God. But I take issue with her about the dangers of "Goddess worship" and the limits she prescribes for modern midrash.

The Red Tent is a sanctuary to which women can retreat when they bleed, either from menstruation or after childbirth. It is a place in which they celebrate womanhood and where they are free to worship as they please. Men are not welcome, knowing "nothing of *The Red Tent* or its ceremonies and sacrifices." When Jacob discovers the goings on in the tent, he smashes all the women's household gods and buries them, sending a clear message: Goddesses cannot co-exist with his ancestral, monotheistic God.

Most Jews do not think deeply about the monotheistic message. We worship one God and declare daily that God is One. Yet Goddess worship seems to fill a need. Rachel clearly valued her father's household God/desses. The prophets ranted and raved against Ashera worship, indicating that Israelites needed more than a male God to lean on. In the same prophetic vein, Samuel Dresner feared that Jews who indulged in Goddess worship were guilty of

---

[298] This article was printed in response to the Review Essay by Simone Lotven Sofian, "Popular Fiction and the Limits of Modern Midrash: *The Red Tent* by Anita Diamant," *Conservative Judaism* 54:3 (Spring 2002): 95-105.

paganism and would eventually cause the Jewish people to self-destruct.[299] Paula Reimers also wrote quite convincingly against the use of God/She language saying that it "leads inevitably to the introduction of alien theological ideas into the heart of monotheistic religion."[300]

All of the above assume that the monotheistic God, who has been portrayed almost exclusively with male metaphors, is a "male God." "HE," the Male God, has become the default in prayer language. This Male God is even considered to be gender neutral![301] This conception and language is a problem for many women. The language used when portraying God as male was given a chance to develop and relate to changing needs. Female metaphors of God were not given equal time.[302] They were not only few, but also remained static, or as Judith Plaskow said a "caricature," and a "distorted portrait."[303]

Some have a difficult time with the concept of "Goddess." "Why not a God which incorporates the dual gender aspects of God?" they say. The answer is that the differences between the sexes are so extreme that invoking a monotheistic God often denies that fact. The danger of "oneness" is that too often it blurs even the most obvious distinctions. Those who represent tradition always speak of "oneness" as the only option for monotheism, and accuse those who don't, or who suggest alternatives, of being divisive. This is done, however, only when those without power and representation recognize and name their exclusion, and begin to speak about their needs for inclusion. If God is non-gendered and incorporates both sexes, why is it so difficult to accept the need to include language and metaphors about the female aspects of God, as well as the male, in worship? Why not? Perhaps because

---

[299] Samuel H Dresner, "The Return of Paganism?" *Midstream* (June/July 1988): 32-38 and "Goddess Feminism," *Conservative Judaism* 46:1 (Fall 1993): 3-23.

[300] Paula Reimers, "Feminism, Judaism and God the Mother," *Conservative Judaism* (Winter 1993): 25.

[301] See Jules Harlow, "Feminist Linguistics and Jewish Liturgy," *Conservative Judaism* (Winter 1997) and the Open Forum reactions to it in The Fall 1997 issue: 72-83.

[302] See Mayer I. Gruber, "The Motherhood of God in Second Isaiah," *Revue Biblique* 3 (July 1983): 351-359.

[303] Judith Plaskow, "Jewish Anti-Paganism," *Tikkun* (6:2): 66-68.

when viewed from the other side, it exposes the imbalance and makes us uncomfortable, forcing us to think!

Is worshiping God in goddess language more idolatrous than "God's mighty arm" illustrated in the Haggada, portraits of the Baba Sali, the Lubavitcher rebbe, or even Mizrach pictures of the Western Wall found in so many Jewish homes? Is focusing on the female side of God really that bad for the Jews? If one believes that God is neither male nor female and that God created both in God's image, it makes no sense to depict God as solely male, and as much sense to depict the Deity in female terms. Yet we do the former, not the latter. Those who would depict God as female or who would praise Goddess-oriented societies, by claiming they were egalitarian and peaceful, are scorned. Diamant has tried to re-imagine and re-create the struggle that took place in a patriarchal era and has been labeled a heretic or anti-Semite.[304] I think we should consider carefully what Rita Gross wrote more than twenty years ago: "When we cannot imagine tampering with the symbols that have come down to us, *our* image of God has become idolatrous."[305]

The roots are ambiguous in our tradition. One can make a good case for God being androgynous from both the passage in Genesis when Elohim created us "male and female" *be-tzelem elohim* and the midrashim about its meaning. Can we not argue that Elohim him/herself, in whose *tzelem* we were created, is as two-sided (*du partzuf*) as Elohim's own creations?[306]

Not only do women need to have more feminine metaphors for God, but we need to create a midrashic environment which cultivates female imagery as normatively as it does male imagery. Diamant has done this. And hats off to her for having written a best-selling novel, which is being read seriously by many religious women. As someone who has studied and written imaginatively about the Dinah story and its repercussions, I am fascinated by

---

[304] In addition to Lotven Sofian's review of Diamant's book, see Benjamin Edidin Scolnic, "When Does Feminist Biblical Interpretation Become Anti-Semitic?" *Women's League Outlook* 72:2 (Winter 2001): 27-30.

[305] Rita M. Gross, "Female God Language in a Jewish Context," in Carol P. Christ and Judith Plaskow (eds.), *Womanspirit Rising: A Feminist Reader in Religion* (New York: Harper & Row, 1979): 167-173 [italics mine].

[306] See discussion in *Lev. Rabba* 14:1 and *Midrash Tehillim* (Buber ed.) 139:5. I would like to thank Shirley Ledermann Graetz for this insight.

Diamant's interweaving of the Bible and traditional midrash.[307] Diamant's work is in counterpoint to classical midrash aggada. It is clear that she is aware of the tradition that Dinah had a baby girl (Asenat) who ended up marrying Joseph.[308]

Diamant is not the first woman to write modern midrash— for it is often a female enterprise. Her interpretation is not the only one of the Dinah story, but it is as legitimate as mine or Carl Van Doren's or Thomas Mann's.[309] The Dinah of the novel gets to raise her son, have a career as a midwife and eventually re-marry. It is the story of the triumph of a good woman of the world who faces harrowing odds over the evil machinations of her brothers. Dinah is forced into exile and anonymity because of her shame. She hides her identity, because of the abhorrence felt by the nations toward the deeds of Simon and Levi after they pillage the town of Shechem.

Prior to this pivotal event, Jacob's wives, Dinah's four mothers (Leah, Rachel, Bilhah, and Zilpah) have a cordial relationship of reciprocity with the townspeople. The political implications are clear. Had Dinah been allowed to marry Shalem, the king's son, we would not be at war with our neighbors. Her use of this name, rather than Shechem, son of Ḥamor, tells all. Jacob's sons kill peace (shalom). It is a brilliant touch. It is not an *atta*ck on circumcision; it is an *atta*ck on the perversion of the use of circumcision to kill peace.[310] Sofian accuses *The Red Tent* of unfairly

---

[307] Naomi Graetz, "A Daughter in Israel is Raped," in Naomi Mara Hyman (ed.), *Biblical Women in the Midrash* (Northvale, NJ: Jason Aronson, 1997): 68-71; and "Dinah the Daughter," in Athalya Brenner (ed.), *A Feminist Companion to Genesis* (Sheffield UK: Sheffield Academic Press, 1993): 306-317.

[308] Louis Ginzberg, *The Legends of the Jews* (Philadelphia: JPS 1910, 1988): vol. 2: 38.

[309] Thomas Mann, "The Story of Dinah," in *The Tales of Jacob: Joseph and His Brothers* (London: Secker and Warburg, 1956); Mark Van Doren, "The Tragic Lovers: Dinah and Shechem," in Edith Samuel (ed.), *In the Beginning Love: Dialogues between Maurice Samuel and Mark Van Doren on the Bible* (NY: John Day Co., 1973): 107-171.

[310] I disagree with Sofian that there is no textual basis for this. The prooftext for this is in Genesis 33.18. One can argue that there was peace or wholeness before the episode. Notice that in 35.2-4 Jacob's entourage still has foreign Gods and only after the episode does he bury them. See workshop sources from Naomi Graetz, "Can There be Peace Between the

depicting the "foundation myth of Jewish men's spiritual life [as] violence, cruelty, misogyny, intolerance and xenophobia." Actually, I think that it is a very fair, if not favorable, image of much of our tradition. For instance if we study Talmudic discussions about women, *b'nai noah* or *am ha-aretz,* we will see that the aforementioned negative characteristics are not alien to Jewish texts.

Sofian points out that *The Red Tent* leads women to question the truth of monotheistic Judaism and that those who would find meaning in Diamant's reading of the matriarchs will find that "Judaism as we have inherited it is meaningless to women, for it is the descendant of a singularly male religion." She thinks that the covert message of the book is that women should be re-establishing a separate but parallel woman's religion. She goes further when she writes "Idolatry or the worship of natural phenomena can not be encouraged by casting it in a positive light. Moreover, it must be condemned with its practitioners punished" because it "undermines the Bible's ultimate sacred character."

A point in Sofian's case is the depiction of Rebecca in *The Red Tent* as the oracle of Mamre, the keeper of woman's religion, the perpetuator of Goddess worship. Sofian fears that Diamant inverts traditional rabbinic midrash and "separates the most spiritual of women from the God of her husband and son." She objects to the suggestion that baking of cakes and burning a piece of lunar cake dedicated to the Queen of Heaven on the seventh day takes away from the real origin of burning the ḥalla to remind us of the dough offering in the Temple. I prefer Diamant's midrashic explanation of women's mitzva of ḥalla to that of *Genesis Rabba*'s answer to the question as to why the precept of dough was given to women: "Because she corrupted Adam who was the dough (ḥalla) of the world" (17.8). In my eyes *The Red Tent* is equally legitimate midrash.

If we look at traditional midrashim about Dinah, we often find a stance which condemns the victim. In *Ecclesiastes Rabba* 10:8, while Jacob and Dinah's brothers were sitting studying Talmud, she went out to see the daughters of the land (Gen 34.1), thus bringing upon herself her violation by Shechem. Or in a much-quoted midrash (*Gen. Rabba* 17:8), when asked: "Why do the women walk

House of Jacob and the House of Shechem?" *CAJE* 13 (Hebrew University): July 31-August 5, 1988.

in front of the corpse at a funeral?," R. Joshua answers that it is "Because they brought death into the world...." With legitimate midrash like this it is easy to see why women feel a need for midrashim of their own.

The problem is modernity. Once you include women as equals, you have to give us our own midrashim and tradition. I do not think the only function of midrash is to preserve a reading of Torah in which teachings about a male God are center-stage. I believe midrash is and should be reader-responsive and thus I view all text-based interpretation as legitimate. Diamant's novel is a good example of what feminist midrash does.

Women have power to express our own voices and must be revisors and revisionists, and with new vision bring new perspectives to the traditional text. If we do this, we reflect women's reality as well as men's and put our voices back where they should have been in the first place. "This kind of midrash does not detract from or undermine the Torah, rather it adds additional dimensions to the Torah by making it contemporaneous, relevant and religiously meaningful."[311] In so doing we continue to contribute to the work of revelation.

---

[311] Most of the above points are taking from Naomi Graetz, "Why I Write Midrash," in Naomi Graetz, *S/He Created Them: Feminist Jewish Retellings of Biblical Stories* (Piscataway, NJ: Gorgias Press, 2003).

AKEDA REVISITED[312]

Choose! Bechor[313]

Why?

I am what I am![314]
You are what you are!

Why choose?

I have put before you
Life and Death,
Blessing and Curse.
Choose Life—
If you and your offspring would live.[315]

One for Life.
One for Death.

My sons! I can not.
The knife, the Agony.
The pain, again
To choose.

---

[312] This poem first appeared in *Judaism* (Summer, 1991): 322-323. It was written just before my son Zvi Yehuda Graetz was inducted into the Israeli Defense Force at age eighteen.

[313] In Hebrew *behor* is to choose; *bekhor* is the elder. Different roots and sounds, yet the associations are there for the discerning reader.

[314] Exod 3.14

[315] Deut 30.19

Father? God? Son?
I lived. Why?
To choose!
No!
You must!
It is not choice if I must.
To choose is to die.

Two nations are in [her] womb.
Two separate peoples…
One people shall be mightier than the other.
And the older shall serve the younger.[316]

It is not the practice in our place
To prefer the younger over the elder.[317]

Give up one.
Divide your heart.

This is my son, the live one.
I am he.
Or am I the dead one—
Lost, abandoned,
On the altar,
On the way to the knife.

A sword was brought before him.
To cut the live child in two.
One shall rule.[318]

No!
I shall choose love.

Let it be.
Give the live child to her.

There will be no glory for you
That the choice will be
In the hands of a woman.[319]

---

[316] Gen 25.22-23
[317] Gen 29.26
[318] I Kings 3.22-26
[319] Judges 4.9

Do not put him to death.
She is his mother.[320]

Choose well my dear.
There are no returns
When destiny means choice.
Send him off if you can.

My son, our sons.

---

[320] I Kings 3.27

VASHTI UNROBED

Straight and proud she stands.
Not for her the Selections.
She has refused
She has objected
She will not subject herself,
Submit to gazing drunken eyes
Boring into her.

The path she has chosen is different.
Not for her the party clothes
The giggling,
The dressing up
For others.

She is other
Anomaly
Threat to
Claims of supremacy.

Vashti bends down.
Not for her Supplications.
She bares her head
For the first
And last time.
The party is over. For her.

A PASSOVER TRIPTYCH

Rabban Gamliel said: "Whoever has not spoken of the following three matters on Passover has not fulfilled the obligation of the holiday: They are *Pesach* (the Paschal Lamb), *Matza* and *Maror*" (The Passover Haggada).

My people! What wrong have I done you? What hardship have I caused you? Testify against Me. In fact, I brought you up from the land of Egypt, I redeemed you from the house of bondage, And I sent before you Moses, Aaron, and Miriam (Micah 6.3-4).

Miriam The Bitter — "Maror"

She stands apart.
One of three.
Separate, different,
Sister to a priest.
Midwife (they say)
To the Leader.

The waters broke.
With song and delicacy
She pulled HIM out
And sweet water
From hard rocks.

As a child I knew
Blood, fear
Endless crying—
He was in my power.

I gave my all.

My reward:
HE has turned God against me.
Whiteness of skin,
Shielded from sun and friends
With no one to listen
To my prophecy.

Moses The Leader — "Matza"

Ill tempered, Hitter of rocks,
Breaker of tablets, parter of
Waves, wrecker of home-life. He
Gets his Way—no Diplomat he.

Leprosy makes his point. Pitiless
Provider of plagues.

He casts his rod and parts the reed
Sea.

SHE stands by his side with her
Timbrels and musical instruments.

Duet: Sing a song of sea, oh!
Moment of glory, togetherness.

The waters broke. SHE saved him
And brought him sweet water from
Hard rocks.

Home-wrecker: jealousy—three
Leaders—only one is chosen.

Abandon ship: women first (wife,
Sister), then the brother.

Aaron The Priest — "Pesach"

Bowed down by sacrifice,
Bleating of lambs,
Mewing of cows, Blood spewed.

Wash, blood, wash, blood,
Wash...the heady rhythm of drums
In background—prayer forgotten,
Sons neglected.

Always a spokesman, never a
Leader—except for one golden
Moment. Sacrificial calf
Transformed to idol. Heady stuff
To be worshipped,
Chosen by People, never by God.

HE was on the mountain
Dialoguing with God; SHE was
Busy with song and healing.

The people needed someone, some
Thing. He fashioned a golden
Symbol; it was rejected—caused
Chaos and death. His sons!
Punishment for arrogance.

Impatience is a family trait

Pontifical remnants: Priests,
Penitence, Prayer. Sacrifice is
Always accepted.

From heavy tongue to eloquence:
eyl na, refa na lah (Please god,
Heal HER).
SHE puts music to his Words.
They wait.

WORKS CONSULTED

"Acquisition," *Encyclopedia Judaica* 2 (Jerusalem: Keter, 1971): 216-221.

Achtemeir, Elizabeth. "The Impossible Possibility: Evaluating the Feminist Approach to Bible and Theology," *Interpretations* 42: 1 (January 1988).

Adelman, Peninah. *Miriam's Well: Rituals for Jewish Women Around the Year* (Fresh Meadows, NY: Biblio Press, 1986).

Adler, Rachel. "Feminist Folktales of Justice: Robert Cover as a Resource for the Renewal of Halakha," *Conservative Judaism* XLV: 3 (1993).

——. "I've had Nothing Yet So I Can't Take More," *Moment* 8:8 (1983): 22-26.

——. *Engendering Judaism: An Inclusive Theology and Ethics* (Philadelphia: Jewish Publication Society, 1998).

Al-Tabiri. *The History of al-Tabari*, Vol II, Prophets and Patriarchs, William M. Brenner (tr.) (Albany: State University of New York Press, 1987): 62-63.

Alpert, Rebecca Trachtenberg. "Sisterhood is Ecumenical: Bridging the Gap between Jewish and Christian Feminists," *Response: A Contemporary Jewish Review* 14: 2 (Spring 1984).

Andersen, Francis I. and David Noel Freedman. *Hosea: A New Translation* (The Anchor Bible, New York: Doubleday, 1980).

Aschkenasy, Nechama. "A Non-Sexist Reading of the Bible," *Midstream*, June/July (1981): 51-55.

Atwood, Margaret. *The Handmaid's Tale* (Toronto, Canada: McClelland and Stewart, 1985).

Azmon, Yael (ed.). *A View into the Lives of Women in Jewish Societies: Collected Essays* (Jerusalem: Zalman Shazar Center for Jewish History, 1995) [Hebrew].

Bach, Alice (ed.). *The Pleasure of Her Text: Feminist Readings of Biblical and Historical Texts* (Philadelphia: Trinity Press International, 1990).

Bach, Alice. "Breaking Free of the Biblical Frame-Up: Uncovering the Woman in Genesis 39," in Athalya Brenner (ed.). *A Feminist Companion to Genesis* (Sheffield UK: Sheffield Academic Press, 1993).

Bal, Mieke. *Death and Dissymmetry: The Politics of Coherence in the Book of Judges* (Chicago: University of Chicago Press, 1988).

———. *Lethal Love: Feminist Literary Readings of Biblical Love Stories* (Bloomington, IN: Indiana University Press, 1987).

Baskin, Judith R. *Midrashic Women: Formations of the Feminine in Rabbinic Literature* (Hanover, NH: Brandeis University Press, 2002).

———. "Rabbinic Reflections on the Barren Wife," *Harvard Theological Review* 82:1 (1989): 101-114.

Beckerman, Cheryl. "Kiddushin and Kesharin: Toward an Egalitarian Wedding Ceremony," *Kerem* 5 (1997): 84-100.

Berger, David. *The Rebbe, the Messiah, and the Scandal of Orthodox Indifference* (London: The Littman Library of Jewish Civilization, 2001).

Biale, Rachel. *Women and Jewish Law* (New York: Shocken Books, 1984).

Bird, Phyllis A. "Male and Female He Created Them," *Harvard Theological Review* 74: 2 (1981): 129-159.

———. "'To Play the Harlot': An Inquiry into an Old Testament Metaphor," in Peggy L. Day (ed.). *Gender and Difference in Ancient Israel* (Minneapolis: Fortress Press, 1989): 75-94.

Bleich, J. David. "Halakha as an Absolute," *Judaism* 29 (1980): 30-37.

————. "The Ketubah: Survey of Recent Halakhic Periodical Literature," *Tradition* 31:2 (1997): 50-66.

Blumenthal, David R. "Many Voices, One Voice," *Judaism* 47:4 (Fall 1998): 465-474.

————. "Who is Battering Whom?" *Conservative Judaism* (Spring, 1993): 72-89.

Boyarin, Daniel. *Unheroic Conduct: The Rise of Heterosexuality and the Invention of the Jewish Man* (Berkeley: University of California, 1997).

Brenner, Athalya. "Pornoprophetics Revisited: Some Additional Reflections," *Journal for the Study of the Old Testament* 70 (1996): 63-86.

Bronner, Leila Leah. *From Eve to Esther: Rabbinic Reconstructions of Biblical Women* (Louisville: Westminster John Knox Press, 1995).

Brueggemann, Walter. "The Costly Loss of Lament," *Journal for the Study of the Old Testament* 36 (1986): 57-71.

Buber, Solomon. *The Midrash on Psalms* (Vilna 1891).

————. *Aggadat Bereshit* (Krakow 1893).

Carmichael, Calum N. *Women, Law, and the Genesis Traditions* (Edinburgh: Edinburgh University Press, 1979).

Chesler, Phyllis. "The Rape of Dina: On the Torah Portion of *VaYishlah*," *Nashim* 3 (2000): 232-248.

Cohen, Aryeh. "Framing Women/Constructing Exile," *The Postmodern Jewish Philosophy Bitnetwork* 3,1 (May, 1994) [bitnet address: pochs@drew.drew.edu].

Cohen, Boaz. "Betrothal in Jewish and Roman Law," *Proceedings of the American Academy for Jewish Research* 18 (1948-49).

Cohen, Gershon. "The Song of Songs and the Jewish Religious Mentality," in *Studies in the Variety of Rabbinic Cultures* (Philadelphia: Jewish Publication Society, 1991).

Cohen, Norman J. "Miriam's Song: A Modern Midrashic Reading," *Judaism* 33 (1984): 179-190.

Cohen, Sharon. "Reclaiming the Hammer: Toward a Feminist Midrash," *Tikkun* 3, 2: 55-57; 94-95.

Cohen, Shaye. "The Modern Study of Ancient Judaism," in Shaye Cohen and Edward L. Greenstein (eds.). *The State of Jewish Studies* (Detroit: Wayne State University Press, 1990).

Cover, Robert. "The Supreme Court, 1982 Term-Foreword: *Nomos* and Narrative," *Harvard Law Review* 97:1 (1983).

Crenshaw, James L. *Story and Faith: A Guide to the Old Testament* (New York: Macmillan, 1986).

Daly, Mary. *Beyond God the Father* (Boston: Beacon Press, 1973).

Darr, Kathryn P. "Ezekiel's Justifications of God: Teaching Troubling Texts," *Journal for the Study of the Old Testament* 55 (1992): 97-117.

Darrand, Tom Craig and Anson Shupe. *Metaphors of Social Control in a Pentecostal Sect* (Lewiston, NY: Edwin Mellen Press, 1983).

De Beauvoir, Simone. *The Second Sex*. H. M. Parshley (ed. & tr.) (New York: Vintage Books, 1989).

Deem, Ariella, "The Goddess Anath and Some Biblical Hebrew Cruces," *Journal of Semitic Studies* 23.1 (1978): 25-30.

Diamant, Anita. *The Red Tent* (New York: Picador USA, 1997).

Diamond, A. R. P. and K. M. O'Connor. "Unfaithful Passions: Coding Women Coding Men in Jeremiah 2-3," *Biblical Interpretation* 4:2 (1990): 75-88.

Dobbs-Allsopp, F. W. *Weep, O Daughter of Zion: A Study of the City-Lament Genre in the Hebrew Bible*, Biblica et Orientalia 44 (Editrice Pontificio Istituto Biblico: Rome, 1993).

Dorff, Elliot N. and Arthur Rossett. *A Living Tree: The Roots and Growth of Jewish Law* (Albany, NY: State University Press of New York, 1988).

Dresner, Samuel H. "Goddess Feminism," *Conservative Judaism* 46:1 (Fall 1993): 3-23.

———. "The Return of Paganism?" *Midstream* (June/July 1988): 32-38.

Edelman, Diana "Huldah the Prophet—Of Yahweh or Asherah?" in Athalya Brenner (ed.). *A Feminist Companion to Samuel and Kings* (Sheffield UK: Sheffield Academic Press, 1994): 231-250.

Etz Hayim: Torah and Commentary (New York: The Rabbinical Assembly, 2001).

Exum, J. Cheryl. "The Ethics of Biblical Violence Against Women," in John W. Rogerson et al. (eds.). *The Bible in Ethics*, JSOT Supplement Series 207 (Sheffield UK: Sheffield Academic Press, 1995): 248-271.

Falk, Marcia T., Drorah Setel, et al. "Roundtable: Feminist Reflections on Separation and Unity in Jewish Theology," *Journal of Feminist Studies* 2:1 (1986).

Falk, Marcia T. *Book of Blessings* (San Francisco: Harper, 1996).

Falk, Ze'ev. *Jewish Matrimonial Law in the Middle Ages* (London: Oxford University Press, 1966).

Feinauer, Leslie. "Rape: A Family Crisis," *The American Journal of Family Therapy* 10:4 (1982): 35-39.

Fetterly, Judith. *The Resisting Reader: A Feminist Approach to American Fiction* (Bloomington and London: Indiana University Press, 1978).

Finkelstein, J. J. "Sex Offenses in Sumerian Laws," *Journal of the American Oriental Society* 86 (1966): 355-372.

Fisch, Harold. "Hosea: A Poetics of Violence," in *Poetry with a Purpose* (Bloomington, IN: Indiana University Press, 1990).

Fishbane, Michael. *The Garments of Torah: Essays in Biblical Hermeneutics* (Bloomington, IN: Indiana University Press, 1989).

————. *The JPS Biblical Commentary: Haftarot* (Philadelphia: Jewish Publication Society, 2002).

Fonrobert, Charlotte Elisheva. "The Handmaid, The Trickster and the Birth of the Messiah: A Feminist Reading of Midrash," at http://www.bet-debora.de/2001/jewish-family/fanrobert.htm.

Freedman, H. and Maurice Simon (eds.). *Midrash Rabba* (London: The Soncino Press, 1983).

Freiman, Avraham. *Seder Kiddushin ve Nissuin* (Jerusalem: Mosad Harav Kook, 1964) [Hebrew].

Friedman, Mordecai A. "Marriage as an Institution: Jewry Under Islam," in David Kraemer (ed.). *The Jewish Family: Metaphor and Memory* (New York: Oxford University Press, 1989): 31-45.

———. "The Ethics of Medieval Jewish Marriage," in S. D. Goitein (ed.). *Religion in a Religious Age* (New York: K'tav, 1973): 83-102.

Frye, Northrop. *The Great Code: The Bible and Literature* (New York: Harcourt Brace Jovanovich, 1982).

Frymer-Kensky, Tikva. "On Feminine God-Talk," *The Reconstructionist* 59:1 (Spring 1994): 48-55.

———. "Ritual for Affirming and Accepting Pregnancy," in Susan Grossman and Rivka Haut (eds.). *Daughters of the King: Women and the Synagogue* (Philadelphia: Jewish Publication Society 1992).

———. "The Bible and Women's Studies," in Lynn Davidman and Shelly Tenenbaum (eds.). *Feminist Perspectives on Jewish Studies* (New Haven: Yale University Press, 1994).

———. *In the Wake of Goddesses* (New York: The Free Press, 1992).

Gellman, Marc. *Does God Have a Big Toe? Stories About Stories in the Bible* (New York: HarperCollins, 1989).

———. *God's Mailbox: More Stories about Stories in the Bible* (New York: Morrow, 1996).

Ginsberg, H. L. "Hosea, Book of," *Encyclopedia Judaica* 8 (Jerusalem: Keter, 1971): 1010-1025.

———. "Studies in Hosea 1-3," in Menachem Haran (ed.). *Yehezkel Kaufmann Jubilee Volume* (Jerusalem: Magnes Press, 1960): 50-69 [English Section].

Ginzberg, Louis. *The Legends of the Jews* (Philadelphia: Jewish Publication Society, 1909, 1968).

Goldstein, Elyse. *Revisions: Seeing Torah Through a Feminist Lens* (Woodstock, VT: Jewish Lights, 1999).

Goodspeed, Edgar J. *The Apocrypha: An American Translation* (New York: Vintage Books, 1959).

Graetz, Naomi. *S/He Created Them: Feminist Retellings of Biblical Stories* (Piscataway, NJ: Gorgias Press, 2003).

———. "A Daughter in Israel is Raped," in Naomi Mara Hyman (ed.). *Biblical Women in the Midrash* (Northvale, NJ: Jason Aronson, 1997): 68-71.

———. "Did Miriam Talk Too Much?" in Athalya Brenner (ed.). *A Feminist Companion to Exodus to Deuteronomy* (Sheffield UK: Sheffield Academic Press, 1994): 231-242.

———. "Dinah the Daughter," in Athalya Brenner (ed.). *A Feminist Companion to Genesis* (Sheffield UK: Sheffield Academic Press, 1993): 306-317.

———. "God is to Israel as Husband is to Wife," in Athalya Brenner (ed.). *A Feminist Companion to the Latter Prophets* (Sheffield UK: Sheffield Academic Press, 1995): 126-145.

———. "Jerusalem the Widow," in Esther Fuchs (ed.). *Women in Jewish Life and Culture*, a special volume of *Shofar* 17:2 (Winter 1999): 16-24.

———. "Response to Popular Fiction and the Limits of Modern Midrash," *Conservative Judaism* 54:3 (Spring 2002): 106-110.

———. "Review Essay: Siddur Va'ani Tefillati," *NASHIM: A Journal of Jewish Women's Studies and Gender Issues* 2 (March 1999): 161-172.

———. "The Haftorah Tradition and the Metaphoric Battering of Hosea's Wife," *Conservative Judaism* XLV (1992): 29-42.

———. *Silence is Deadly: Judaism Confronts Wifebeating* (Northvale, NJ: Jason Aronson, Inc., 1998).

———. *Genesis Retold: Aggadot on Sefer B'reshit* (Beersheba: Schichpul Press of Ben Gurion University, 1985).

Greenberg, Blu. "Marriage in the Jewish Tradition," *Journal of Ecumenical Studies* 22:1 (1985): 3-20.

Greenstein, Edward L. "A Jewish Reading of Esther," in Jacob Neusner et al. *Judaic Perspectives on Ancient Israel* (Philadelphia: Fortress Press, 1987).

————. "Biblical Studies in a State," in Shaye J. D.Cohen and Edward L. Greenstein (eds.). *The State of Jewish Studies* (Detroit MI: Wayne State University Press, 1990).

Gross, Rita M. "Female God Language in a Jewish Context," in Carol P. Christ and Judith Plaskow (eds.). *Womanspirit Rising: A Feminist Reader in Religion* (New York: Harper & Row, 1979): 167-173.

Gruber, Mayer I. "The Motherhood of God in Second Isaiah," *Revue Biblique*, 3 (1983): 251-259.

Gubkin, Jennifer. "If Miriam Never Danced… A Question for Feminist Midrash," *Shofar* 14:1 (Fall 1995).

Halbertal, Moshe and Avishai Margalit. *Idolatry*, Naomi Goldblum (tr.) (Cambridge, MA: Harvard University Press, 1992).

Halivni Weiss, David. "The use of KNH in Connection with Marriage," *Harvard Theological Review* (July 1964): 244-248.

Halkin, Hillel. "Feminizing Jewish Studies," *Commentary* (February 1998).

Hammer, Jill. *Sisters at Sinai: New Tales of Biblical Women* (Philadelphia: The Jewish Publication Society, 2001).

Harlow, Jules. "Feminist Linguistics and Jewish Liturgy," *Conservative Judaism* (Winter 1997).

Hasan-Rokem, Galit. "The Voice is the Voice of My Sister: Feminine Images and Feminine Symbols in Lamentations Rabba," in Yael Azmon (ed.). *A View into the Lives of Women in Jewish Societies: Collected Essays*, The Zalman Shazar Center for Jewish History (Jerusalem, 1995): 95-111 [Hebrew].

Herman, Judith. *Trauma and Recovery: The Aftermath of Violence from Domestic Abuse to Political Terror* (New York: Basic Books, 1992).

Hertz, J. H. *The Pentateuch and Haftorahs* (London, 1938).

Heschel, A. J. *The Prophets* (Philadelphia: Jewish Publication Society, 1962).

Heschel, Susannah (ed.). *On Being a Jewish Feminist: A Reader* (New York: Schocken Books, 1983).

———. "Anti-Judaism in Christian Feminist Theology," *Tikkun* 5: 3 (1990): 25-28, 95-97.

———. "Configurations of Patriarchy, Judaism, and Nazism in German Feminist Thought," in T. M. Rudavsky (ed.). *Gender and Judaism* (New York: New York University Press, 1995): 135-154.

Holtz, Barry. *Back to the Sources: Reading the Classic Jewish Sources* (New York: Summit Books, 1984).

Jacobs, Joseph. "Triennial Cycle," *The Jewish Encyclopedia* 12 (New York: Funk and Wagnalls, 1916): 254-257.

Kadushin, Max. *Worship and Ethics: A Study in Rabbinic Judaism* (Evanston, IL: Northwestern University Press, 1964).

Katz, David A. and Peter Lovenheim (eds.). *Reading between the Lines: New Stories from the Bible* (Northvale, NJ: Jason Aronson, 1996).

Koltun, Elizabeth (ed.). *The Jewish Woman: New Perspectives* (New York: Schocken, 1976).

Kramer, Samuel Noah. "The Weeping Goddess: Sumerian Prototypes of the Mater Dolorosa," *Biblichal Archeologist* 46: 69-80.

Kuzmack, Linda. "Aggadic Approaches to Biblical Women," in Elizabeth Koltun (ed.). *The Jewish Woman: New Perspectives* (New York: Schocken Books, 1976): 248-256.

Lakoff, George and Mark Turner. *More than Cool Reason: A Field Guide to Poetic Metaphor* (Chicago: University of Chicago Press, 1989).

Laytner, Anson. *Arguing With God: A Jewish Tradition* (Northvale, NJ: Jason Aronson Inc., 1990).

Lefkovitz, Lori Hope. "When Lilith Becomes a Heroine," *Melton Journal* (Spring, 1990): 7.

———. "Eavesdropping on Angels and Laughing at God: Theorizing a Subversive Matriarchy," in Tamar Rudavsky (ed.). *Gender and Judaism* (New York: New York University Press, 1995): 157-168.

Leifer, Daniel I. "On Writing New Ketubot," in Elizabeth Koltun (ed.). *The Jewish Woman: New Perspectives* (New York: Schocken, 1976): 50-61.

Leith, Mary Joan Winn, "Verse and Reverse: The Transformation of the Woman, Israel, in Hosea 1-3," in Peggy L. Day (ed.). *Gender and Difference in Ancient Israel* (Minneapolis: Fortress Press, 1989): 95-108.

Levenson, Alan. "Jewish Responses to Modern Biblical Criticism," *Shofar* 12:3 (Spring, 1994).

Levinson, Edward R. Zweiback. "Sexegesis: Miriam in the Desert," *Tikkun* 4/1 (Jan./Feb., 1989): 44-46, 94-96.

Levitt, Laura S. "Reconfiguring Home: Jewish Feminist Identity/ies," in Tamar Rudavsky (ed.). *Gender and Judaism* (New York: New York University Press, 1995): 39-49.

Magnus, Shulamit S. "Re-Inventing Miriam's Well: Feminist Jewish Ceremonials," in Jack Wertheimer (ed.). *The Uses of Tradition: Jewish Community in the Modern Era* (New York: Jewish Theological Seminary, 1992): 331-347.

Mann, Thomas. "The Story of Dinah," in *The Tales of Jacob: Joseph and His Brothers* (London: Secker and Warburg, 1956).

McFague, Sallie. *Metaphorical Theology* (Philadelphia: Fortress, 1982).

Meiselman, Moshe. *Jewish Woman in Jewish Law* (New York: K'tav Publishing House, 1978).

Metzger, Deena. *What Dinah Thought* (New York: Viking Penguin, 1989).

Meyers, Carol. "Procreation, Production and Protection: Male-Female Balance in Early Israel," in Charles E. Carter and Carol L. Meyers (eds.). *Community, Identity and Ideology* (Winona Lake IN: Eisenbrauns, 1996): 489-514 [Reprinted from 1983].

————. "The Roots of Restriction: Women in Early Israel," *Biblical Archeologist* 41 (1978): 91-103.

————. *Discovering Eve: Ancient Israelite Women in Context* (New York: Oxford University Press, 1988).

Moran, Richard. "Seeing and Believing: Metaphor, Image, and Force," *Critical Inquiry* 16:1 (1989): 107-109.

Neubauer, Jacob. *The History of Marriage Laws in the Bible and Talmud* (Jerusalem: The Magnes Press, 1994) [Hebrew].

Newsome Carol A. and Sharon H. Ringe (eds.). *The Women's Bible Commentary* (Louisville, KY: Westminster/John Knox Press, 1992).

Niditch, Susan. *War in the Hebrew Bible* (New York: Oxford University Press, 1993).

Nye, Andrea. *Words of Power: A Feminist Reading of the History of Logic* (London: Routledge, 1990).

O'Connor, Kathleen M. "Lamentations," in Carol A. Newsom and Sharon Ringe (eds.). *The Women's Bible Commentary* (Louisville, KY: Westminster/John Knox Press, 1992).

Ochshorn, Judith. "Sex Roles and the Relation of Power to Gender: Biblical Narratives," *The Female Experience and the Nature of the Divine* (Bloomington, IN: Indiana University Press, 1981): 181-226.

Osiek, Carolyn. "The Feminist and the Bible: Hermeneutical Alternatives," in Adela Yarbro Collins (ed.). *Feminist Perspectives on Biblical Scholarship* (Chico, CA: Scholars Press, 1985).

Ozick, Cynthia. "Torah as Feminism, Feminism as Torah," *Congress Monthly* (September/ October 1984).

Pardes, Ilana. *Countertraditions in the Bible* (Cambridge, MA: Harvard University Press, 1992).

Paul, Shalom. *Studies in the Book of the Covenant in the Light of Biblical and Cuneiform Law* (Leiden: Brill, 1970).

Peskowitz, Miriam and Laura Levitt. *Judaism Since Gender* (New York and London: Routledge, 1997).

Plaskow, Judith. "Decentering Sex: Rethinking Jewish Sexual Ethics," presented at the Jewish Feminist Research Group of Ma'Yan, The Jewish Women's Project (January 19, 1999).

———. "Jewish Anti-Paganism," *Tikkun* 6:2 (April, 1991): 66-68.

———. *Standing Again at Sinai: Judaism from a Feminist Perspective* (San Francisco: Harper & Row, 1990).

———. "Blaming the Jews for the Birth of Patriarchy," in Evelyn Beck (ed.). *Nice Jewish Girls: A Lesbian Anthology* (Watertown, MA: Persephone Press, 1982).

Plaut, Gunter. *The Torah: A Modern Commentary* (New York: Union of American Hebrew Congregations, 1981).

Rabinowitz, Louis I. "Haftara," in *Encyclopedia Judaica* 6 (Jerusalem: Keter, 1971): 1342-1345.

Ravitsky, Ruth. *Reading from Genesis* (Tel Aviv: Yediot Aharonot, 1999) [Hebrew].

Reimers, Paula. "Feminism, Judaism and God the Mother," *Conservative Judaism* (Winter, 1993).

Reinhartz, Adele. "Anonymity and Character in the Books of Samuel," *Semeia* 63 (1993): 117-141.

Richards, I. A. *The Philosophy of Rhetoric* (London: Oxford University Press, 1936).

Ricoeur, Paul. *Freud and Philosophy: An Essay on Interpretation* (New Haven: Yale University Press, 1970).

Riskin, Shlomo. "The Song of Hol Hamo'ed," *The Jerusalem Post*, Friday, April 13, 1990.

Rose, Phyllis. *Parallel Lives: Five Victorian Marriages* (New York: Alfred A. Knopf Inc., 1983).

Rosenstock, Bruce. "Inner-Biblical Exegesis in the Book of the Covenant," *Conservative Judaism* (Spring, 1992).

Russell, Letty (ed.). *Feminist Interpretation of the Bible* (Philadelphia: Westminster Press, 1985).

Salkin, Jeffrey. "Dinah, the Torah's Forgotten Woman," *Judaism* (Summer, 1986): 284-289.

Sasson, Jack M. *Ruth: A New Translation with a Philological Commentary and a Formalist-Folklorist Interpretation,* 2nd Edition (Sheffield UK: Sheffield Academic Press, 1989, 1995) [First published in 1979 at John Hopkins University Press].

Schechter, Solomon. "Higher Criticism—Higher Anti-Semitism," *Seminary Addresses* (New York, 1959).

Scholz, Susanne. *Rape Plots: A Feminist Cultural Study of Genesis 34* (New York: Peter Lang, 2000).

Schussler Fiorenza, Elisabeth. *Bread Not Stone* (Boston: Beacon Press, 1984).

———. *In Memory of Her* (New York: Crossroad, 1989).

Scolnic, Benjamin Edidin. "Bible Battering," *Conservative Judaism* 45 (Fall, 1992): 43-52.

———. "When Does Feminist Biblical Interpretation Become Anti-Semitic?" *Women's League Outlook* 72:2 (Winter, 2001): 27-30.

Segovia, Fernando F. and Mary Ann Tolbert (eds.). *Reading from this Place,* Vol. 2 (Minneapolis: Fortress, 1995).

Selvidge, Marla. "Mark 5:25-34 and Leviticus 15:19-20," *Journal of Biblical Literature* 103: 4 (1984).

Setel, T. Drorah. "Feminist Insights and the Question of Method," in Adela Yarbro Collins (ed.). *Feminist Perspectives of Biblical Scholarship* (Chico, CA: Scholars Press, 1985).

———. "Prophets and Pornography: Female Sexual Imagery in Hosea," in Letty Russell (ed.). *Feminist Interpretation of the Bible* (Philadelphia: Westminster, 1985): 86-95.

Shanks, Hershel. "Dever's 'Sermon on the Mound,'" *Biblical Archaeology Review* 13:1 (March, April 1987): 54-57.

Shaviv, Yehuda. *Beyn Haftara le-Parasha* (Jerusalem: Reuven Mass, 2000) [Hebrew].

Sheres, Ita. "The Other Story: The Unredacted Version," in *Dinah's Rebellion: A Biblical Parable for our Time* (New York: Crossroad, 1990): 129-138.

Shields, Mary E. "Circumcision of the Prostitute," *Biblical Interpretation* 3:1 (1995).

Simpson, Catherine R. "The Future of Memory: A Summary," Women and Memory. *Michigan Quarterly Review* 26.1 (1987): 259-265.

Spender, Dale (ed.). *Men's Studies Modified: The Impact of Feminism on the Academic Disciplines* (New York: Pergamon, 1981).

Steinmetz, Devora. "A Portrait of Miriam in Rabbinic Midrash," *Prooftexts* 8 (1988): 35-65.

Stern, David. *Parables in Midrash—Narrative and Exegesis in Rabbinic Literature* (Cambridge: Harvard University Press, 1991).

Sternberg, Meir. "A Delicate Balance in the Rape of Dinah," *Ha-Sifrut* 4, 2 (1973): 193-231.

Tanakh: A New Translation of the Holy Scriptures (Philadelphia: Jewish Publication Society, 1985).

Teugels, Lieve. "'A Strong Woman, Who Can Find?' A Study of Characterization in Genesis 24," *Journal for the Study of the Old Testament* 63 (1994): 89-104.

———. *Aggadat Bereshit. Translated from the Hebrew with an Introduction and Notes* (Leiden: Brill, 2001).

The Torah: A Modern Commentary (New York: The Union of American Hebrew Congregations, 1981).

Tolbert, Mary Ann. "Defining the Problem: The Bible and Feminist Hermeneutics," *Semeia* 28 (1983): 113-126.

Trenchard, Warren. "Woman as Daughter," *Ben Sira's View of Women: A Literary Analysis* (Chico, CA: Brown Judaic Studies 38, 1982): 129-166.

Trible, Phyllis. "Bringing Miriam Out of the Shadows," *Bible Review* 5/1 (February, 1989): 14-34.

———. "Depatriarchalizing in Biblical Interpretation," *Journal of the American Academy of Religion* (March 1973): 30-48.

————. "Depatriarchalizing in Biblical Interpretation," in Elizabeth Koltun (ed.). *The Jewish Woman: New Perspectives* (New York: Schocken Books, 1976): 217-240.

————. *Texts of Terror: Literary-Feminist Readings of Biblical Narratives* (Philadelphia: Fortress Press, 1984).

————. *God and the Rhetoric of Sexuality* (Philadelphia: Fortress, 1978).

Tucker, Gordon. "The Sayings of the Wise are Like Goads: An Appreciation of the Works of Robert Cover," *Conservative Judaism* XLV: 3 (1993).

Umansky, Ellen M. and Diane Ashton (eds.). *Four Centuries of Jewish Women's Spirituality: A Sourcebook* (Boston: Beacon Press, 1992).

————. "Beyond Androcentrism: Feminist Challenges to Judaism," *Journal of Reform Judaism* (Winter 1990): 25-35.

Van Dijk-Hemmes, Fokkelien. "The Imagination of Power and the Power of Imagination: An Intertextual Analysis of Two Biblical Love Songs: The Song of Songs and Hosea 2," *Journal for the Study of the Old Testament* 44:6 (1990): 1342-1345.

Van Doren, Mark. "The Tragic Lovers: Dinah and Shechem," in Edith Samuel (ed.). In *the Beginning Love: Dialogues between Maurice Samuel and Mark Van Doren on the Bible* (New York: John Day Co., 1973): 107-171.

Waldman, Nahum M. "The Designation of Marital Status in the Ketubah," *Conservative Judaism* 38 (3), Spring, 1986: 80-81.

Walker, Lenore. "Battered Women and Learned Helplessness," *Victimology* 2:3-4 (1977-78): 525-534.

————. *The Battered Woman* (San Francisco: Harper & Row, 1979).

Waskow, Arthur. *These Holy Sparks: The Rebirth of the Jewish People* (San Francisco: Harper & Row, 1983).

Weems, Renita J. "Gomer: Victim of Violence or Victim of Metaphor?" *Semeia* 47 (1989): 87-104.

Wegner, Judith Romney. *Chattel or Person? The Status of Women in the Mishnah* (New York: Oxford University Press, 1988).

Weinfeld, Moshe. *Deuteronomy and the Deuteronomic School* (Oxford: Clarendon Press, 1972).

Westphal, Merold. *Suspicion and Faith: The Religious Uses of Modern Atheism* (New York: Fordham University Press, 1998).

Wheelwright, Philip. *Metaphor and Reality* (Bloomington, IN: Indiana University Press, 1962).

Wiesel, Elie. A*ni Maamin: A Song Lost and Found Again*, M. Wiesel (tr.) (New York: Random House, 1973).

Williamson, Nancy. "Daughter Preference," in *Sons or Daughters: A Cross-Cultural Survey of Parental Preferences* (Beverly Hills, CA: Sage Publications, 1976): 103-115.

Wisse, Ruth. "The Feminist Mystery," *The Jerusalem Report*, January 9 (1992), 40.

Yee, Gale A. "Hosea," in Carol A. Newsom and Sharon H. Ringe (eds.). *The Women's Bible Commentary* (Louisville, Kentucky: Westminster, 1992): 195-202.

Yerushalmi, Yosef Hayim. *Zakhor: Jewish History and Jewish Memory* (New York: Schocken, 1989).

Zones, Jane Sprague (ed.). *Taking the Fruit: Modern Women's Tales of the Bible* (San Diego: Women's Institute for Continuing Jewish Education, 1st edition, 1981, 2nd edition, 1989).

Zornberg, Aviva. *The Beginning of Desire: Reflections on Genesis* (New York: Doubleday, 1995).

ABOUT THE AUTHOR

Naomi Graetz (b. 1943, NYC) has been living in Israel since 1967 and in the Negev since 1974. She is the author of *The Rabbi's Wife Plays at Murder* (Beersheva: Shiluv Press, 2004), *S/He Created Them: Feminist Retellings of Biblical Stories* (Professional Press, 1993; second edition Gorgias Press, 2003), and *Silence is Deadly: Judaism Confronts Wifebeating* (Jason Aronson, 1998).

Her many book reviews and articles on women and metaphor in the Bible and Midrash have appeared in such journals and edited books as *Conservative Judaism*, *Shofar*, *Nashim*, *Judaism*, *Hagar*, *A Feminist Companion to the Bible* (ed. Atahlyah Brenner), *Gender and Judaism* (ed. Tamar Rudavsky), *Jewish Mothers Tell Their Stories* (ed. Rachel Josefowitz Siegel et al.), *All the Women Followed Her* (ed. Rebecca Schwartz), *Biblical Women in the Midrash* (ed. Naomi M. Hyman), *The Women's Seder Sourcebook* (ed. Tara Mohr) and *Jewish Feminism in Israel: Some Contemporary Perspectives* (eds. Kalpana Misra and Melanie Rich).

Graetz has been teaching critical reading skills to a generation of students at Ben Gurion University and has integrated articles on feminist thought, pluralism, civil rights and Judaism into her courses. Her conscious use of these materials has greatly increased awareness of women's place in Jewish history, but also of the potential for women in Israeli society. For her course on "Women and Judaism from a Feminist Perspective" to the Overseas Students at Ben Gurion (1993-1996) she prepared a four volume anthology of readings.

Graetz is a Feminist Jew who is grounded both in Jewish tradition and feminist thought. She continues to grapple with problems of modernity while seeing the value of tradition.